IMAGES
of America

ERATH COUNTY

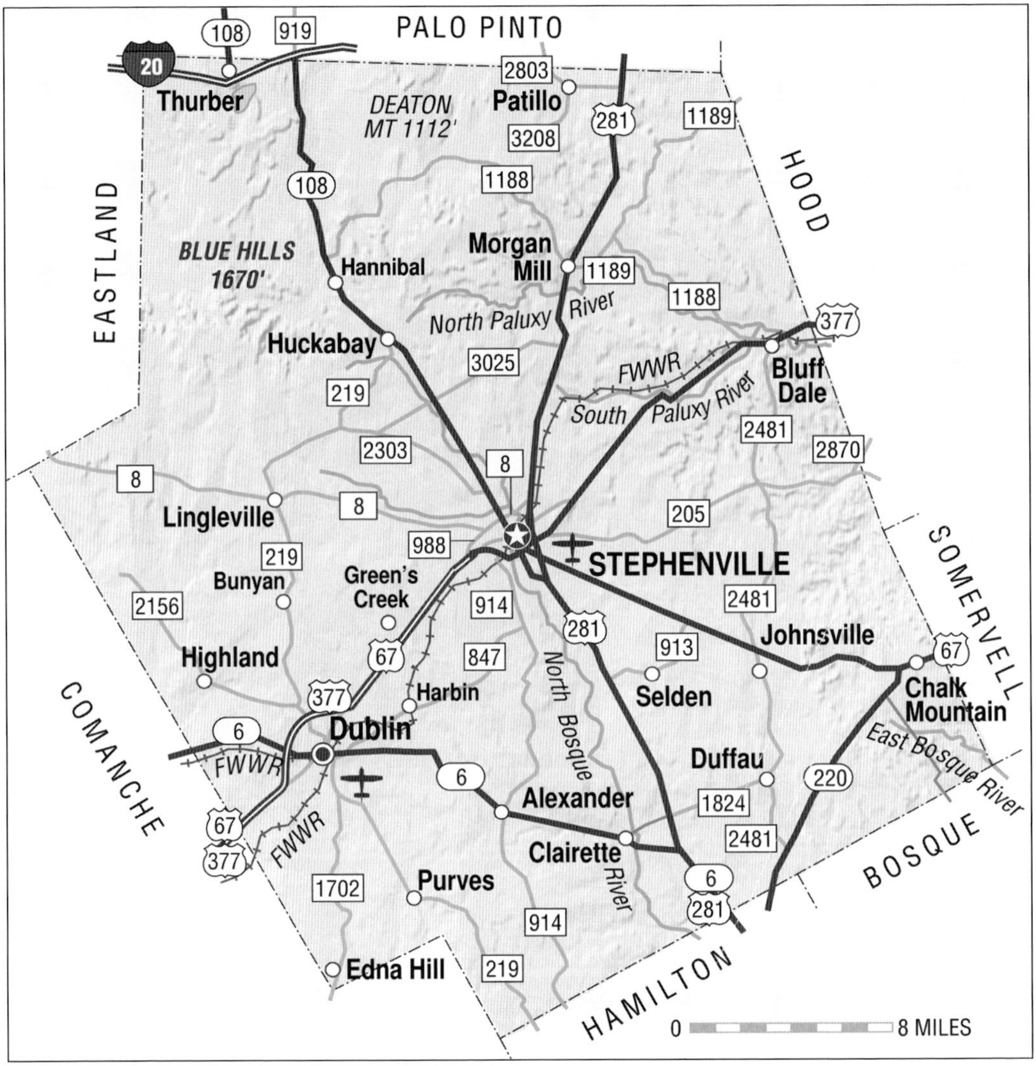

Streams, roads, railways, and highways are thoroughfares connecting the rich history of Erath County, which was established in 1856. The communities seen here, along with dozens more, gave birth to this "Dairy Capital of Texas" and "Cowboy Capital of the World." (Texas Almanac and the Texas State Historical Association.)

On the Cover: Men, women, and children pose in front of a makeshift chalkboard that reads "Post Oak Singing School closed July 28, 1902. J.J. Day, teacher. Miss Myrtie Squyres, Organist." A touring music company held a two-week school to teach music-reading and vocal harmony; this was considered by some to be the primary social opportunity of the year, and people saved their money to pay the tuition. (Stephenville Historic House Museum.)

IMAGES
of America

ERATH COUNTY

Sheryl Reed Rascher

ARCADIA
PUBLISHING

ISBN 978-1-4671-0845-4

Published by Arcadia Publishing
Charleston, South Carolina

Printed in the United States of America

Library of Congress Control Number: 2022935968

For all general information, please contact Arcadia Publishing:
Telephone 843-853-2070
Fax 843-853-0044
E-mail sales@arcadiapublishing.com
For customer service and orders:
Toll-Free 1-888-313-2665

Visit us on the Internet at www.arcadiapublishing.com

For my grandparents,
Clarence and Clara Dixon Reed
and L.B. and Opal Langley Skiles.

Contents

ACKNOWLEDGMENTS

I am humbled by the kindness of those who shared materials and information.

I cherish the friendship of Nelda Blankenship Keever, who long ago responded to my interest with an apprenticeship as a keeper of local lore.

I treasure the tutelage of Thomas Ralph Rogers, who conserves the work of his parents, Ralph and Dossie Rogers—a compilation of 19th- and 20th-century photography. Unless otherwise noted, all images in this book appear courtesy of the Ralph and Dossie Rogers Historic Image Collection.

Other images in the book are courtesy of the Stephenville Historic House Museum (SHHM). No one has been more supportive or offered more tireless assistance than SHHM and Erath County Historical Commission (ECHC) devotee Cindy Shipman. Janella Bramlett Hendon (JBH), of the Dublin Public Library (DPL) board, ECHC, and Erath County Genealogical Society (ECGS), has shared photographs, knowledge, and friendship. I am one of many whom she mentors.

ECGS membership offers steady exposure to regional narratives. I am indebted to Connie Conatser McSpadden, Lola Fry Elrich, Ruth Graves Fletcher, Sandra Shoup Hammons, Patti Hirst, Barbara Dalton Jones, Evelynn Hill Kelly, Judith Robbins Lemons, Pamela Kile Pollock McDuff, Mary Sue Shafer Peacock, Diana Bryan Quinn, Catherine Rampley, Martha Hancock Starnes, Marion L. Stewart, Suzanne Cook Taylor, Linda Tolston, Carla Stacy Trussell, Betsy Reid Ward, and unnamed others.

I thank Jan Jennings for her ECGS donation from the collection of her grandparents John Archibald Guthrie Sr. and Edna Wallace Guthrie.

I appreciate encouragement by author James Pylant; Dr. Dannah Procter Bays, Lingleville ISD, retired; Dr. Ron Bradberry, Tarleton State University, retired; Adina Dunn, DPL director; Cathey Hartmann, past ECHC chair; Phyllis Kinnison and Amanda Pape, Dick Smith Library; and Ben Pate, Dublin Historical Museum director.

I wish to thank Arcadia Publishing's Caroline Anderson Vickerson for her patient guidance, as well as Lindsey L. Givens for her invitation and proposal support.

Mere words fall short of conveying the kindness shared by each of these people. I am thankful.

INTRODUCTION

Erath County is centrally located in Texas about 100 miles southwest of Dallas. Stephenville, the county seat, is named for visionary John Miller Stephen, who donated land for the city. The northwest two thirds of the area are covered by the Western Cross Timbers region of hardwoods, red clay, and sand. The southeast portion lies in the western edge of the Grand Prairie. Some 75 creeks feed the Bosque and Paluxy Rivers, which are tributaries of the Brazos River.

Spain, France, Mexico, the Republic of Texas, and the United States each claimed tenancy without residence. Stephen F. Austin and Samuel May Williams received but did not settle a land grant including this region. Legislators plotted it as part of the Milam district, then Bosque and Coryell Counties. In 1856, at the urging of John Stephen, Erath County was created.

The bounty of the land sustained indigenous peoples for thousands of years. Caddo, Anadarko, and other groups, pressured from the east, settled along local waterways. As European settlers moved into the area, the native peoples were forced out of it. The Comanche ranged the region, calling it Teha Lanna, meaning "land of beauty." In spite of Comancheria, westward expansion persisted. Cognizant of the threat to their way of life, the Comanche were intolerant of the encroachment. The prospect of gaining wealth by gathering wild cattle from the open range brought risk-takers to the area. The Comanche resisted annihilation. The Erath County area remained a violent frontier for two decades, and clashes between the new invaders and the indigenous peoples were ongoing until the mid-1870s.

Herdsmen battled the elements, wild animals, and antagonistic natives. Free-range ranching meant steady migration from one area of open grassland to the next. Stockmen owned no acreage but drove their animals in one region until the grass and water supplies were exhausted, then moved on. The grass, water, and descendants of Spanish cattle were free, and there were no fences.

By 1860, when the county was just four years old, it had 2,300 residents, including a dozen merchants and a half dozen ministers. Ten blacksmiths were complemented by 25 mechanics, meaning machine operators or repairmen. Other labor at hand ("not upon the field") occupations included a carpenter, a bricklayer, a stonemason, and a cabinetmaker. A tailor, shoemaker, tavern steward, and tobacconist were in Stephenville. The county was served by four physicians, four midwives, and a nurse. John Stephen had the first store, and was followed in the merchant business by Granville Jackson Carter, William Leonidas Bateman, Valentine Thomas Dalton, B. Toliver, Martin Leibman, and John A. Frey. Gristmill owners Benjamin Franklin Bates, Hugh Brown Gotcher, and Samuel J. Durnett were not local in 1870, but the Bates and Gotcher families remained near Tolar and Gorman, respectively.

The Civil War halted westward advances, and frontier folk suffered terribly. The 1861 exodus of US Army troops from the already sparse military installations left settlers at the mercy of marauders. Raiding deserters, outlaws, and Native Americans could easily hit and run and escape unfollowed. Men not pressed into Confederate service formed minutemen units. Families pulled back or joined others in civilian strongholds like Desdemona's C.C. Blair fort. The Texas frontier recoiled eastward some 100 miles. Erath's 1860 population of approximately 2,500 dropped to about 1,800 by 1870. However, the influx of war survivors swelled the 1880 count to almost 12,000.

In the late 1860s, surviving soldiers returned to find treacherous bandits, renegades, and thugs in their midst. People feared that the courts could not be successful in punishing and deterring crime. When the US Army and Texas Rangers failed to end horse and cattle rustling, neighbors organized watches that meted out night-rider justice. Vigilantism became so profuse that the Texas governor eventually intervened. Declaring martial law helped end the mob rule of intimidation and lynching. But some Texas Ranger local recruits were, in fact, night riders, so it was the populace that finally incorporated change. As key members changed sides, a legal rabble cleanup ensued.

As war obstructed Union markets, small numbers of Texas cattle were driven to Confederate troops. But generally, unattended herds grew in number on the sparsely populated Texas grasslands. With Northern beef depleted by war, 500-to-1,000-mile cattle drives established routes such as the Chisholm and Loving-Goodnight Trails. Local feeder trails to Waco, Fort Worth, and elsewhere connected with the larger east or west paths to railhead or market. One branch to the Chisholm Trail ran between Hico and Carleton.

Open-range grazing meant that subsistence farmers needed fencing for their truck patches or fruit and vegetable gardens. Prior to the mid-1880s, fencing was commonly limited to split rail or stacked rock to protect a few animals and living quarters. In Maryland, 17th-century lawmakers determined that the adequate fence should be "pig tight, horse high, and bull strong." As barbed wire arrived in the area, many began confining their stock to their own property. This was an impediment for open rangers without land, and fence-cutting became pervasive; after it became a felony in 1884, the open-rangers relocated.

The war-torn South brought thousands to the area in search of a fresh start. The untilled earth of Erath County was a call to those desperately in need. The population grew. Tenant farming escalated. Those unable to buy land could lease a farm and house for cash or, in the case of sharecropping, with a contracted portion of the harvest. One poor crop meant financial ruin. Failed croppers moved on to try again.

A common belief was that high supply costs and low market prices were driven by bank and railroad monopolies. Collective organizations—sometimes referred to as the Grange—asserted that cooperative practices could improve their potential for success. Patrons of Husbandry, Agricultural Wheel, and Farmers' Alliance were three post-Reconstruction agrarian institutions that shared best practices among farmers. The intent behind these organizations was to address economic, educational, and social hardships. The people involved in them conducted cooperative buying and selling and scheduled schools and traveling lecturers, as well as gatherings like picnics and dances. Such groups eventually dissolved into the Populist Party (also known as the People's Party).

The Texas Pacific Coal Company mined bituminous coal near Thurber from 1888 until 1921. From 1918 to 1933, local shale was exploited by the Thurber Brick company for use in the making of brick, pipe, and tile. Erath County's population peaked at over 30,000 around 1918 primarily due to the discovery of petroleum in the region. The Desdemona oil boom brought business to and through Erath townships. Huge amounts of lumber, pipe, supplies, and manpower were freighted from Erath railheads. All support businesses thrived. But over-drilling of the Desdemona field, the closure of the Thurber coal mines and brickyards, and a prolonged drought began a steady 50-year decline that would take almost as long for the county to recover from. By 1930, more than half of the 1918 population was gone. Miners and drillers found work in West Texas, New Mexico, and Arizona. Many farmers migrated to nearby counties or Oklahoma. The Dust Bowl pushed some to West Coast agricultural fields. Mining, logging, and farming drew Erath Countians to California, Oregon, and Washington state.

As farming implements increased in size, efficiency, and affordability, motorized units made it possible for one man to do more with less. In the 1930s, implement dealers went from farm to farm demonstrating equipment. Today's Bramlett Implement is a fourth-generation business started by D.R. Barbee. In 1937, Barbee relocated his Edna Hill horse and mule trade to Dublin and became a John Deere dealer. Barbee's willingness to accept horse and mule teams as payment enabled his customers to modernize.

Even when financial prosperity was negligible, communities in the county flourished. Churches and schools were ideally within walking distance, thus many small villages existed. At least 140 individual churches have existed in the county at one time or another. These sites are often recognizable by the surviving cemeteries. Over 200 separate schools opened, consolidated, or closed. Education has always been important to Erathians. Paluxy Baptist Association had a college in the area in the late 1870s. At the end of the 19th century, Lingleville had colleges sponsored by the Church of Christ and the Farmers' Alliance. The predecessor to Tarleton State University was the 1899 John Tarleton Agricultural College. Dr. Marshall McIlhaney, of Stephenville's bankrupt McIlhaney College, was hired as Tarleton's first president. Huckabay Academy, in operation from about 1902 to 1914, was a high school that expanded to include first-year college courses.

Name changes were common, and if a community faded, the land did not move, but the address was altered. Barton Creek, Hannibal, and Liberty were near Huckabay. Berlin, Corinth, Pleasant Home, School Hill, and Topaz evaporated to "out near Lingleville." In 1877, Bluff Springs became Bluff Dale, with a new post office, as there was already a Bluff Springs in the state. A location might reflect the name of the postmaster or one of the earliest settler families. When the Texas Central Railroad came through, Clairette was named for a soap product that was popular at the time. Locals did not like the Fitzgerald school name, so they called it Unity. More than 50 post offices opened in the county between 1857 and 1930. Bluff Dale, Dublin, Lingleville, Morgan Mill, and Stephenville remain.

Safe travel via bridges and roadways, a secure water supply via windmills and reservoirs, and communication via newspapers and radio are all indicative of progress. But fossil-fueled transportation and higher-income employment in urban areas eliminated the need for schools and stores within a 10-minute walk.

More than 100 communities thrived in Erath between the 1860s and 1930s. Some had only a school or church, but each embodied a set of households that identified with one another. A few of Erath's lost communities not mentioned here include Atkinson, Box, Colbert, DeAlva, Hurley Grove, Moccasin Rock, Palm Rose, Rose, and Union Grove.

These were the stalwart souls who turned Texas and the United States into what they are today. Throughout lives of hardship, giving of themselves to the betterment of their environment and its future, they tamed—and saw the passing of—the frontier. Politicians and money coffers had much to do with advancement in the county, but it was the faith and fortitude of these "lost" communities that bequeathed a rich heritage and auspicious future to their successors.

A study of the history of Erath County from its 1850s inception to the early 1930s reveals an explosion of small communities that developed in the area. Most of those local centers have vanished. No photographs have surfaced from earlier than the 1880s, but records offer an idea of the setting that greeted those who arrived in the 19th century. Maps made prior to 1856, when the county was established, charted the region as "Large Droves of Wild Cattle and Horses." Hunters and stockmen of European descent intruded upon this Native American hunting ground. A few intrepid interlopers passed beyond the border of civilization, gathering livestock without displacing more than a bedroll and fire. But for a population expanding westward, the lure of cheap land brought stock-raisers and nesters regardless of hazard. Living off the land was what they knew, so that was what they pursued. Trade and commerce followed. The blacksmith repaired the wagon. The carpenter needed nails. Bridges connected roads and people. Law and order were expected, and men died for their country. People gathered in worship and educated their children. Societies united to help their fellow man. Today, those villages have disappeared. This book endeavors to honor the existence and experiences of those lost communities. It is the unique personality of such rural townships that laid the foundation of this place named Erath.

One

Early Erath

Fertile loam soil and verdant banks along clear streams teemed with wild game such as antelope, deer, prairie chicken, and turkey. Vast herds of bison, cattle, and mustangs roamed the land filled with waist-high grass. For two decades, the confrontations between the unconquerable Comanche and the indomitable pioneers resulted in unimaginable brutality. The newly arrived European descendants trespassing on central Texas plains suffered relentless retribution. The full moon became known as the "Comanche moon" as warriors took advantage of the brightly lit night sky to steal horses.

To ensure fresh water for family and livestock, early settlers followed the waterways. Land speculators marketed Texas as nature's paradise. Promotional material led immigrants to believe water was available; in fact, it was often seasonally contingent. Newcomers relied on streams until a well could be dug and cisterns could collect rain. Hauling barrels of water by wagon for several miles was a common necessity. Although rain was plentiful in 1885, an 1886 drought led many to withdraw from the area. People quenched their thirst using the gourd or tin dipper kept in the water bucket. Bluff Dale, Dublin, Huckabay, Lingleville, and Stephenville had public wells. Developed in the 1890s, the Aermotor windmill was standard by 1915.

A.C. Dobkins and his brothers-in-law Will and Tom Holland brought their families to the area in 1854. Their outpost, located near the current site of Dublin, served as a frontier fort, stage stop, and camp for buffalo hunters. In 1855, Thomas Arendell, George B. Erath, a Mr. Henley, John Jones, and John Stephen brought their families, later establishing Stephenville. Settling several miles south of present-day Dublin, Sabra Rose and Chesley Turnbow brought their extended family wagon train, which included Chesley B. Caudle, Andrew Jackson Gilbreath, William Henry Gilbreath, and John R. Maloney. Resley Creek provided cool, clear water for drinking and timber for building and burning. In 1857, Frances Lloyd and James Jones Barbee brought their family from Arkansas after their daughter Mary's marriage to Rev. Thomas Crockett Capell.

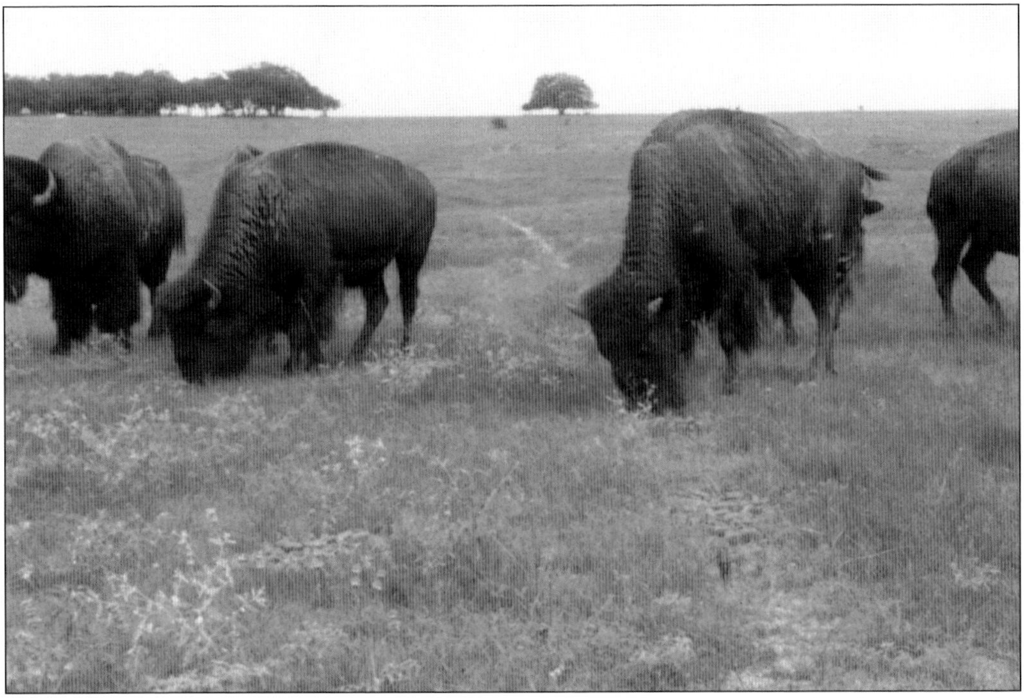

Immense herds of buffalo—the lifeblood of the Native Americans—roamed within a few miles of what became Stephenville. Wagon trains of hunters procured supplies and lodged in town between hunts. Extensive slaughter in 1873 pushed the bison to the brink of extinction and the Comanche to starvation. (SHHM.)

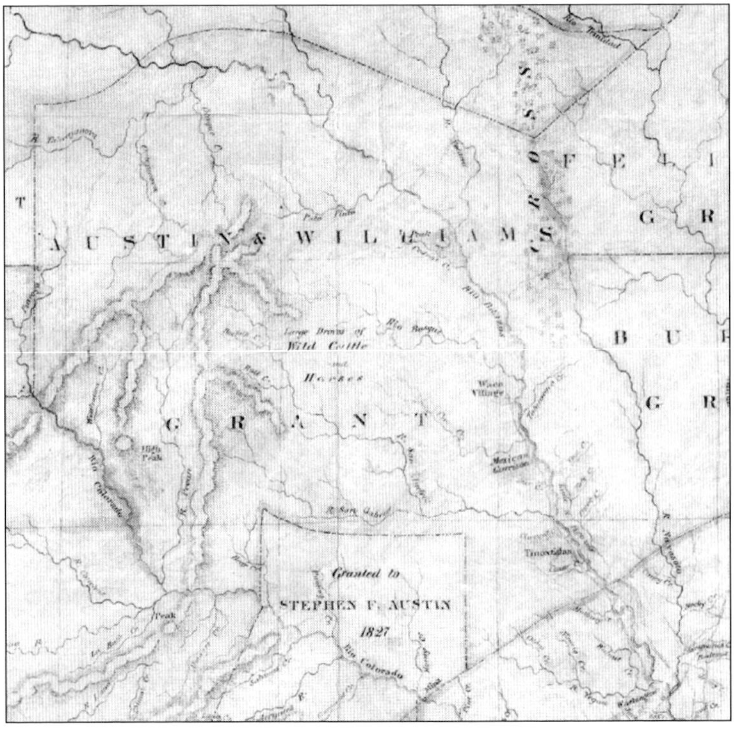

Stephen F. Austin's 1837 map labeled the area where Erath County now exists as "Large Droves of Wild Cattle and Horses." The 1831 Austin and Williams contract did not issue land to settlers, but sold permits to speculators. Migrating from southeast to northwest, the new arrivals traversed waterways upstream along the Brazos River and its tributaries—the Bosque, Paluxy, and Palo Pinto Rivers. (Texas General Land Office.)

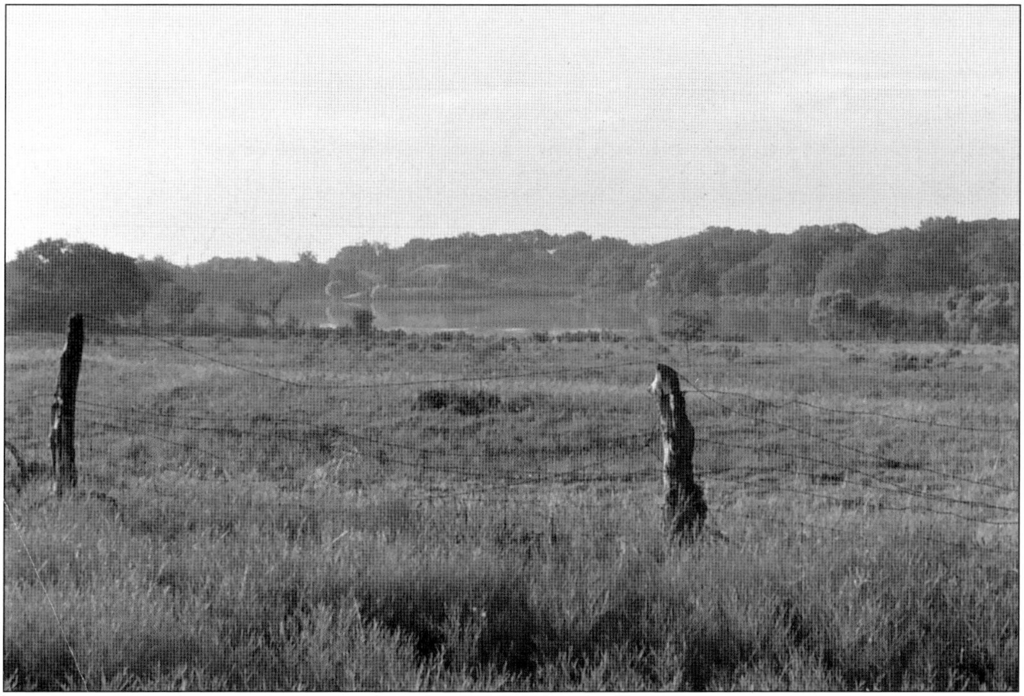

First mapped as Indian Creek, then Little Green Creek, today's Bell Branch runs beyond this 130-year-old barbed wire fence. A Native American village once existed in this flatland near the high stone knoll along the far bank. By 1860, the peaceful Anadarko and Caddo tribes had left the area. (Judith Robbins Lemons.)

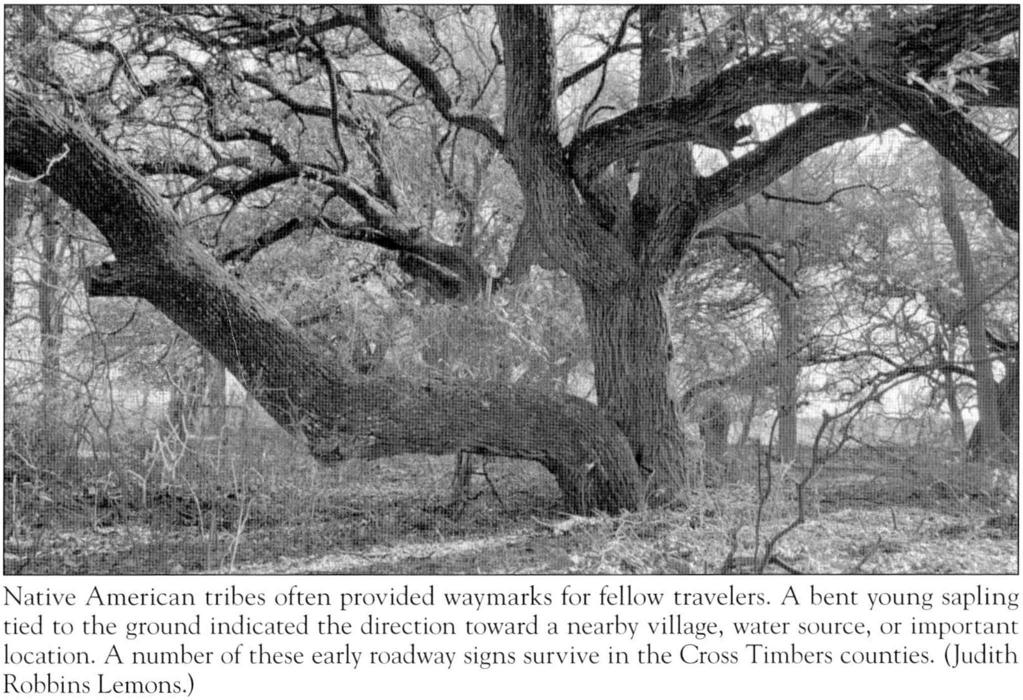

Native American tribes often provided waymarks for fellow travelers. A bent young sapling tied to the ground indicated the direction toward a nearby village, water source, or important location. A number of these early roadway signs survive in the Cross Timbers counties. (Judith Robbins Lemons.)

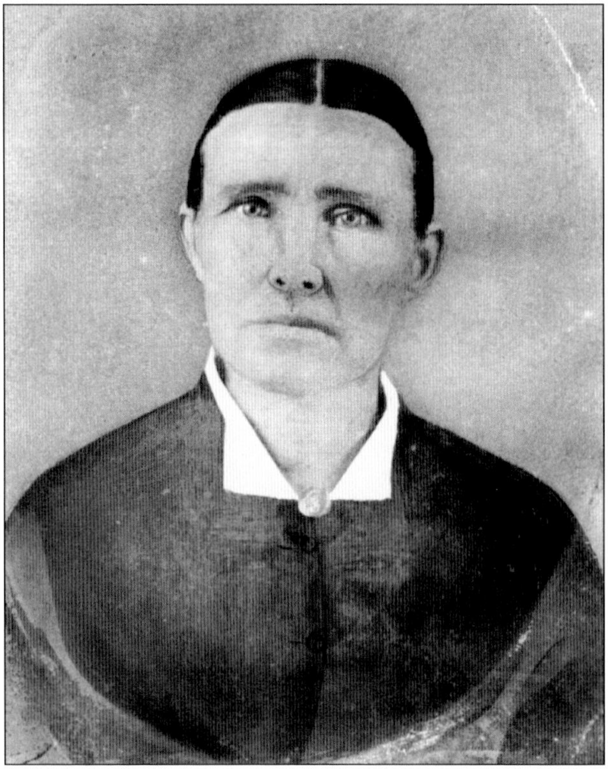

Warned of Gen. Antonio López de Santa Anna's approaching army, in the Runaway Scrape, Emily Ann Howard's mother led an oxcart of belongings and her three children to the river. Because the weight of wet feather mattresses could sink a barge, filling was removed to save the ticking. The riverbanks appeared to be blanketed in snow. Howard's family were settlers in Austin's Second Colony, and Emily's father, John, received a land grant for his military service. (JBH.)

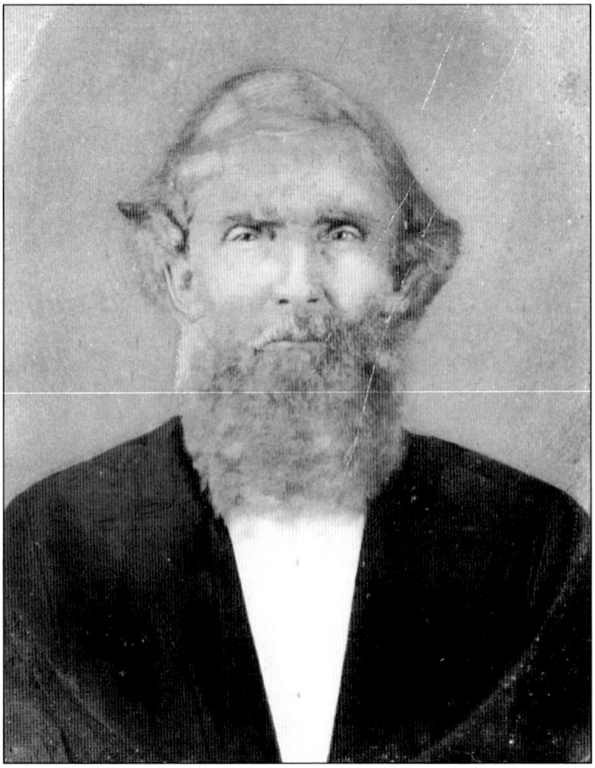

Many people who arrived before 1860 took advantage of open-range grazing to raise livestock. Emily Ann Howard (pictured above) and Rufus Bean White (pictured here) came to the area in 1855 with the J.M. Stephen group. White, Stephen, and about 45 others were canvased as stock raisers in 1860, while some 25 were reported to be farmers. Because these newcomers were encroaching on Comanche hunting grounds, a group of minutemen were utilized to counter attacks. (JBH.)

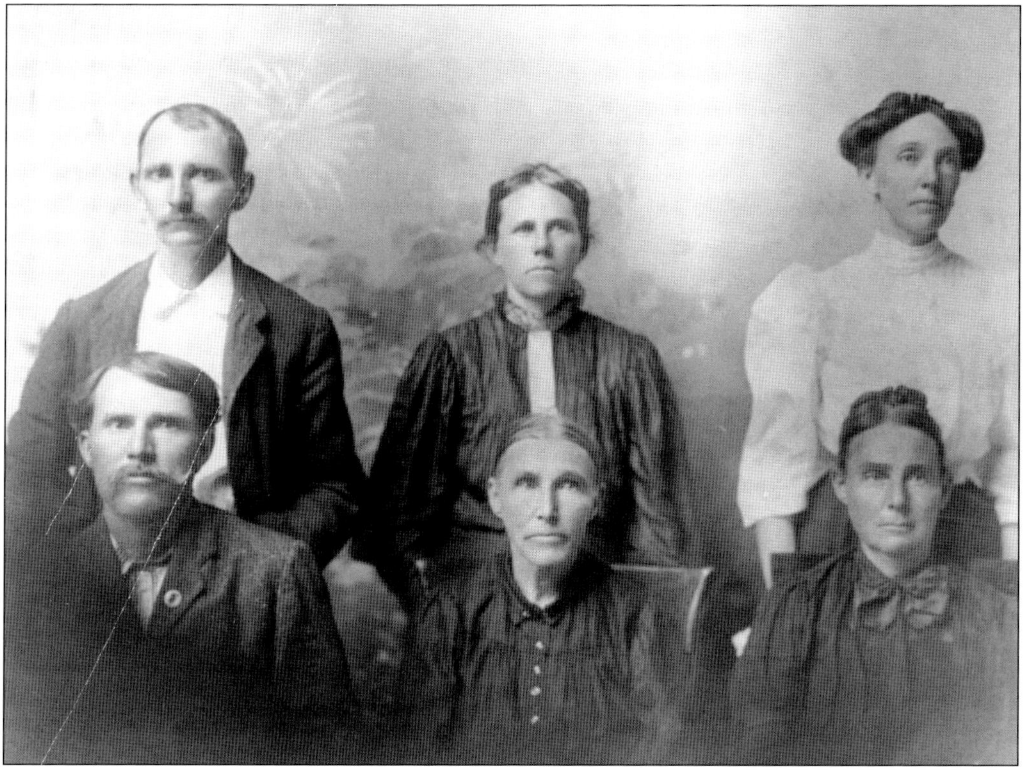

Emily Ann Howard, daughter of Sarah Gage Burleson and John Howard, gave birth to 12 of Rufus White's 13 children. Emily was 10 years his junior and outlived Rufus and six of their children. From left to right are (first row) Samuel Black White, Emily Ann Howard White, and Sarah Frances "Sallie" White Burnett; (second row) Leander Jackson White, Louisa Jane White Barbee, and Panola Octavia "Nola" White Mason. (JBH.)

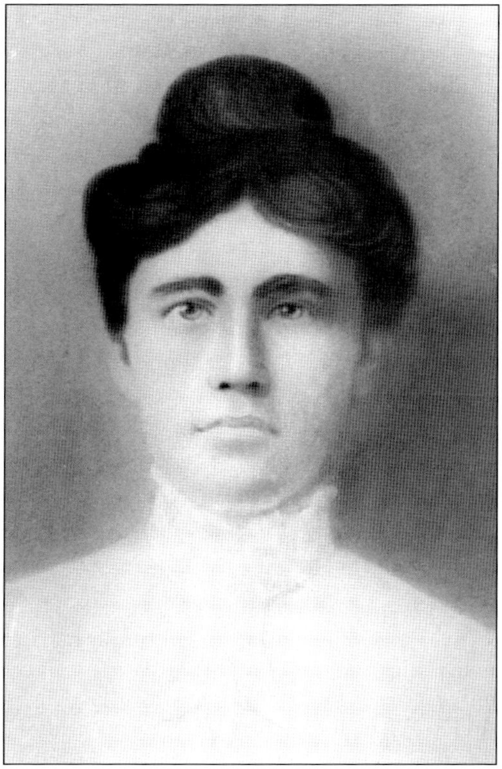

Before her marriage to William Henry Mason, Panola owned a place in Edna Hill. Her mother, Emily Ann Howard, came to care for her and the children. At age 47, when she knew she was dying of breast cancer, Panola entrusted her youngest son, six-year-old John Henry Mason, to her sister Louisa Jane White Barbee to raise. (JBH.)

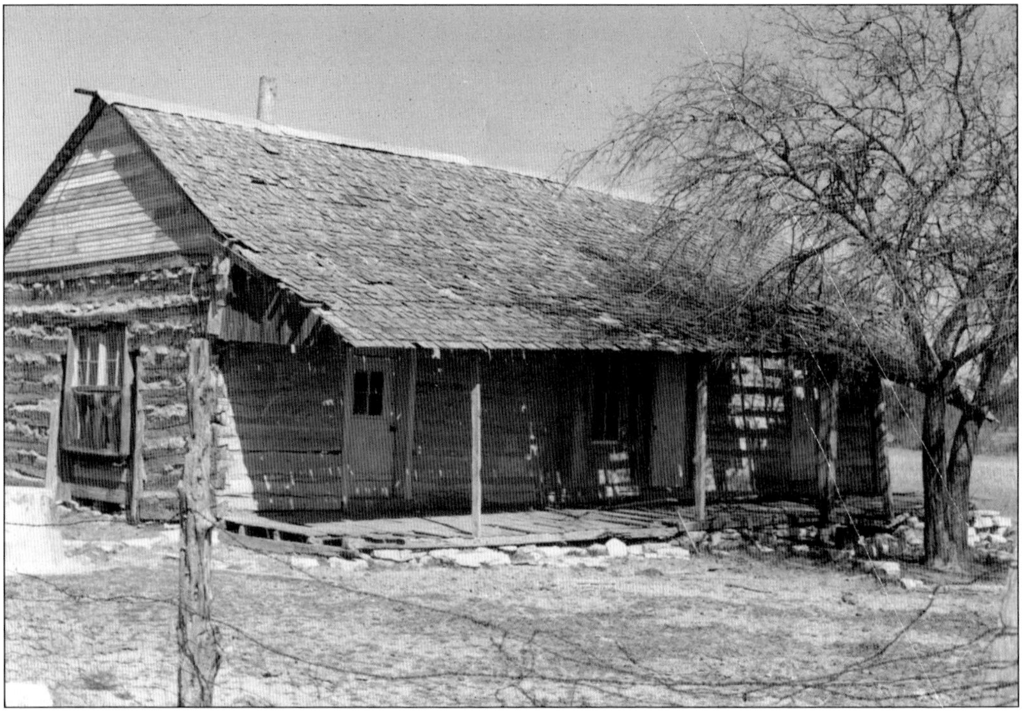

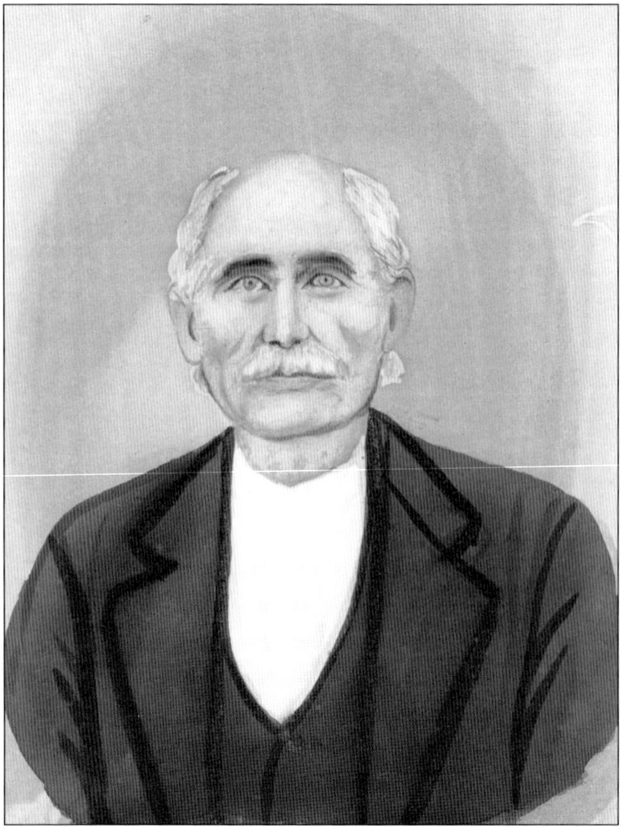

Chesley Turnbow traded two Tennessee mares—valued at $500—to James Stephen for 500 acres on Resley Creek. Turnbow built a double cabin with a central breezeway and immense fireplaces at the east and west ends. After Turnbow's best horses were stolen, assumedly by Native Americans, he moved about 15 miles east and rebuilt on Greens Creek. Others in the Turnbow-Gilbreath clan stayed on Resley Creek. Jones Barbee (left) bought the Turnbow cabin and acreage in 1858. The Turnbow-Barbee cabin served as a place for school, church, weddings, and safety. In 1859, when 10-year-old Sidney Barbee died of scarlet fever, his was the first burial at what became Barbee Cemetery. Killed by Native Americans, teenager Sam Houston Kuykendall was buried there in the summer of 1861. The cabin served as a residence for 100 years. (Both, JBH.)

Hiram, the oldest son of Jones Barbee, was a wagon train scout, Texas Ranger, Confederate soldier, rancher, vigilante, land dealer, and deacon. Having purchased an East Texas Railroad land grant, he donated a portion for the Lone Star school, where both Baptists and Methodists met. Hiram and his first wife, Orlena Emmiline Jeffries, had two children, Mary Jane Barbee Landes and John Franklin Barbee. Orlena died of yellow fever in 1862. (JBH.)

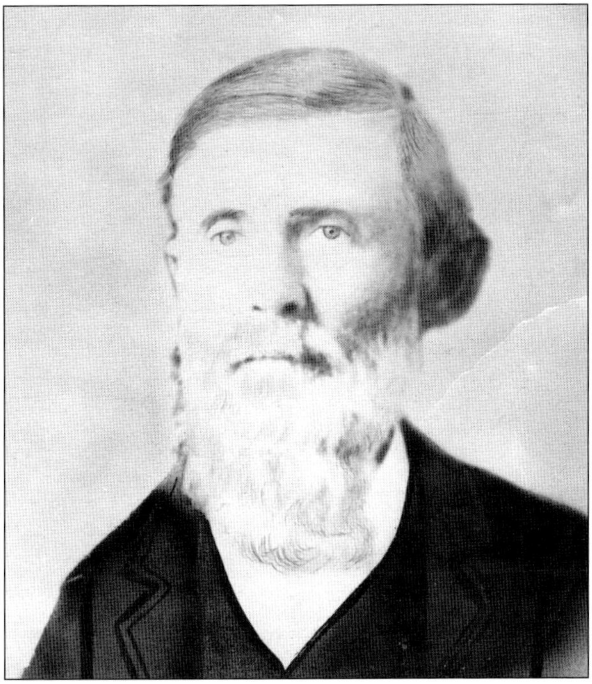

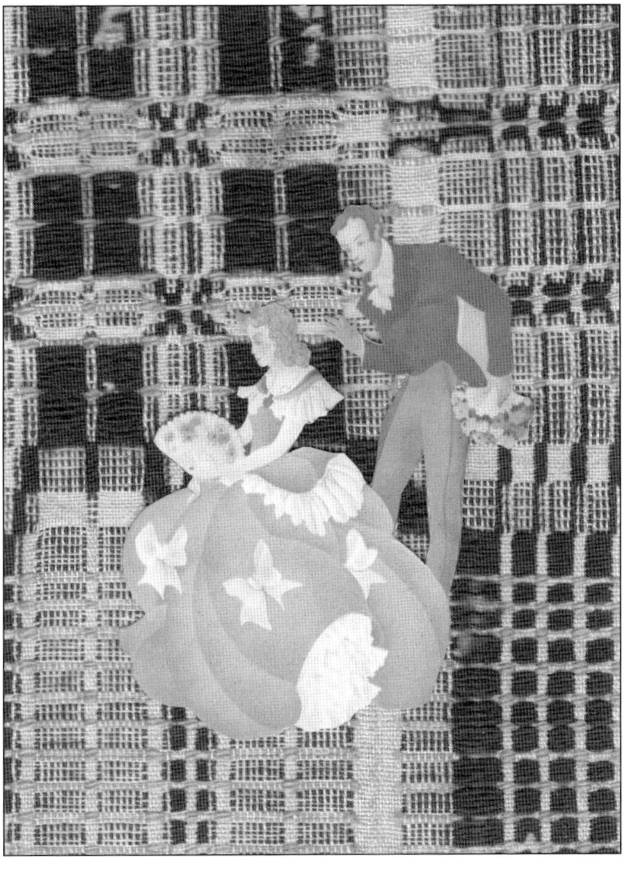

Orlena Barbee raised sheep, spun wool, weaved cloth, cast dye, and sewed a bed comforter. Local women made an annual trip to a spot on the Leon River to gather red clay for red dye. Cuttings of the old, worn comforter were framed with decorative cut paper silhouettes and shared with descendants. (JBH.)

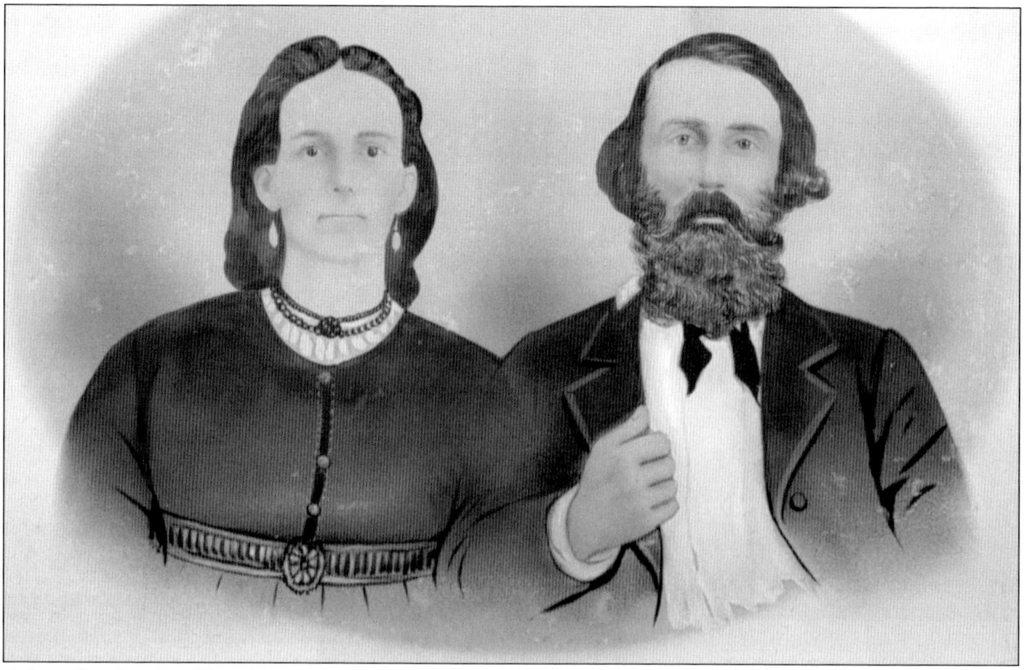

After the death of his first wife, Orlena, Hiram Barbee left to serve with the Confederate 30th Texas Cavalry, Company G. His sister Mary Capell cared for his toddler, Mary Jane, and his parents, Frances Lloyd and Jones Barbee, kept his baby, John Franklin. In 1867, Hiram married Candace Durham Powers (left) who taught at the Cora school. She was a great cook, and her family operated a bakery in Comanche. She had her own cattle brand. (JBH.)

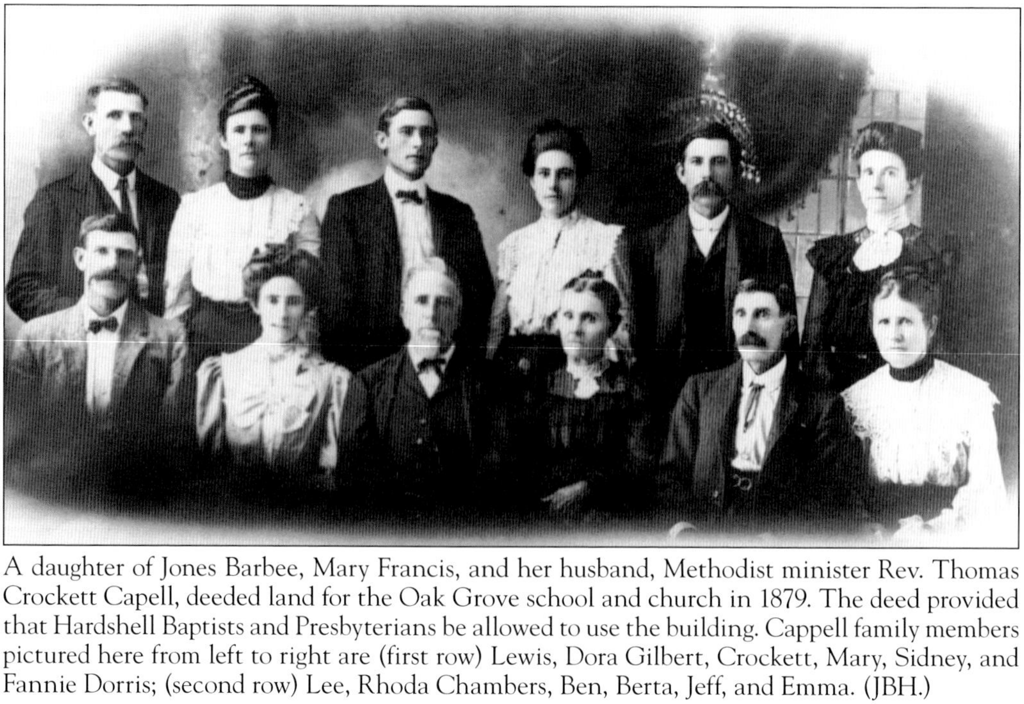

A daughter of Jones Barbee, Mary Francis, and her husband, Methodist minister Rev. Thomas Crockett Capell, deeded land for the Oak Grove school and church in 1879. The deed provided that Hardshell Baptists and Presbyterians be allowed to use the building. Cappell family members pictured here from left to right are (first row) Lewis, Dora Gilbert, Crockett, Mary, Sidney, and Fannie Dorris; (second row) Lee, Rhoda Chambers, Ben, Berta, Jeff, and Emma. (JBH.)

In 1864, eighteen-year-old Walter Kern Barbee, son of Frances Lloyd and Jones Barbee, served with the Second Frontier District Home Guard, commanded by Maj. George B. Erath. Walter and his first wife, Sarah Elizabeth Martin, had 11 children. Walter had one son with his second wife, Lily Luda Smoot. Walter frequently served on district court juries, ran for office, and was a recognized community leader. (JBH.)

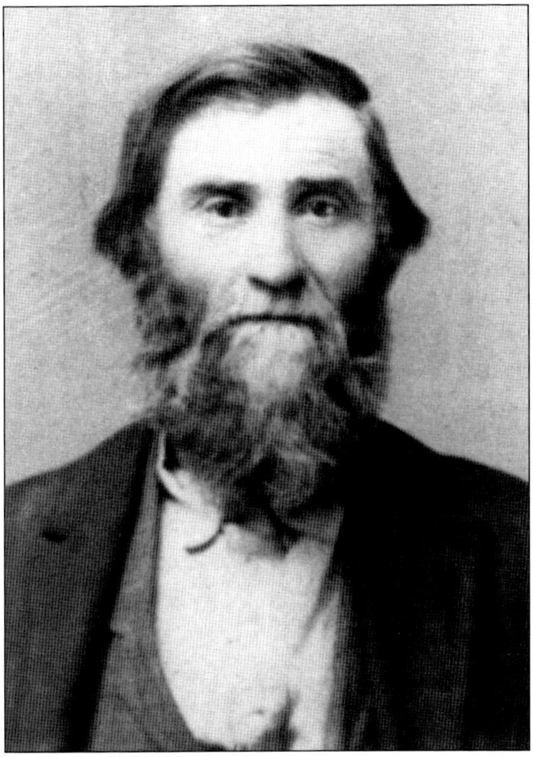

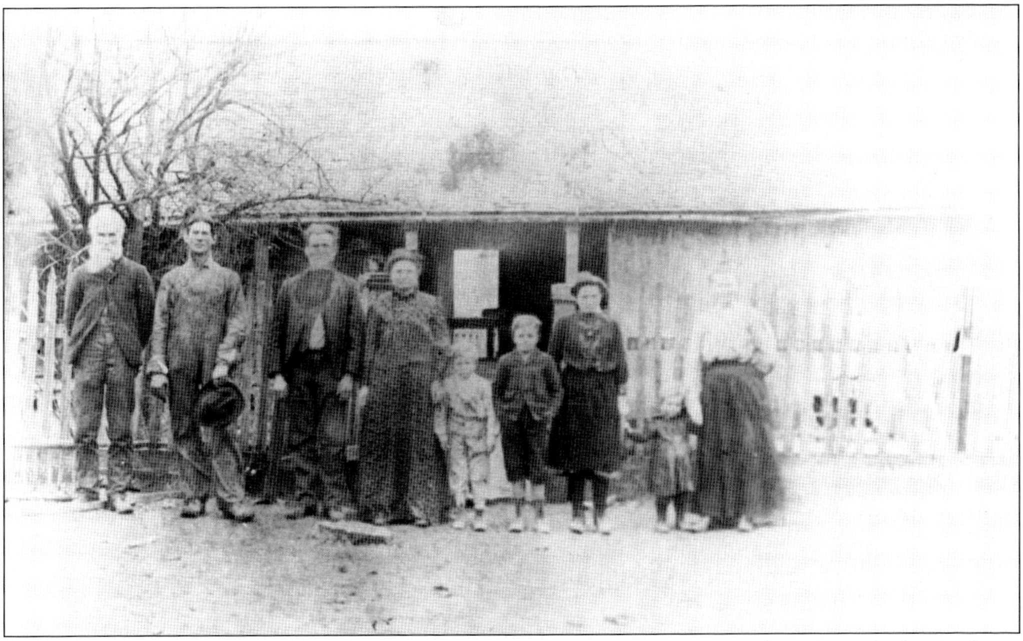

In 1877, extended family and neighbors formed a cooperative gin at Walter Kern Barbee's place. Seeded cotton was removed from the wagon by basket to a platform eight feet above the ground. Cotton was hand-fed into a stand to separate seed from lint. Lint was carried by basket to the press, which was powered by a steam engine using the water of Resley Creek. The gin closed in 1903. (JBH.)

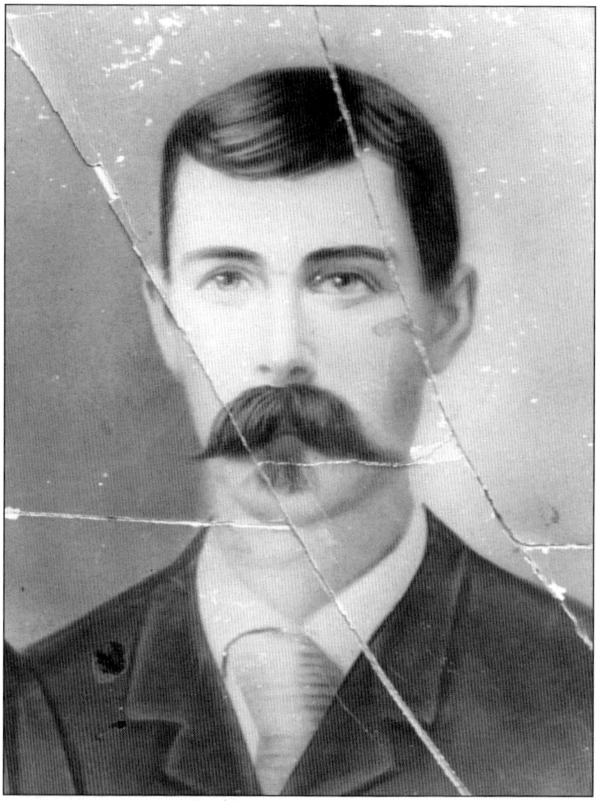

In the mid-1860s, while hidden in the barn loft, young John Franklin Barbee watched as Comanche raiders stole his first pony. In 1867, John's grandfather Jones Barbee sent five-year-old John on their fastest horse to warn neighbors that "Indians" were in the area. As children, John and his sister Mary Jane hid beneath the riverbank when their fishing was interrupted by a passing band of Native Americans. (JBH.)

John Franklin Barbee was a landowner, merchant, and storekeeper in Edna Hill. He and his wife, Louisa Jane White, had eight children. From left to right are (first row, seated) John Franklin, Clayton (first grandchild), Zora Octavia "Tava," and Louisa Jane; (second row, standing) Orlena Candace, Dee Rufus, Ernest H. "Johnnie," Minnie (married to son Walter), Walter, Naoma "Oma" Ethel, and Annie Pearl. (JBH.)

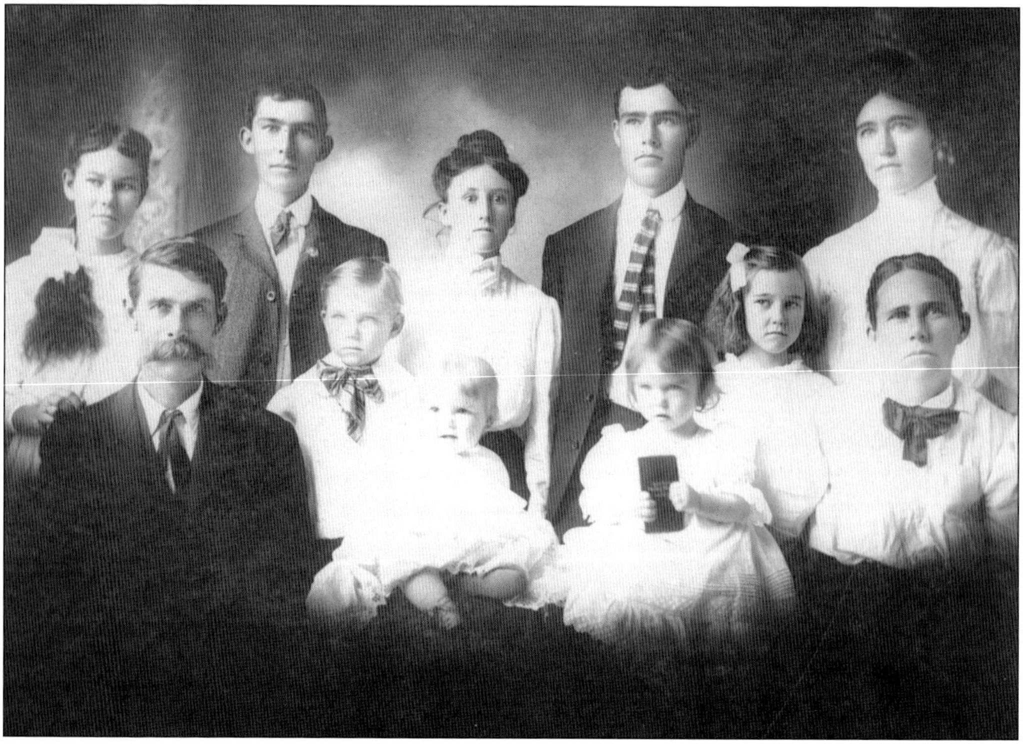

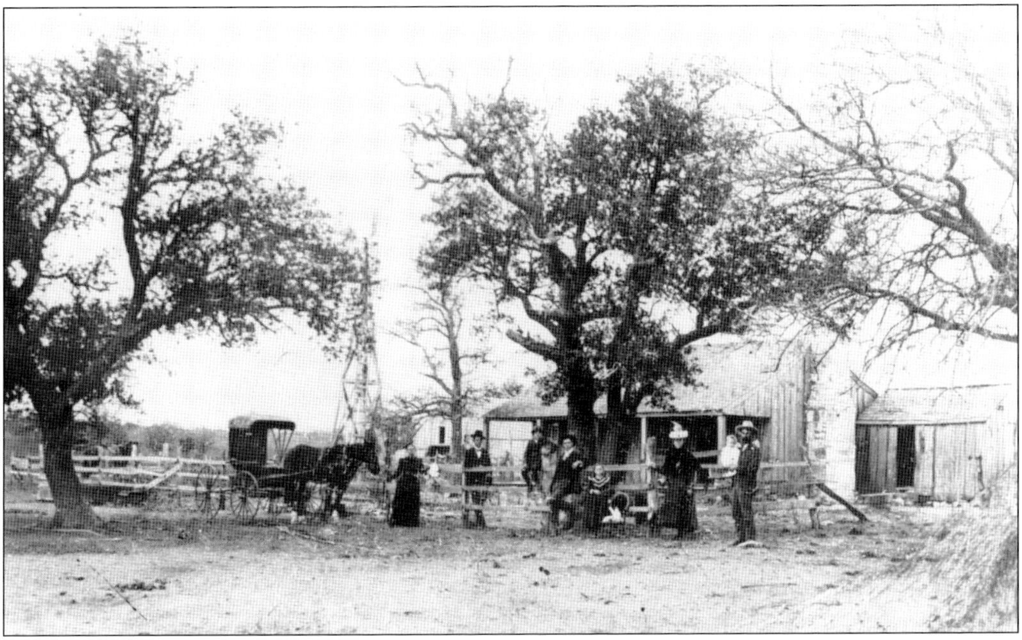

John Franklin Barbee bought land adjoining the holdings of his father, Hiram Barbee. Walter Barbee's saddle horse Nickels is standing in the corral at far left. Louisa Jane is holding the reins of buggy horse Blackhawk. A neighbor, Arthur Woods, is behind the fence. Dee Rufus is sitting on the fence next to Walter. Orlena "Lena" Candace poses beside her doll. Annie Pearl is wearing a hat. John Franklin is holding baby Naomi "Oma" Ethel. (JBH.)

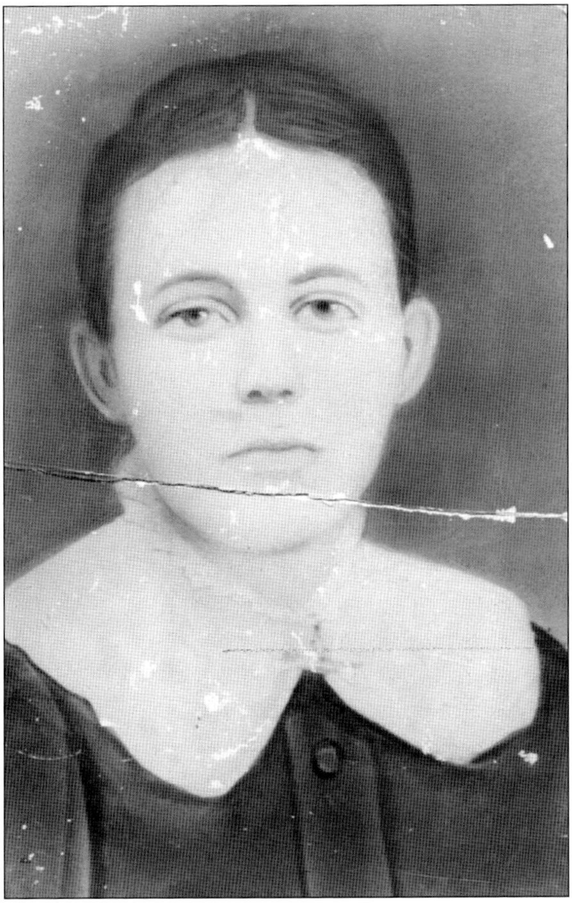

In their younger years, John and Louisa Jane Barbee (pictured) attended round games (square dancing). In their senior years, when their grandchildren were trying to polka in the living room, the youngsters were shocked when their lifelong Baptist grandparents demonstrated how it was done. John and Louisa danced until both were winded and fell on the couch laughing. (JBH.)

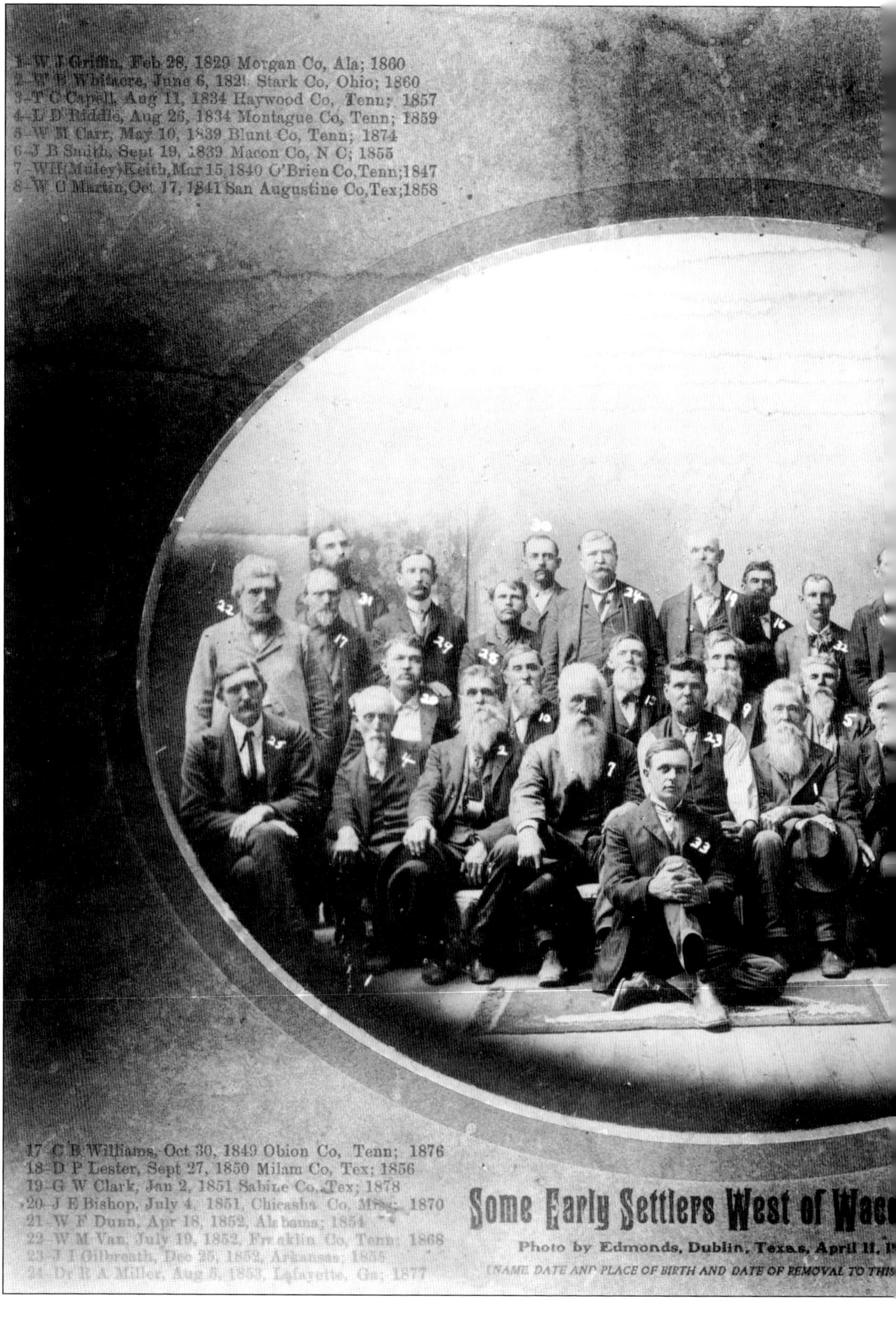
1-W J Griffin, Feb 28, 1829 Morgan Co, Ala; 1860
2-W E Whitacre, June 6, 1829 Stark Co, Ohio; 1860
3-T C Capell, Aug 11, 1834 Haywood Co, Tenn; 1857
4-L D Riddle, Aug 26, 1834 Montague Co, Tenn; 1859
5-W M Carr, May 10, 1839 Blunt Co, Tenn; 1874
6-J B Smith, Sept 19, 1839 Macon Co, N C; 1855
7-WH(Muley)Keith, Mar 15, 1840 O'Brien Co, Tenn; 1847
8-W C Martin, Oct 17, 1841 San Augustine Co, Tex; 1858
17-C B Williams, Oct 30, 1849 Obion Co, Tenn; 1876
18-D P Lester, Sept 27, 1850 Milam Co, Tex; 1856
19-G W Clark, Jan 2, 1851 Sabine Co, Tex; 1878
20-J E Bishop, July 4, 1851, Chicasha Co, Miss; 1870
21-W F Dunn, Apr 18, 1852, Alabama; 1854
22-W M Van, July 19, 1852, Franklin Co, Tenn; 1868
Some Early Settlers West of Wac
Photo by Edmonds, Dublin, Texas, April 11, 1
NAME, DATE AND PLACE OF BIRTH AND DATE OF REMOVAL TO THIS

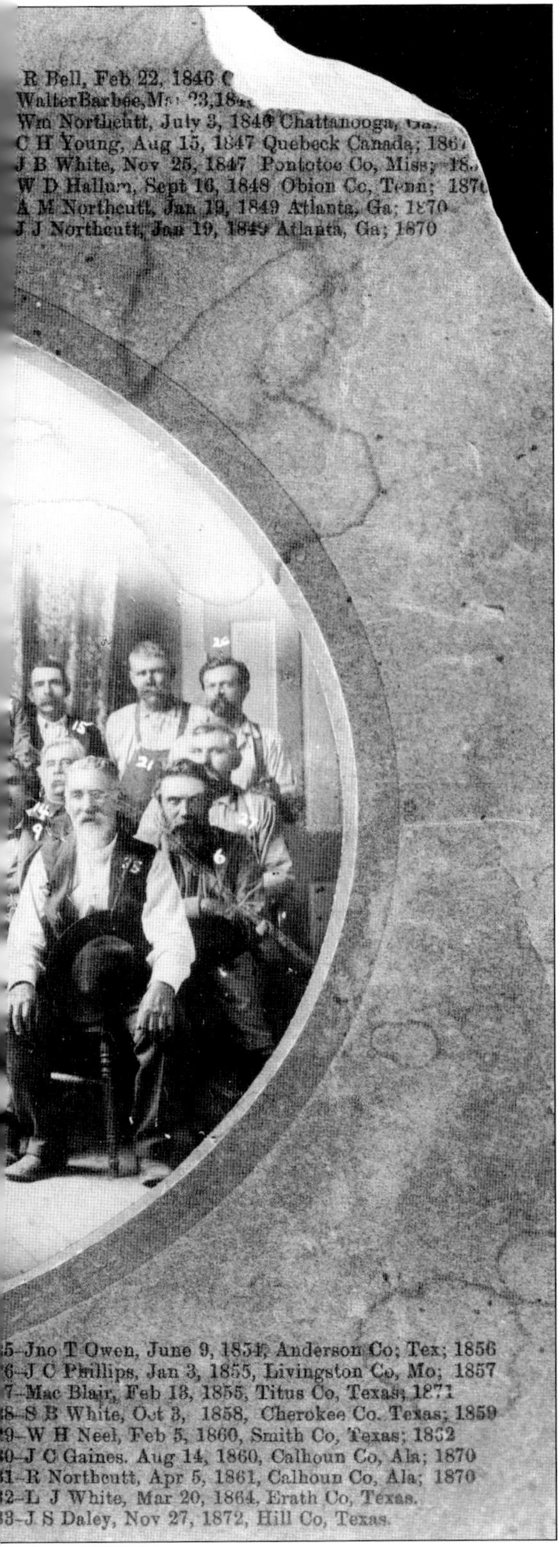

At the urging of William Harrison "Muley" Keith, early settlers were invited to a Dublin gathering on April 11, 1903. A souvenir photograph was taken by J.F. Edmonds and made available for 50¢. The date and place of birth is recorded for each person pictured, followed by the year of their arrival in Erath County. The significance of being in the area before 1870 may be attributable to the fact that the last Native American raids in Texas occurred in the early 1870s, before the Red River War. Those in the region prior to that date lived under constant threat of attack.

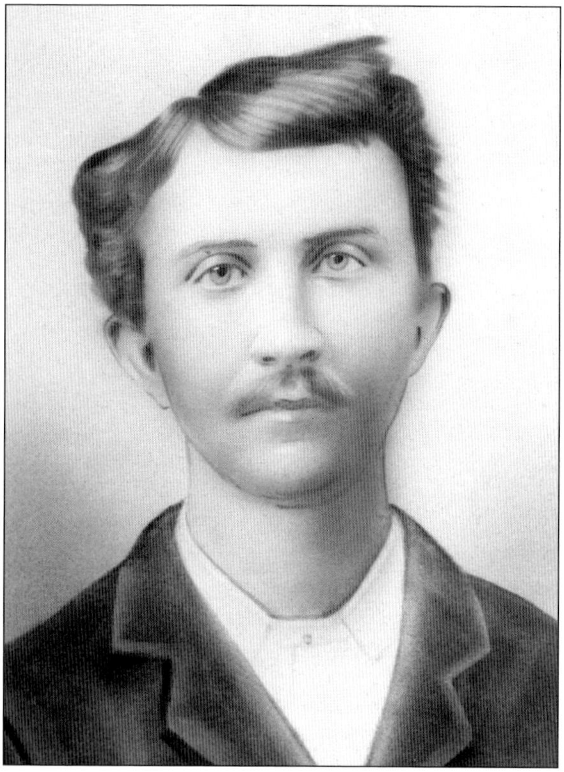

Jesse Absolom Looney (pictured) and his wife, Ella Elizabeth Sharp, had four children: Helen Alma, Lula Lee, Lucia Florence, and Carl Gordon Looney. Jesse worked as a veterinarian and owned a blacksmith shop in Comanche. He told customers that if he did not heal their horses, they did not have to pay. In their senior years, Jesse and Ella lived in Erath's Little Mexico community. (JBH.)

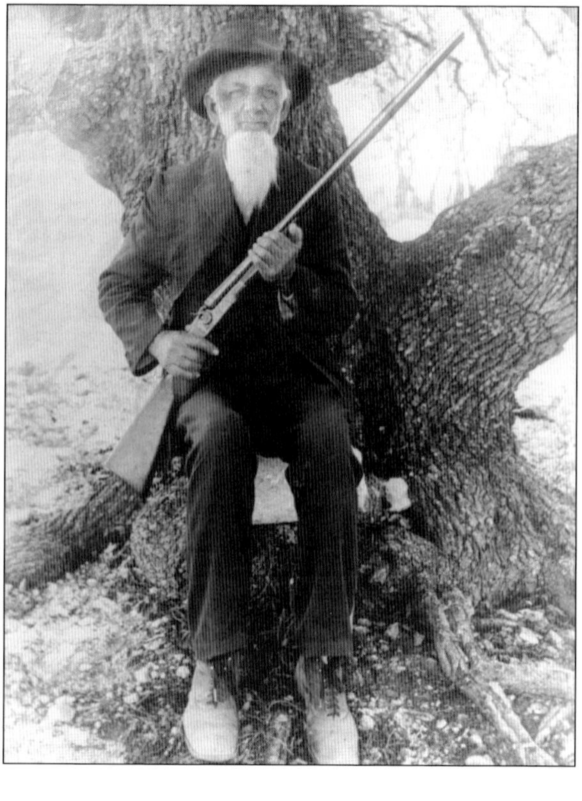

Married in 1858, Tennessee born Lucinda McNatt and Harold Wiggins Daniel (pictured) had seven daughters and one son. After serving with Company E of the Union's Sixth Missouri Cavalry, Harold moved his family to Arkansas. By 1890, the Daniel family was farming near Purves, where the Daniel daughters married into the Ascue, Brazille, Jones, Lincoln, and Turney families. Several of them are buried at Live Oak Cemetery.

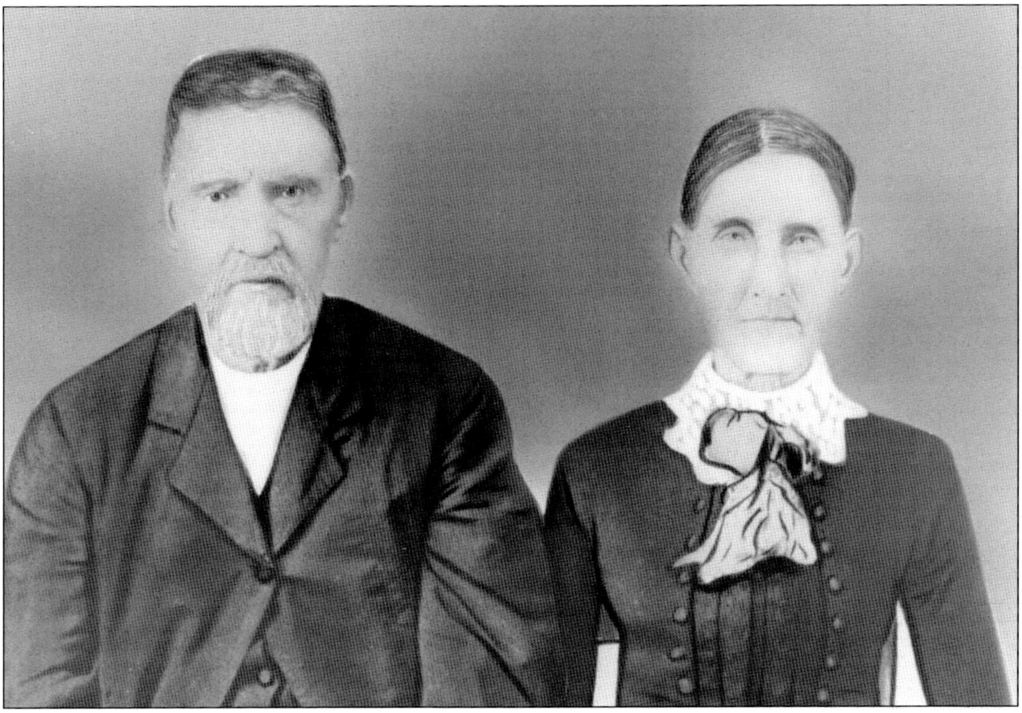

Mary Norred and John Sanders Howell left Alabama for post-Reconstruction Texas. After more than 10 years in Hill County, they moved to the Edna Hill community. John's February 1891 obituary cited him as a lifelong Methodist and a Mason for over 30 years. Mary and John are buried at the Barbee Cemetery. (JBH.)

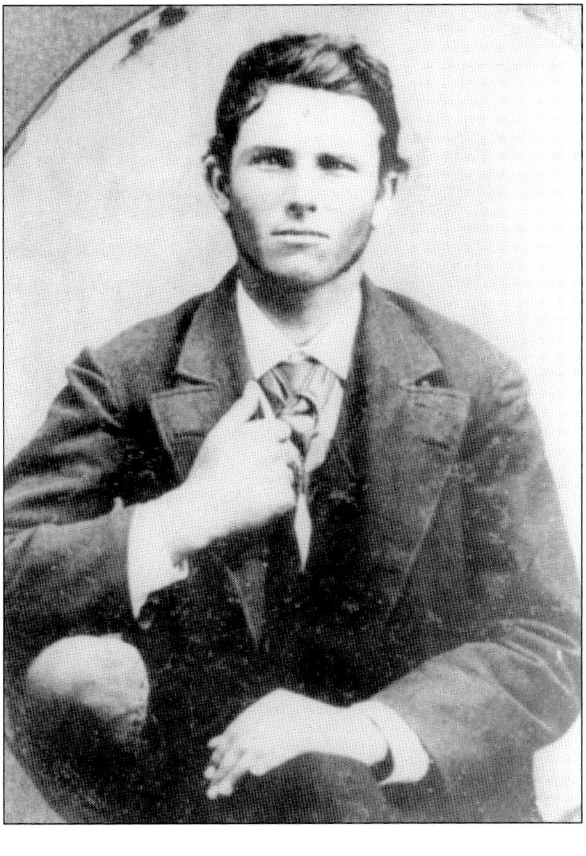

Named for his paternal grandfather, John Archibald McNeill was the son of Mary Abrilla Stephen and Dr. William W. McNeill. John's maternal grandfather, John Miller Stephen, the founder of Stephenville, led 30 people to establish the county and donated land for the county seat. Around age 50, John Archibald moved his family to Oregon, where he owned and managed a fruit farm. (SHHM.)

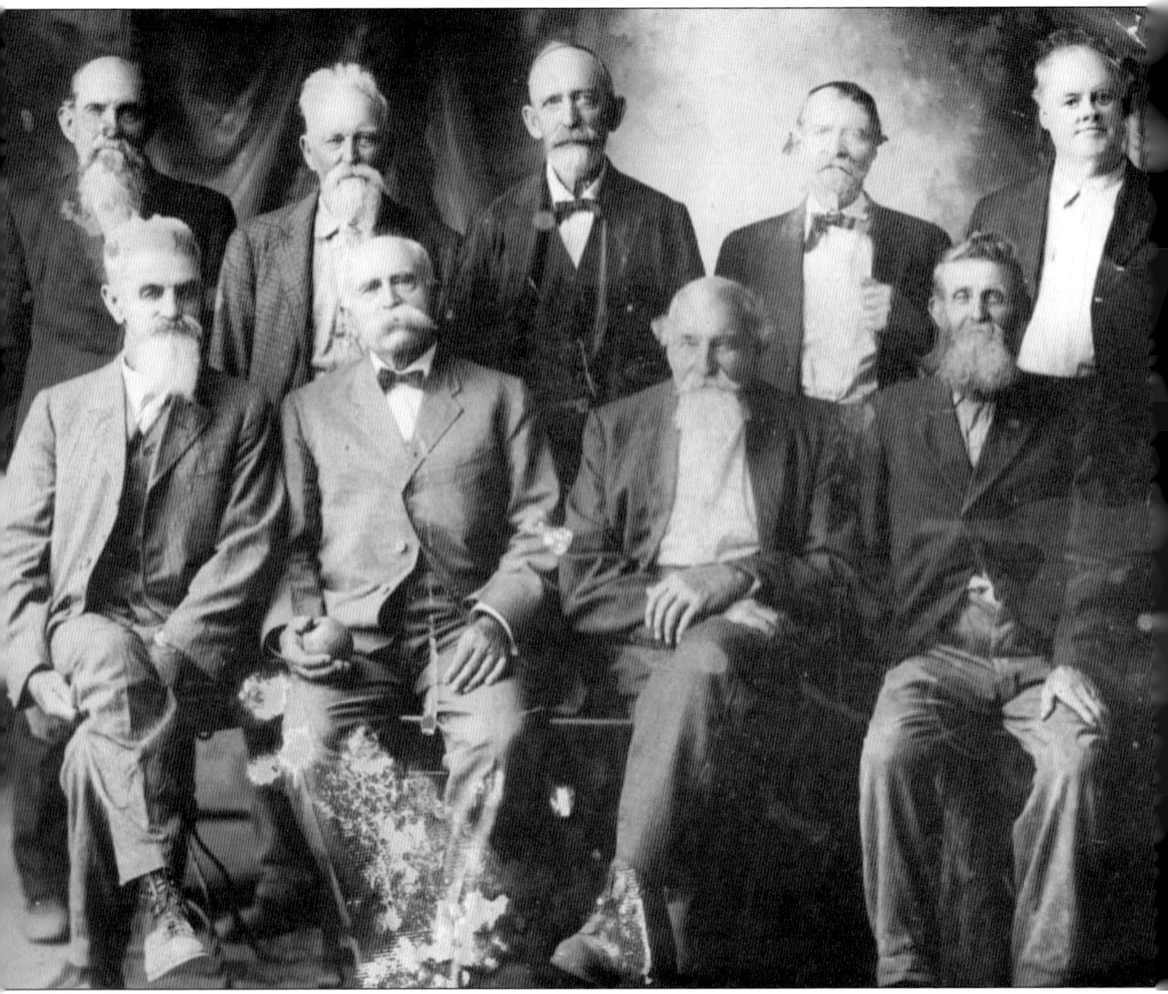

Representing those who arrived in the area before 1865, these men came as youngsters with their parents. From left to right are (first row) John James Kelly, James Miller Stephen, William Jasper Mefferd, and unidentified (possibly Tom Arnold or Lindsay Pickney "L.P." Evans); (second row) Samuel Vaughn "Pete" Edwards, George Washington Lidia, Isaac Newton Roberts, Jimmy Roberts, and Condy Toliver. A stonemason by occupation and member of the Masons, Kelly was an alderman, county treasurer, and charter member of Stephenville's Masonic lodge. Edwards, Evans, Kelly, Mefferd, I.N. Roberts, and Stephen served with the local militia. Toliver rode with the deputy sheriff. Arnold was a cotton ginner on Sims Creek at Selden. I.N. and Jimmy Roberts served as county commissioners. Evans, son of Baptist reverend Silas Evans of Pony Creek and Johnsville, was a Democratic Party leader. Clairette stockman Edwards served as a school trustee. Lidia was a wheat farmer who ran an Oak Dale granary. Here, Stephen holds a cannonball, and the unidentified man may be missing his right arm. (SHHM.)

Two

Living off the Land

Boards cut from native oak trees covered one- or two-room log structures. Floors were dirt or rough lumber planks. Lime and sand mortar, or clay, filled the gaps between logs. A large cooking fireplace provided indoor warmth. Some kitchens were separate or outdoors. A fire was always burning in the hearth, or someone went to borrow fire from a neighbor, as matches were a nonexistent luxury. Candle or coal oil provided light at night. Each item was utilized. Wood ashes were saved to make lye, and lye was used to make soap. Corn shucks and straw were used to fill mattresses. A duck or goose feather bed was an achievable refinement. A dry year meant no feed crop and livestock having to graze freely. Wandering stock chanced encounters with Native Americans. The winters of 1884 through 1887 were severe. An estimated 50 percent loss of livestock followed the blizzard of 1887.

Walking was the primary means of transportation. A buggy or carriage was convenient, but a wagon was a necessity. The wagon was used to gather crops, bring in forage for livestock, haul water and wood from the stream, and carry goods to and from town. A reliable ox wagon was essential to haul goods to and from Fort Worth or Waco.

One man with one horse could furrow the soil with a steel plow. A second pass or second individual dropped the seed. Another pass by the plow would cover the seed. At harvest, a cotton field worker dragged an eight-foot sack that could hold 25 pounds of cotton.

Women spun wool to make yarn and carded cotton to weave cloth. Hand-sewing continued until the financially fortunate could purchase a 20th-century machine. Although authorities urged crop rotation, it was the boll weevil, exhausted soils, and unprofitable prices that led to change. Drought and disease brought depression to regional agriculture in the 1920s and 1930s. Growers transitioned to orchards, nurseries, peanuts, poultry, and dairy. Poultry was a major crop in the 1930s. By the mid-1940s, ranching was again the primary means of livelihood in Erath County. Dairy rose to the top as the chief industry in the 1950s.

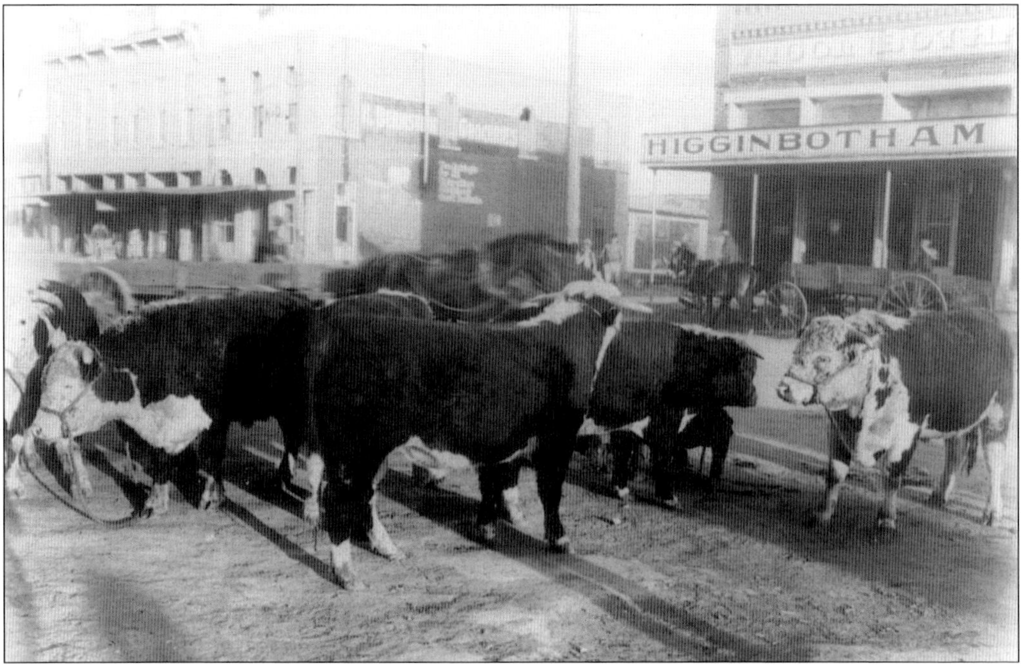

The earliest entrepreneurial settlers sought to make a living by raising livestock on the acres of open range. Wandering cattle required minimal care compared to farmed crops. Fencing was sparse to nonexistent until the late 1880s. Livestock roamed free on public lands until 1889. Marks and brands were registered at a county courthouse. Cattle roamed across multiple counties until roundup time. Calves were branded according to the brand of their mother. Stock raisers drove their cattle along a feeder trail between Carlton and Hico that made its way to the main Chisholm Trail. Some cowboys hired out until they could purchase livestock of their own.

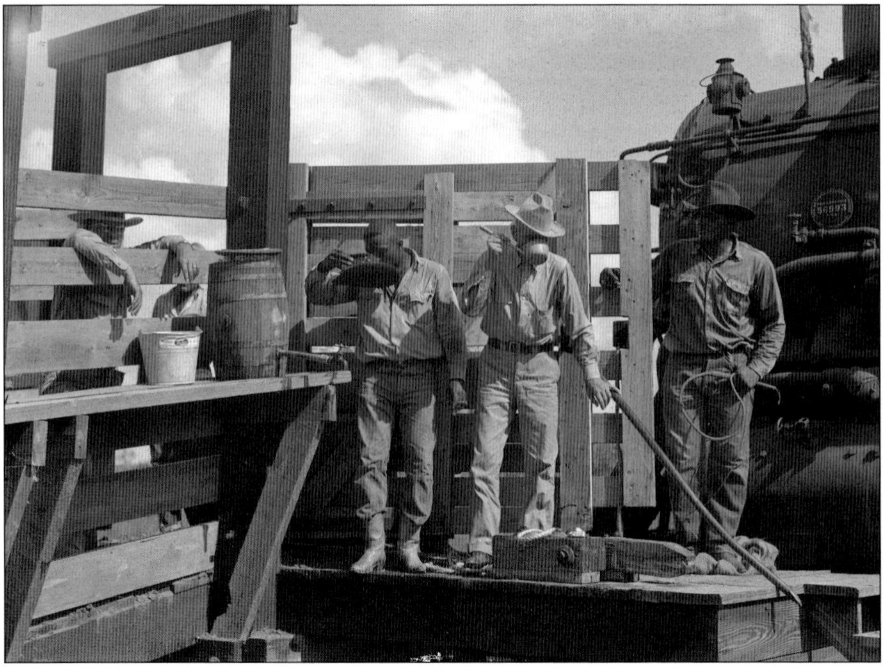

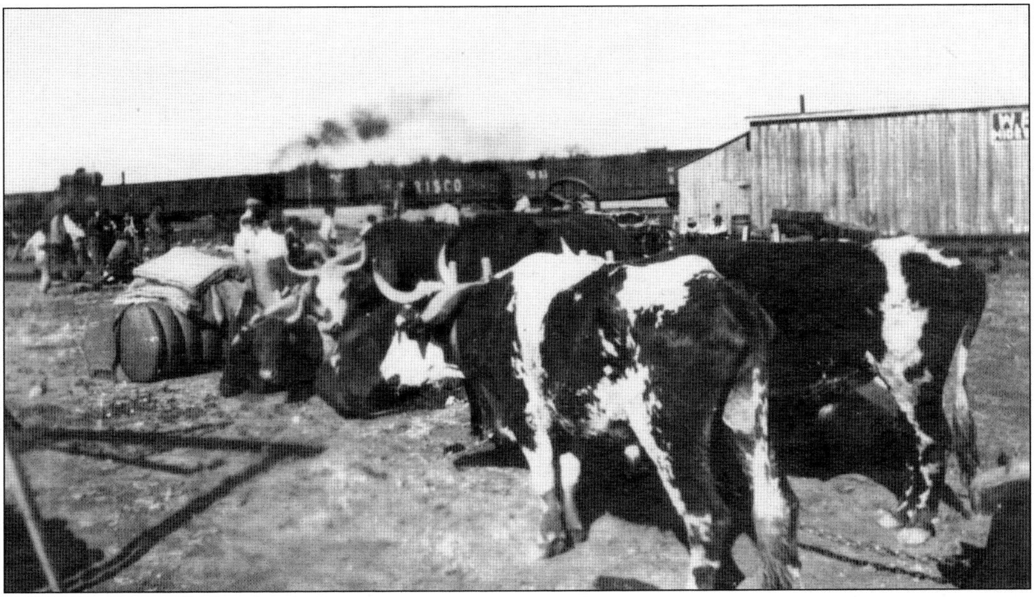

Wagon trains traversed the countryside at oxen speed. While slow, an ox was strong, ate less, and cost less than a horse or mule. Frontier newcomers learned that Native Americans were less likely to steal oxen than horses. When the Lone Star school was mistakenly built on land other than that donated by Hiram Barbee, John Knox pulled the schoolhouse to Barbee property using his oxen team.

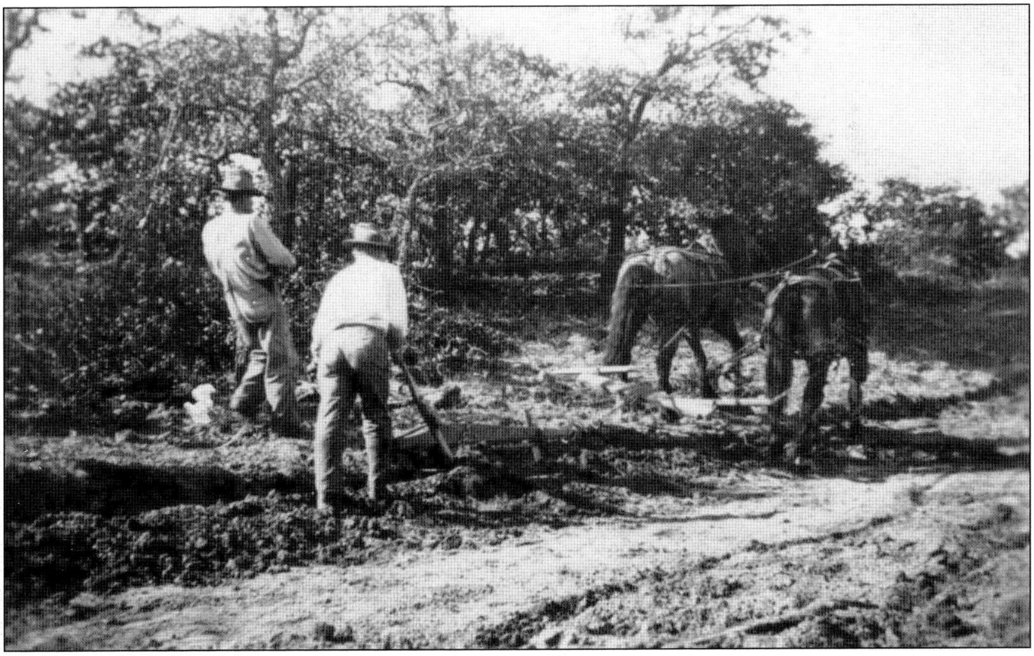

Families continued to live from their wagons indefinitely, as laying in a crop took priority. A wooded area near fresh water had to be cleared. The soil needed to be tilled or "improved." The farmer hitched the oxen or mules to plow. The financial depression of the 1930s delayed the overtaking of horsepower by tractors until the mid-1940s. (Linda Tolston.)

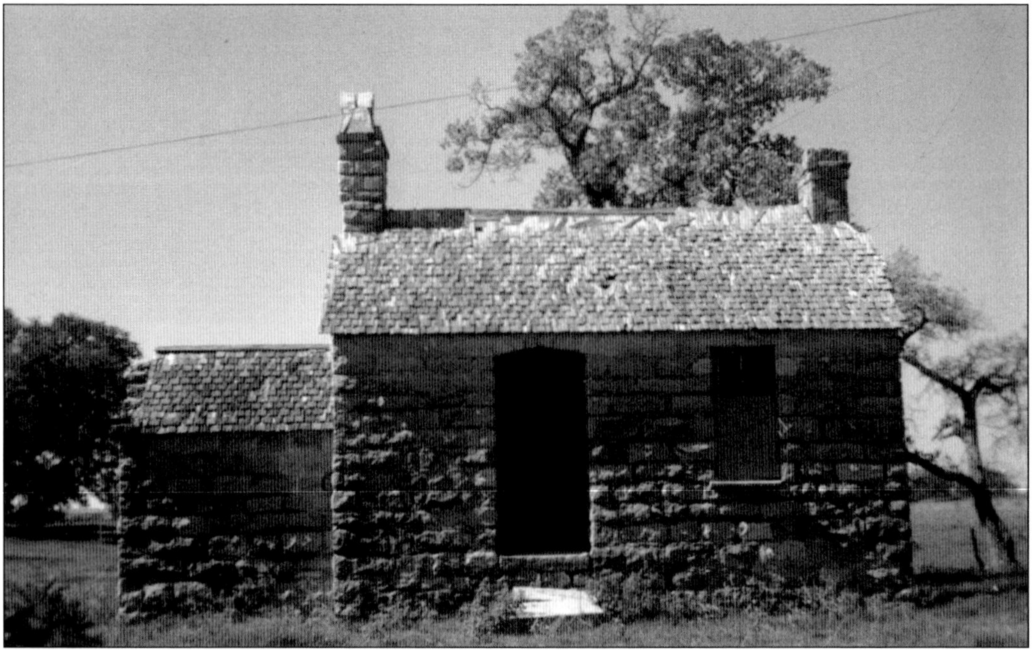

Before refrigeration, a cellar—often called the root cellar—and smokehouse were essential for food storage. Carrots, garlic, onions, potatoes, and turnips are examples of foods kept in the cellar to prevent them from freezing in winter and keeping them cool during the summer heat. The smokehouse was used as a place to season, cook, and store meat as well as protect it from theft. Salt-curing and smoking preserved the meat for a short while. (SHHM.)

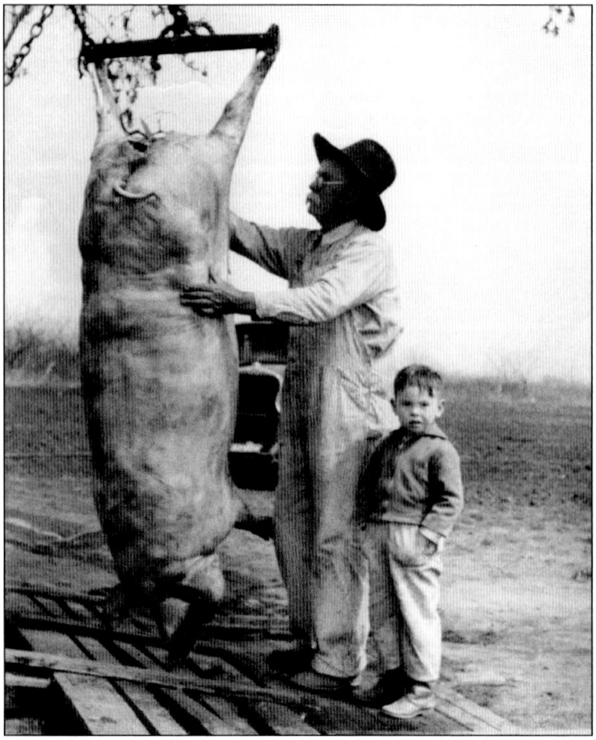

Excess food and milk were fed to the hogs until the weather cooled. In this March 1936 photograph, James Thomas Gilbreath is butchering a fattened swine for bacon, ham, and ground sausage as his grandson Thomas Ralph Rogers watches. Neighbors often staggered the task of butchering and shared raw meat to avoid spoilage. Salt used for preservation was rinsed off before cooking. Lard was rendered for cooking and making soap.

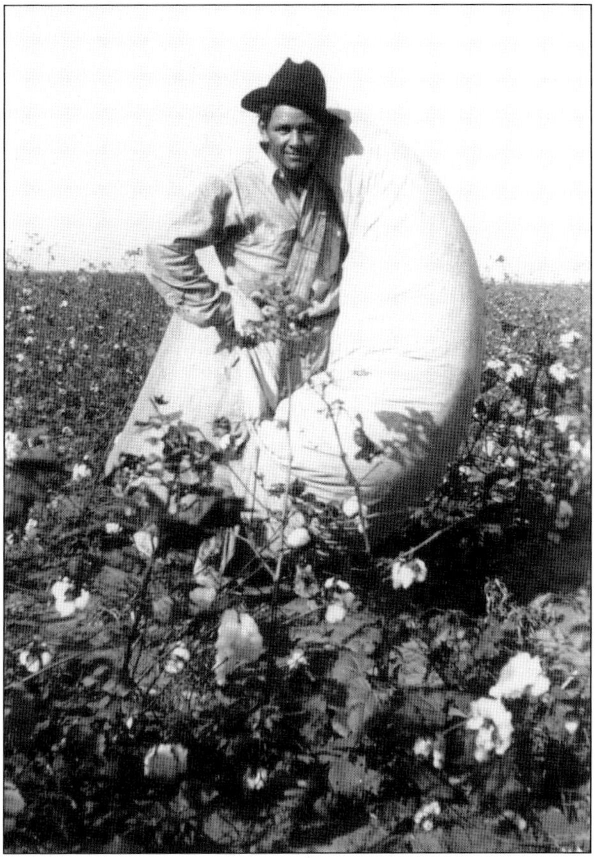

James Thomas "J.T." Gilbreath lived his entire life in the Edna Hill community except for the six years that he served as sheriff of Comanche County. The son of Erath County sheriff John Chesley Gilbreath, J.T. was elected for three terms and served from 1925 to 1931. In his Edna Hill farm bookkeeping ledger, he recorded the number of pounds of cotton picked and wages paid for each worker and family member. Picked cotton was carried by mule or horse-drawn wagon to the nearest cotton gin for processing. In the c. 1934 image below, J.T.'s three-year-old grandson Thomas Ralph Rogers is sitting on his lap on the cotton wagon.

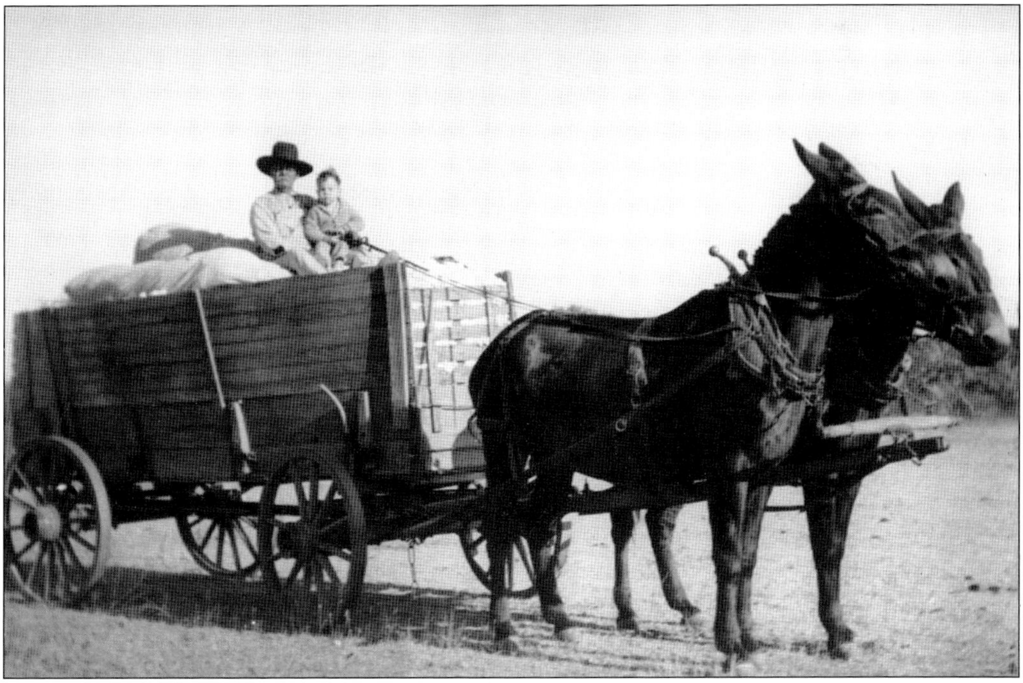

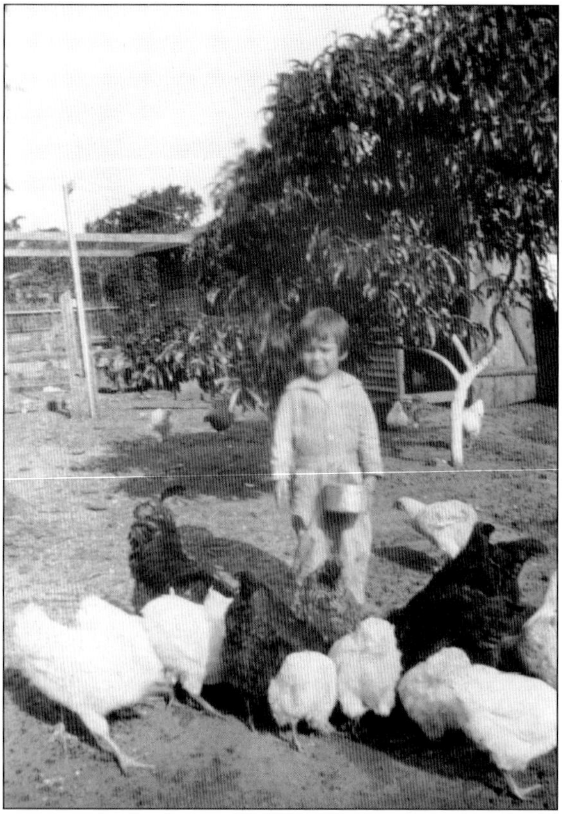

Orpah Iantha Jeanette Howell and Cornelious Samuel Watson, from Alabama, arrived with extended family in Erath just a few years apart and got married in 1886. Making their home near Bluff Dale, they reared nine children. Each family member on the farm has assigned tasks. In 1935, Orpah and Cornelious's granddaughter Betty Jean Kile helped by feeding the chickens on the family farm. (Pamela Kile Pollock McDuff.)

Hard work on the farm could be rewarded with a rich bounty of fresh fruits, vegetables, and meats. When assisted by average temperatures and adequate rainfall, much of the soils of Erath and nearby counties provide the ideal environment for growing produce. In this c. 1915 photograph, from left to right, Bess, Hazel, and Fern Hickey from the Lingleville area cool off on a hot afternoon as they enjoy the season's watermelon. (Connie Conatser McSpadden.)

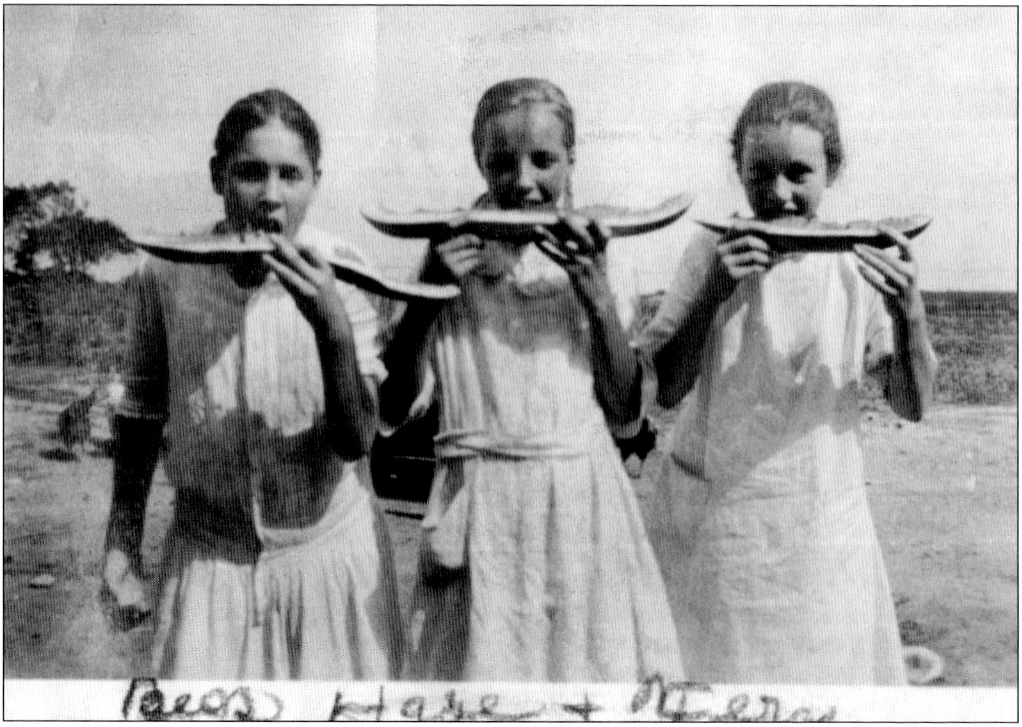

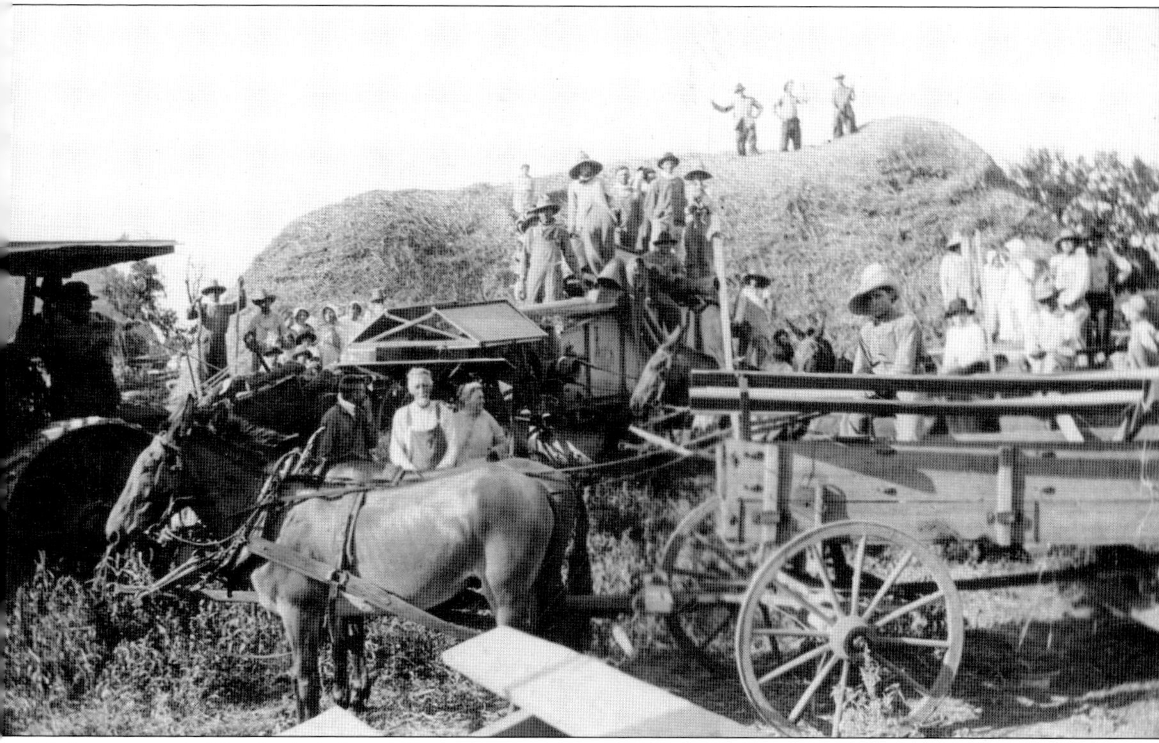

Alabama couple Elizabeth Sides and Marcus Lafayette Dowdy traveled to Texas by covered wagon by 1852 and arrived in Erath in 1871. Not long after settling on the fertile banks of the Bosque River, a band of Comanche raiders stole their horses. By 1878, they moved to a sandy spot south of Clairette and not far from the Hamilton County line. Marcus was an ordained deacon of Hopewell Baptist Church and always ready to help anyone in need. Their oldest son, William Albert Dowdy, married Mary Elizabeth Salmon. Mary was the daughter of Martha Ann Green and Thomas R. Salmon, who arrived in Erath in time for Mary's birth in 1857. In this photograph created by Wiseman Studio, located in nearby Hico, the extended Dowdy and Salmon families are shown threshing hay. (Suzanne Cook Taylor.)

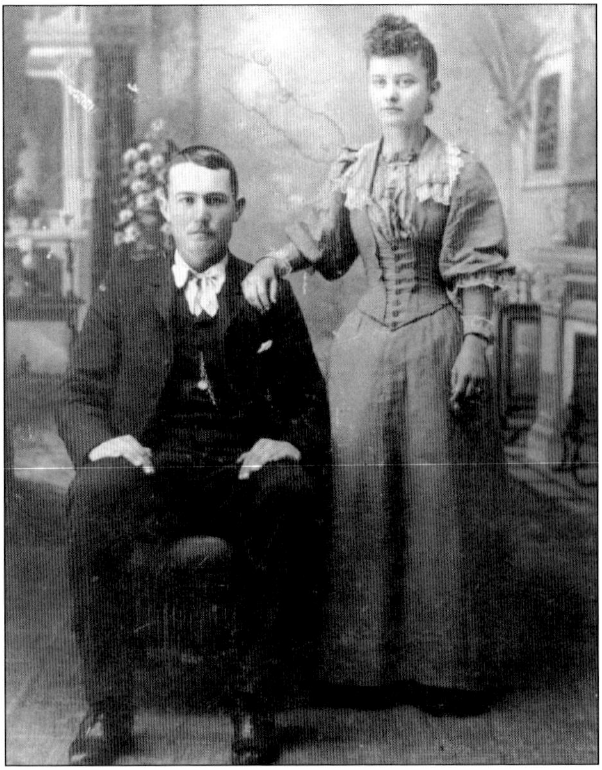

Allie Mae Mason and Washington Percy Hancock grew up on nearby farms in the mid- to late 19th century. Hancock's extended family migrated from Flynn's Lick, Tennessee. His father, Jefferson Blufford, was a charter member of the Morgan Mill Masonic lodge and owned a mercantile store. Married in 1893, Percy and Allie reared five children while maintaining their farm. The Hancocks are buried at the Morgan Mill cemetery.

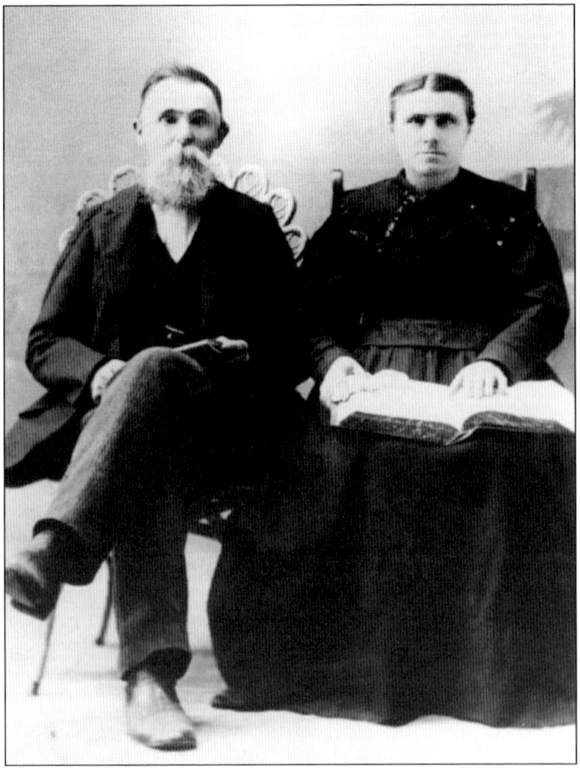

Arriving around 1872 from Limestone County, Mary Elizabeth and William Thomas "Tommy" Hancock reared 11 children while raising cattle, corn, and cotton near Purves. Active with their church and community, the Hancocks were two of the first members of Bynum Methodist Church, which was established in 1895 on the outskirts of Purves. After it was moved, the church was renamed Purves Methodist Church. (Martha Hancock Starnes.)

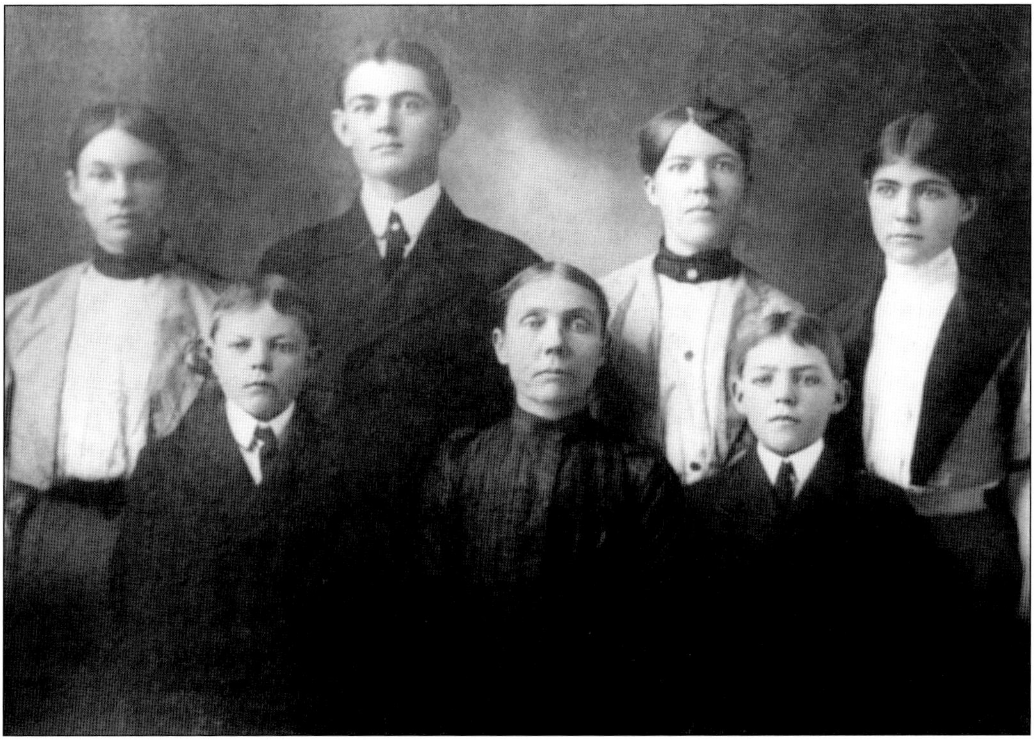

Purves pioneers Ella Frances McNeil and James Henry Coppedge married in 1882. Widowed at age 39, Ella embodied the stalwart pioneer woman devoted to church and community while farming and raising children. From left to right in this 1905 Coppedge family photograph are (first row) Simeon "Sim" Benjamin, Ella, and James "Jim" Warren; (second row) Effie Izora Hancock, William Thomas "Tom," Alma Pearl Hancock, and Mary Cathyrn "May" Licett. (Martha Hancock Starnes.)

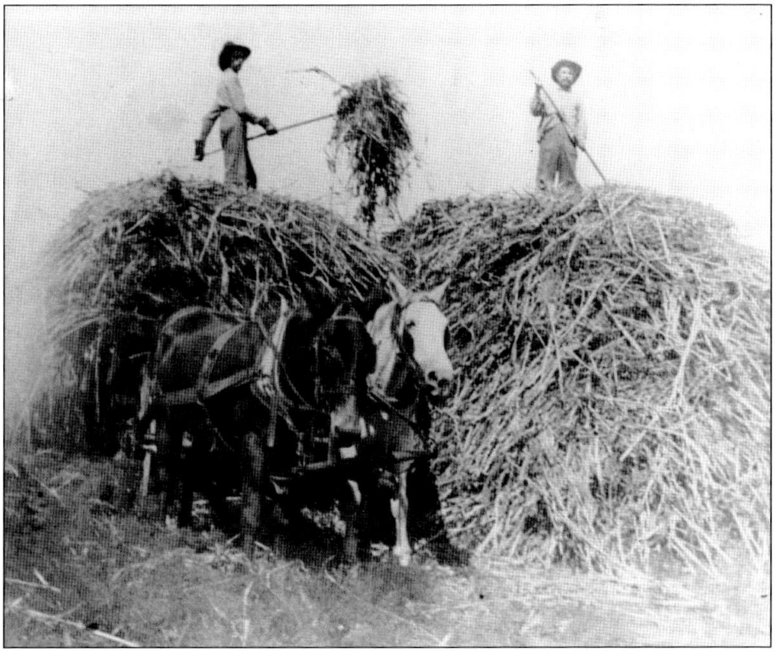

Neighboring farmers George W. Johnson (left) and Luther Leo Cook work together near Purves to put up hay. Hay was cut, raked, and gathered by hand into a wagon. A horse- or mule-drawn wagon transported the hay to a stationary bailing machine or a location selected for storage. (Linda Tolston.)

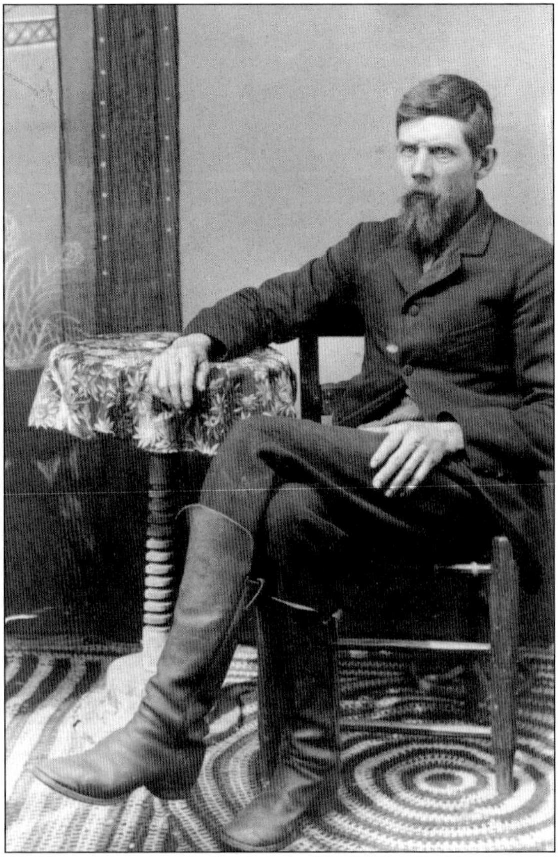

After Margaret Jane Dowdy and James Houston Sides (pictured) married in 1870, Margaret's father, Marcus Lafayette Dowdy, assisted with the construction of their Clairette farm house, seen in the next image. By 1895, James and Margaret owned 127 acres, a buggy, a wagon, 4 horses, 10 cattle, and 9 hogs. James was possibly the first Clairette farmer to grow and sell peanuts. (SHHM.)

Four miles southeast of Alexander, the James Houston Sides log house had rough lumber walls and walnut shingles. This was where the Sides children were born between 1871 and 1888. Pictured in 1888 are, from left to right, Jim (in the doorway), Nellie, Oder, Emry (seated with baby Dennis), and Ira. Not shown is Alexander, who died at age eight. Logs from this house were later used to build a barn. (SHHM.)

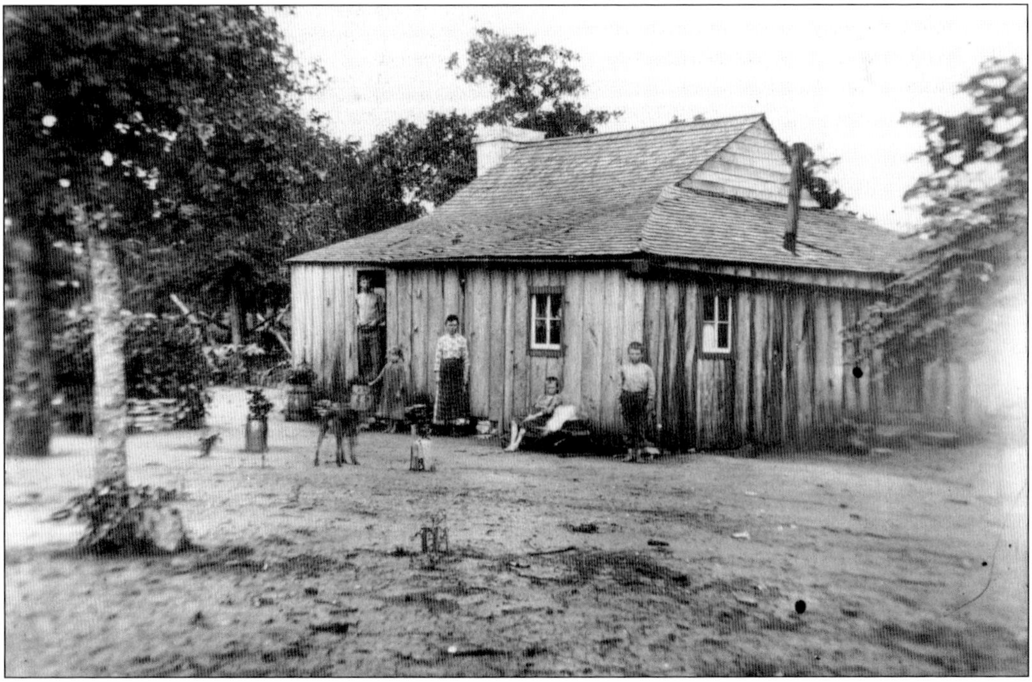

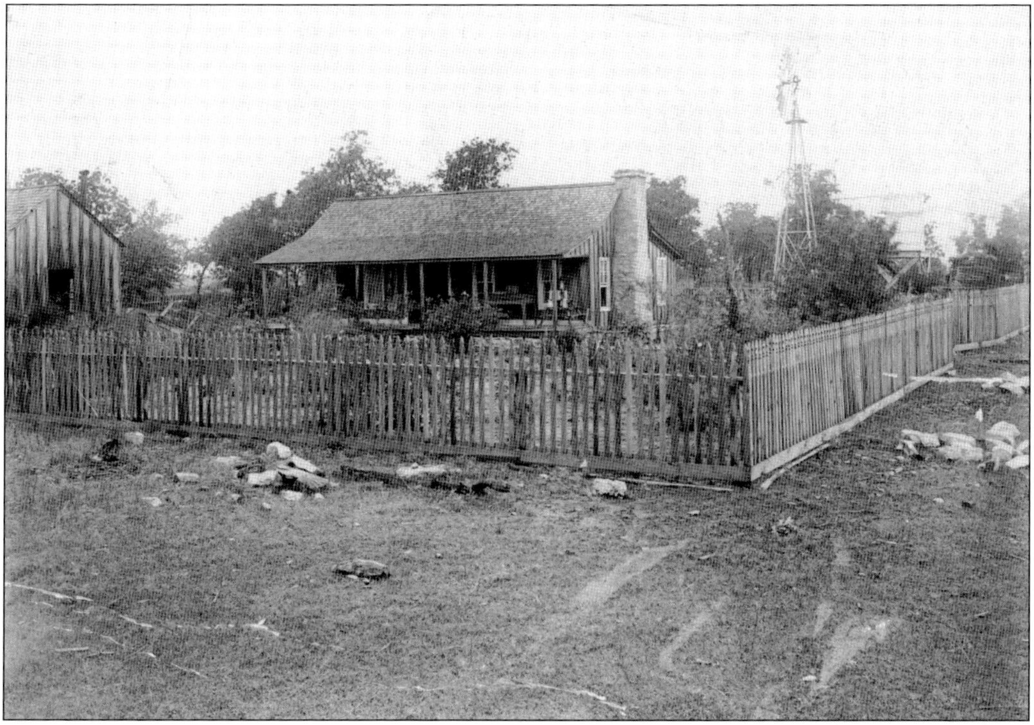

By 1890, James Houston Sides had built a new home for his family. Note the smoothly milled lumber, tall and airy windows, long porch with a work bench under the roof, windmill, water tower, and barn, all surrounded by protective and decorative picket fencing. In 1895, James's son Jim and daughter Ira organized the Clairette Literacy and Debating Society. (SHHM.)

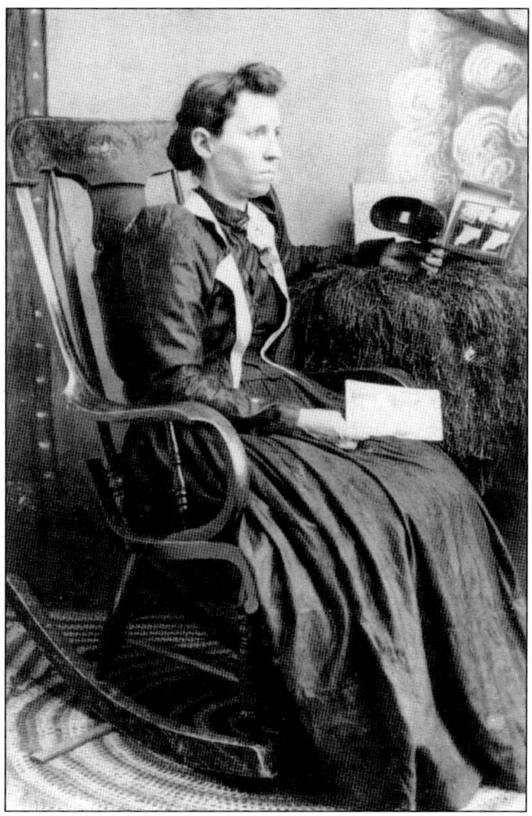

Shown sitting in a rocking chair holding a Holmes stereoscope, Margaret Jane Dowdy Sides was the daughter of Primitive Baptists Elizabeth Sides and Marcus Lafayette Dowdy. Upon her mother's death, Margaret wrote, "My dear precious mother . . . she has lain her armor by and is sweetly sleeping by the side of our dear father in Clairette graveyard." (SHHM.)

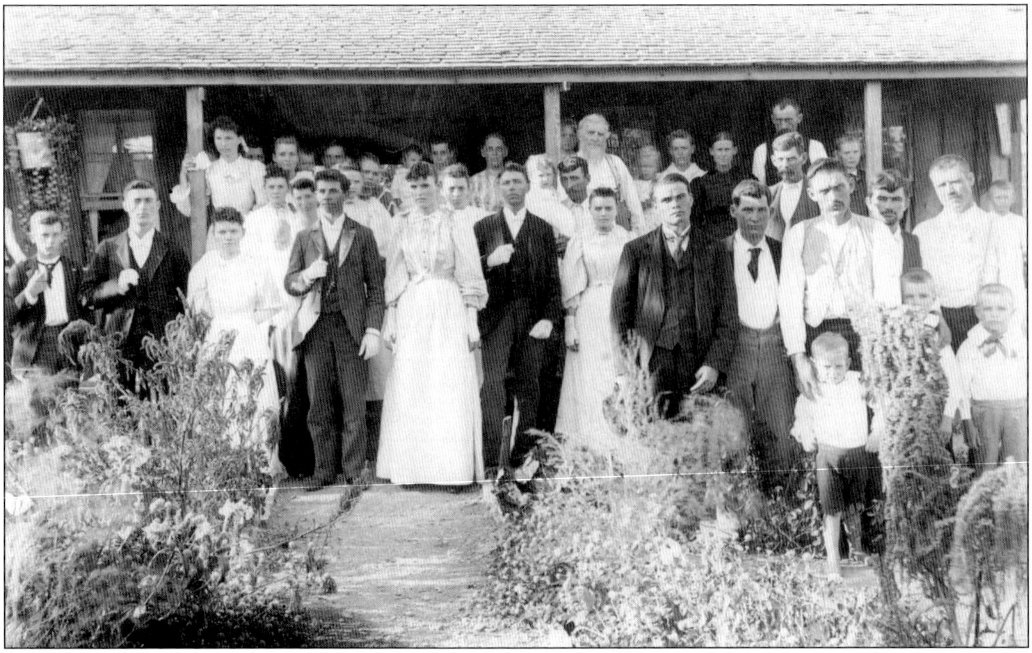

Extended family and friends wore their Sunday best for the gala home wedding of Oder Jane Sides and William Jesse Wilbanks. Oder and Jesse took on the farming there after the 1915 death of Oder's father, James Houston Sides. Wilbanks also worked for the Missouri, Kansas, & Texas Railroad before moving to farm with his father in Crosby County. (SHHM.)

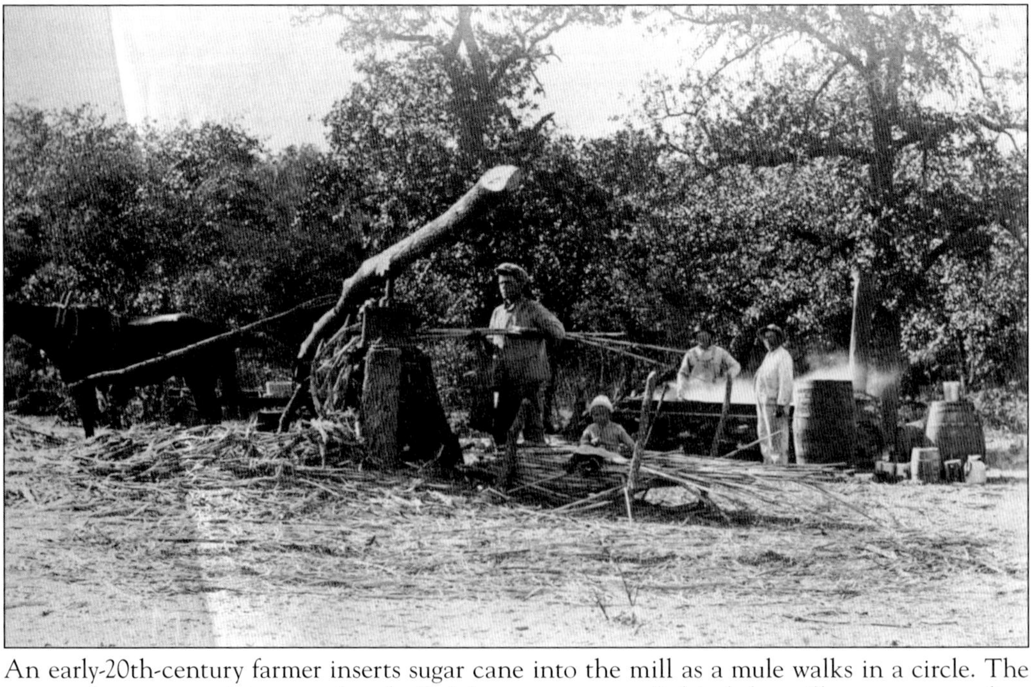

An early-20th-century farmer inserts sugar cane into the mill as a mule walks in a circle. The squeezed sugar cane juice was then boiled down to a syrup. Behind the mill, men are standing by a vat of boiling juice that will eventually become syrup. This mill was located near Wilson in Comanche County, just a short walk from Erath County's Edna Hill and Purves.

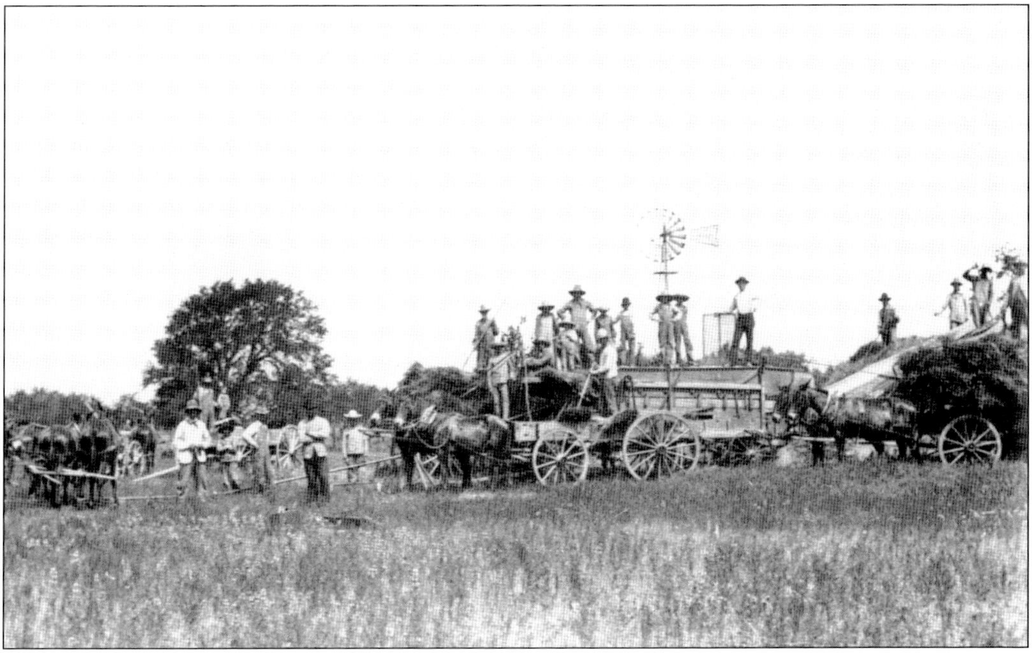

Harvested grain, such as oats or wheat, was hand-fed into the horse-powered threshing machine. The threshing motion separates the seeds from the stalks. This 1904 scene occurred on the farm of William James "Billy" and Lanora "Nora" McCraw Meador near Johnsville, where they had farmed since 1888. The thresher was owned by Owen Riggs. (SHHM.)

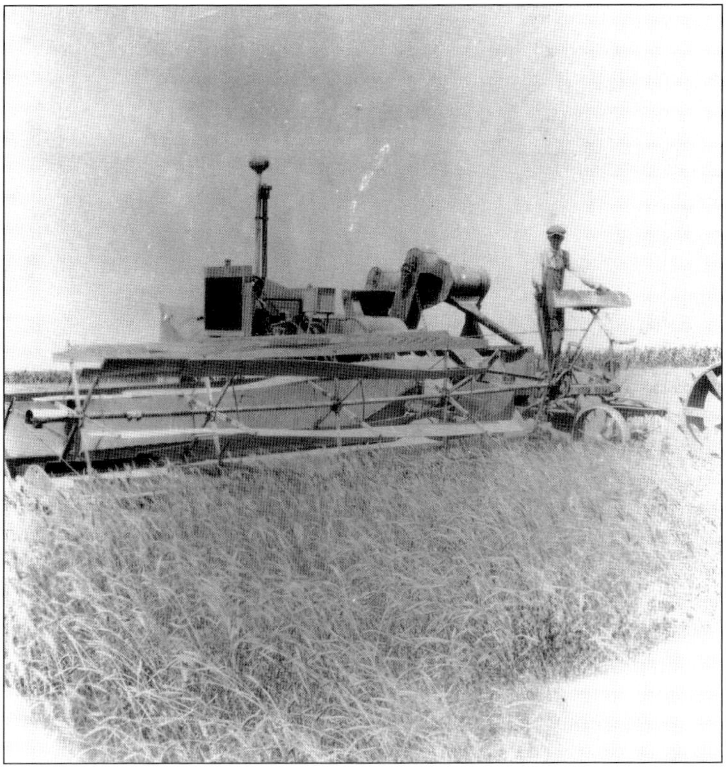

Nape Oxford is demonstrating the combine harvester, which cut, threshed, and sacked grain in one operation. Equipped with a 60-horsepower gas motor to pull a separator and cycle, a Fordson tractor dragged the machine in the field. Two men could harvest 50 acres in 10 hours. Oxford commented, "To make bread is only necessary to grind in hand-grist mill and cook. This could all be done in 30 minutes." (SHHM.)

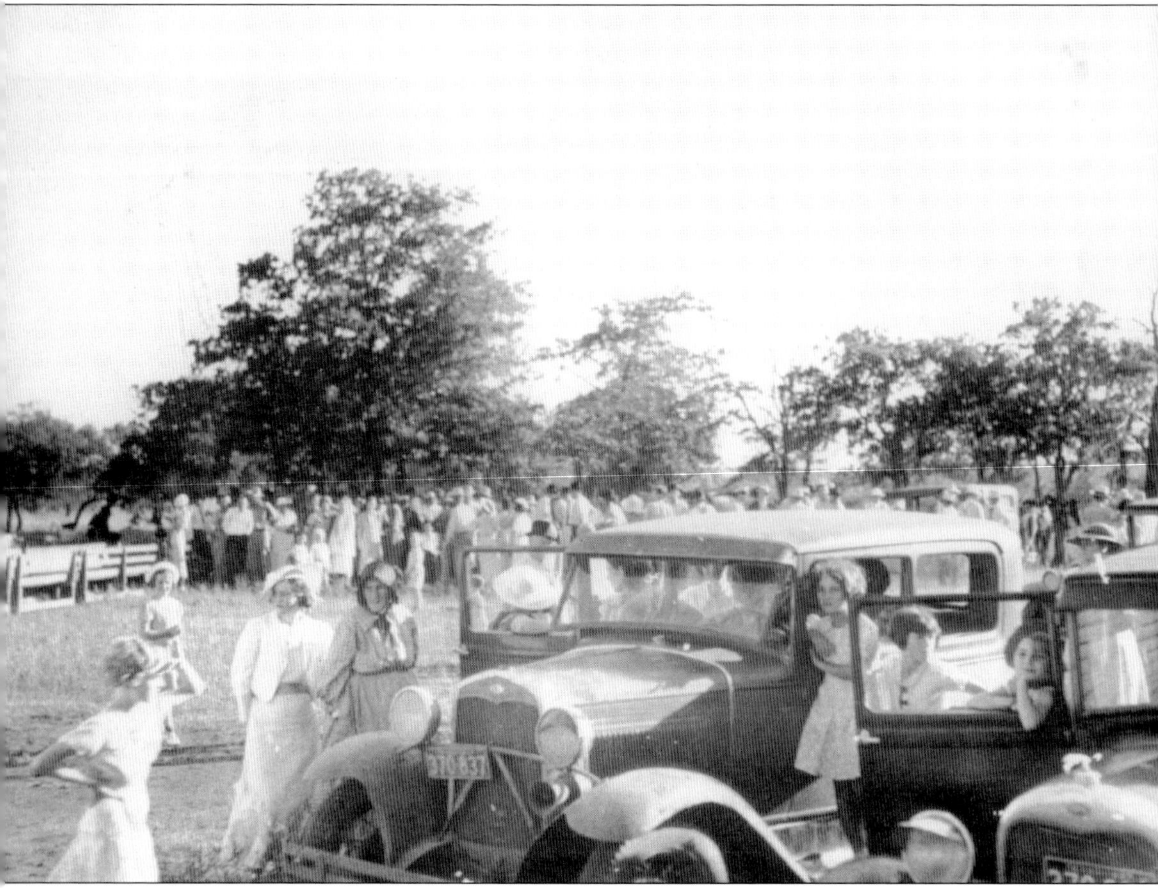

Crop disease and drought ignited the Great Depression in north central Texas long before the stock market crash of 1929, as times were already tough for central Texas root farmers. The Texas State Department of Agriculture reported that Texas sweet potato growers lost $1.8 million in 1917 due to insect infestation. In the fall of 1929, the West Texas Potato Growers Association organized in neighboring Eastland County. Thirteen counties—including Brown, Callahan, Comanche, Eastland, Erath, Stephens, and Taylor—faced quarantine for the sweet potato weevil. Erath's School Hill community is near the Eastland County line. Shown is a 1935 barbecue gathering for the West Texas Potato Growers Association at School Hill Baptist Church. H.H. Tudor of Lingleville cooked the barbecue in a washpot. In the left foreground from left to right are Juanita Yardley, Opal Brock, and Amanda Hair. Other families in the community included Bays, Christian, Dixon, Elston, Fair, Huffman, Tate, Wells, and Wilcoxson. (Nelda Blankenship Keever.)

Three

TRADE AND COMMERCE

Pioneers went shopping for supplies once or twice per year. Brown sugar, coffee, and tobacco were commodities that could be acquired if one had cash or trade. After the Civil War, a steady ingress of people arrived hoping to rebuild their lives. The great buffalo slaughter that took place from 1874 to 1877 led to full boardinghouses, livery stables, and saloons. Mercantile stores provided supplies. Sawmills, corn and flour mills, and cotton gins were powered by oxen, horses, water, or steam. Most cotton gins also had a gristmill set up for grinding grain crop into meal and flour. A farmer could pay with a portion of the meal, which the miller could sell.

A November 1876 Stephenville *Tribune* article reported voting boxes at Billingsley's Mill, Harper's Mill, and Wylie's store. J.R. Billingsley later sold his mill to Frank P. Morgan. According to Henry Grady Perry's book *Grand Ol' Erath*, Charles Walker set up the first cotton gin in 1873. Tom and Lawrence Wood had the first Stephenville flour mill and gristmill, selling to Quine and Bassel in 1874. John Sinclair set up a gristmill and sawmill about 1875. When the Texas Central Railroad arrived in 1881, John D. St. Clair moved his Little Green Creek sawmill from Harper's Mill to establish the depot town of Alexander. The railways allowed for the export of cotton, which led to it being the dominant area crop into the 1910s. Mills and gins existed at Alarm Creek, Armstrong, Bunyan, Chalk Mountain, Clairette, Dublin, Duffau, Edna Hill, Exray, Harbin, Highland, Huckabay, Liberty, Lingleville, North Bosque, Purves, Resley Creek, Selden, Topaz, Victor, and elsewhere.

Several towns had banks, including Alexander State Bank, Bluff Dale State Bank, Farmer's State Bank at Clairette, Farmers and Merchants Bank of Duffau, Huckabay's West Texas State Bank, First State Bank at Lingleville, and First State Bank of Morgan Mill. Faster transportation brought some of civilization's comforts to the area. The Texas & Pacific Railway advertised artesian wells and mineral waters at Duffau Springs, Hico, and Thurber. Hotel accommodations were popularized with the advertising of treatments for internal and external disease and chronic illness.

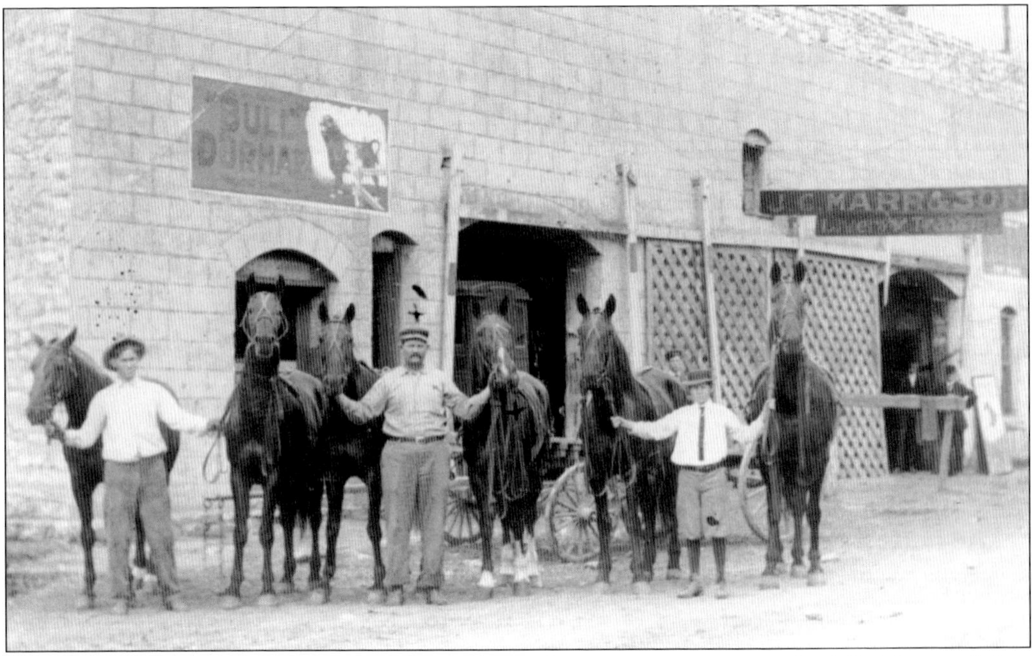

In 1912, Joseph Columbus Marr and his son Joseph Lee were operating the J.C. Marr and Son Livery and Transfer Stable in Stephenville. A traveler could store at the livery (or hire from it) a horse, team, carriage, or wagon. Equipment repair and veterinary care were also available. Within a few years, the Marrs transitioned to Model T Fords, eventually providing transfer service to and from the Desdemona oil fields. Below, Everett Cline stands between two horses in front of Eli A. Powell's livery around 1900. Powell operated a livery and transfer line in Dublin from around 1895 to 1910. Railroad companies contracted Powell to transfer passengers to and from the depot. (Both, SHHM.)

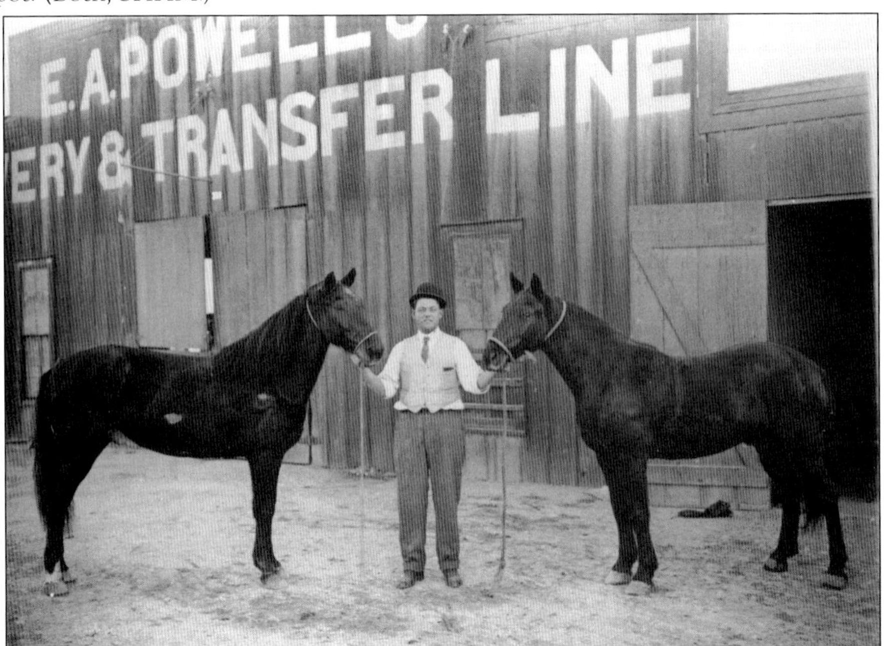

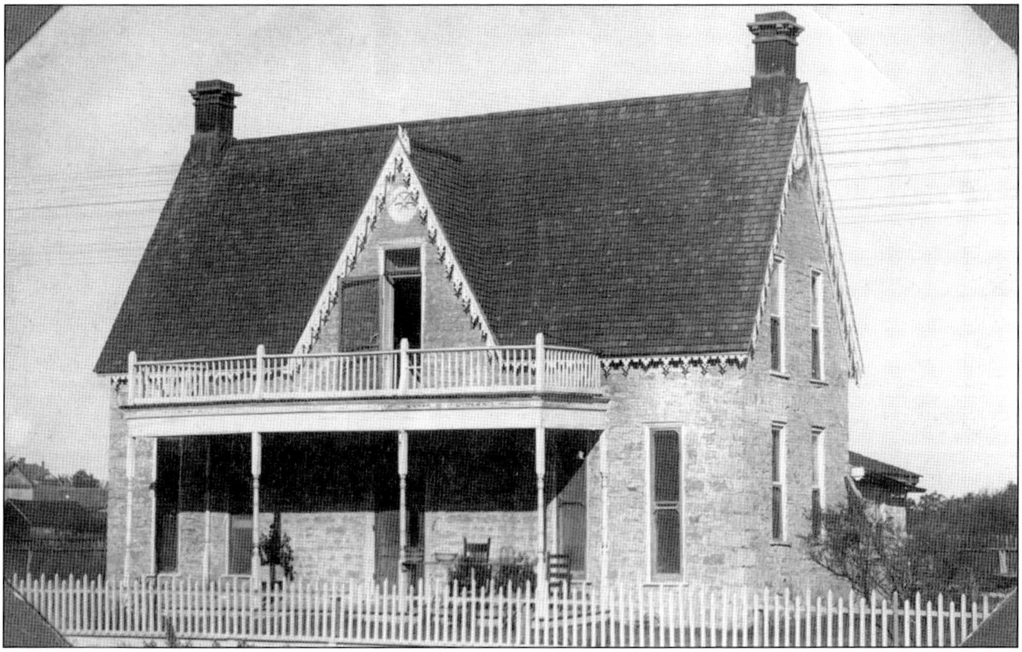

Built in 1869 by attorney J.D. Berry, the distinctive Berry Cottage is listed in the National Register of Historic Places. Cypress gingerbread fringes the steep roof on the native limestone Gothic Revival structure. This landmark is nestled along the Bosque River within sight of the courthouse tower. Also known as Hill House and the D.D.H. Moore Home, it was restored in 1965 as the Stephenville Historical House Museum. (SHHM.)

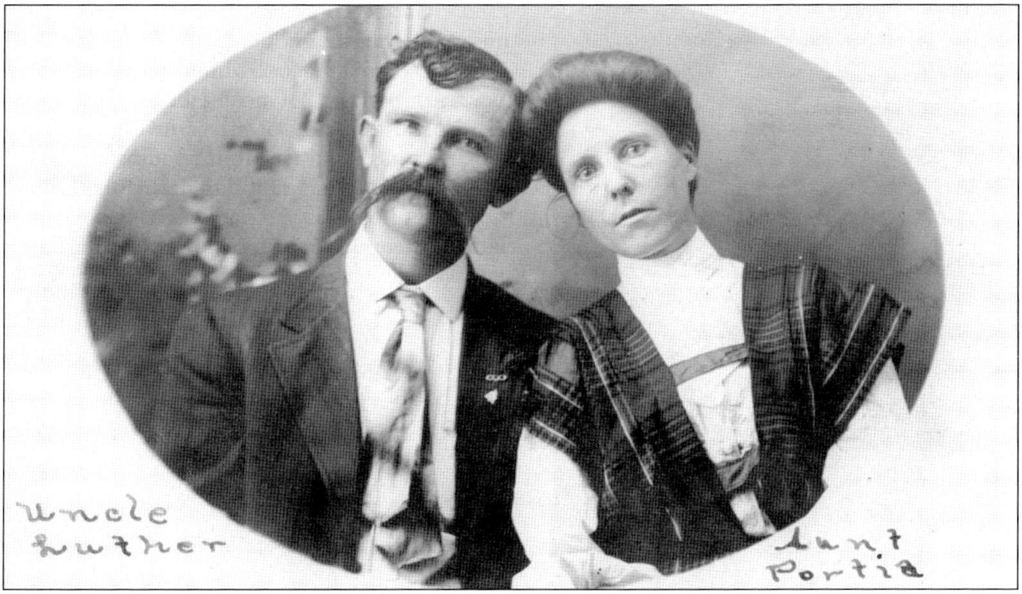

After purchasing property in 1889, banker C.J. Shapard subdivided it, with his business partner Emmie Paddock creating the Shapard and Paddock Addition. Portia Ellen Bellomy (right) and James Luther Hill (left) were living at Berry Cottage in 1911. Portia owned the property until 1922. In August 1916, James Luther Hill and Tennie Hawk were proprietors of the Palace Café on the west side of the courthouse square. (SHHM.)

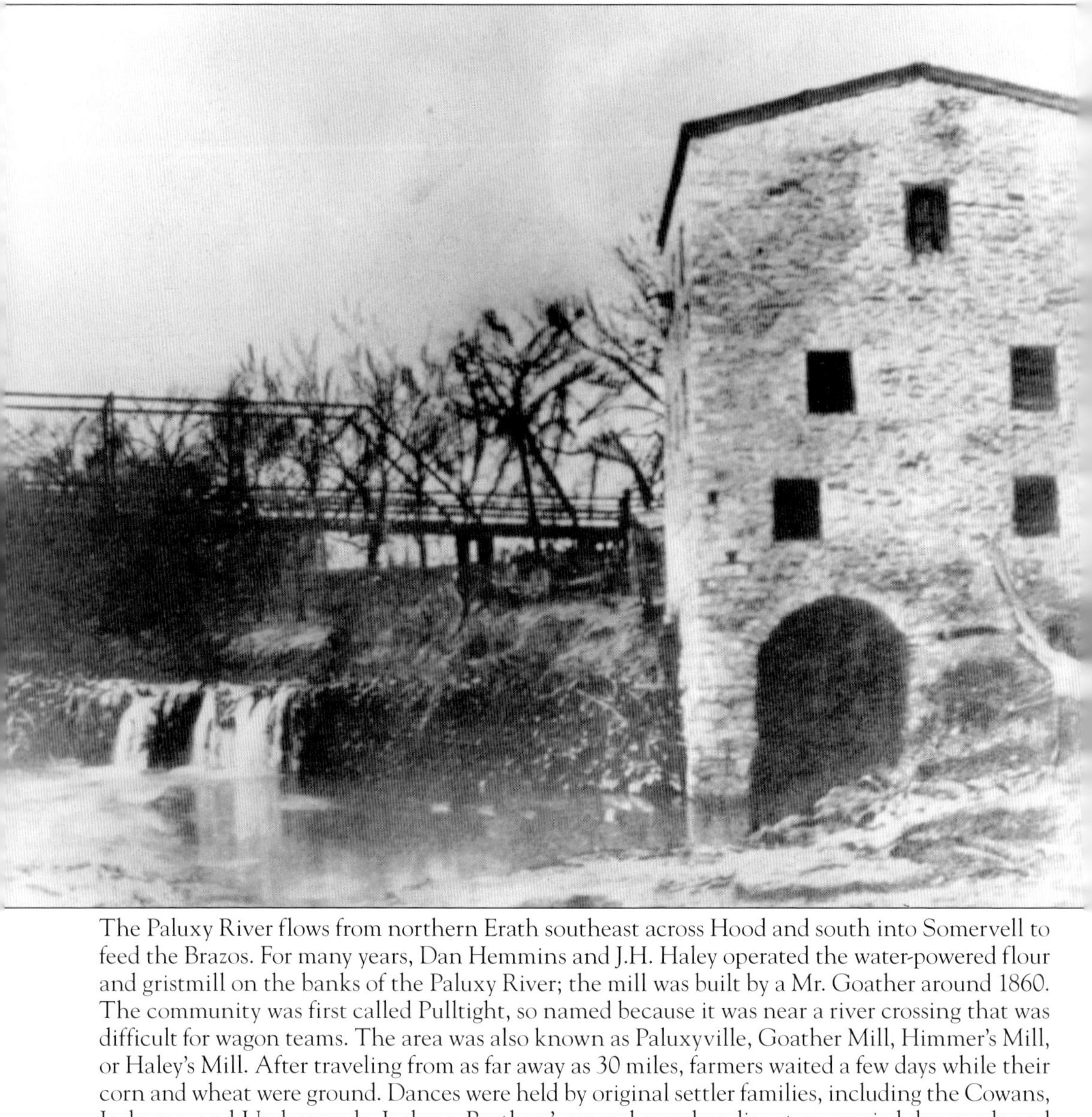

The Paluxy River flows from northern Erath southeast across Hood and south into Somervell to feed the Brazos. For many years, Dan Hemmins and J.H. Haley operated the water-powered flour and gristmill on the banks of the Paluxy River; the mill was built by a Mr. Goather around 1860. The community was first called Pulltight, so named because it was near a river crossing that was difficult for wagon teams. The area was also known as Paluxyville, Goather Mill, Himmer's Mill, or Haley's Mill. After traveling from as far away as 30 miles, farmers waited a few days while their corn and wheat were ground. Dances were held by original settler families, including the Cowans, Jacksons, and Underwoods. Jackson Brothers' general merchandise store carried dry goods and druggist supplies. School was held at Paluxy, Rock Church, and downriver at the short-lived Vinegar Hill village. With his wagon team, Capt. P.H. Thrash hauled his Paluxy Mill yield to Fort Worth, carrying merchandise on the return trip. The mill never reopened after a disastrous 1906 flood swept away the waterwheel. (SHHM.)

Mary Branch and Isaac F. "Ike" Cowan settled in the Paluxy valley about 1857. Cowan was a Mason and served as justice of the peace during the 1860s and early 1870s. He rode with the frontier minutemen during the Civil War. After the war, Cowan went back east to procure a steam engine gin. Shipped to Galveston and then hauled by ox and wagon, the equipment was in use by 1867. (SHHM.)

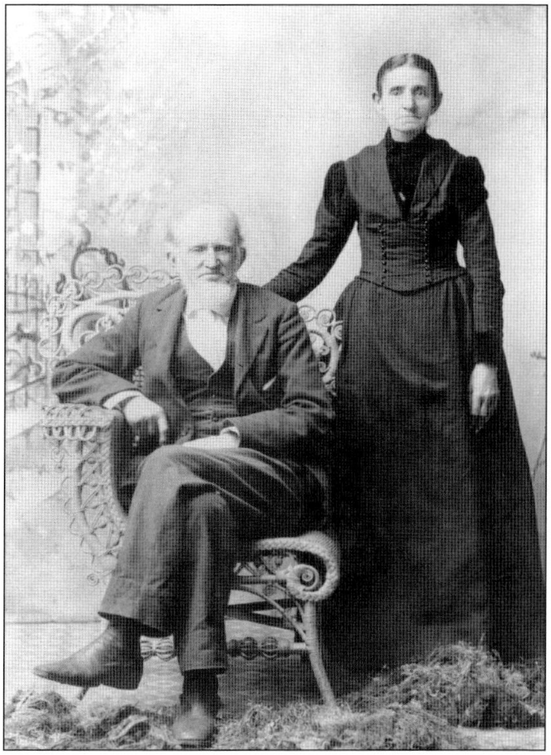

Married in 1897 in Coosa County, Alabama, Martha Minerva "Mattie" Castleberry and Andrew Jackson "Jack" Smith followed her family to Texas. They were living at the Underwood House Hotel in Paluxy when their second daughter, Myrtle Jane, was born on July 2, 1902. Here, unidentified tenants watch from upstairs as the young family poses in 1902. From left to right are Mattie, Martha Ruby, Myrtle Jane, and Jack Smith. (Sandra Shoup Hammons.)

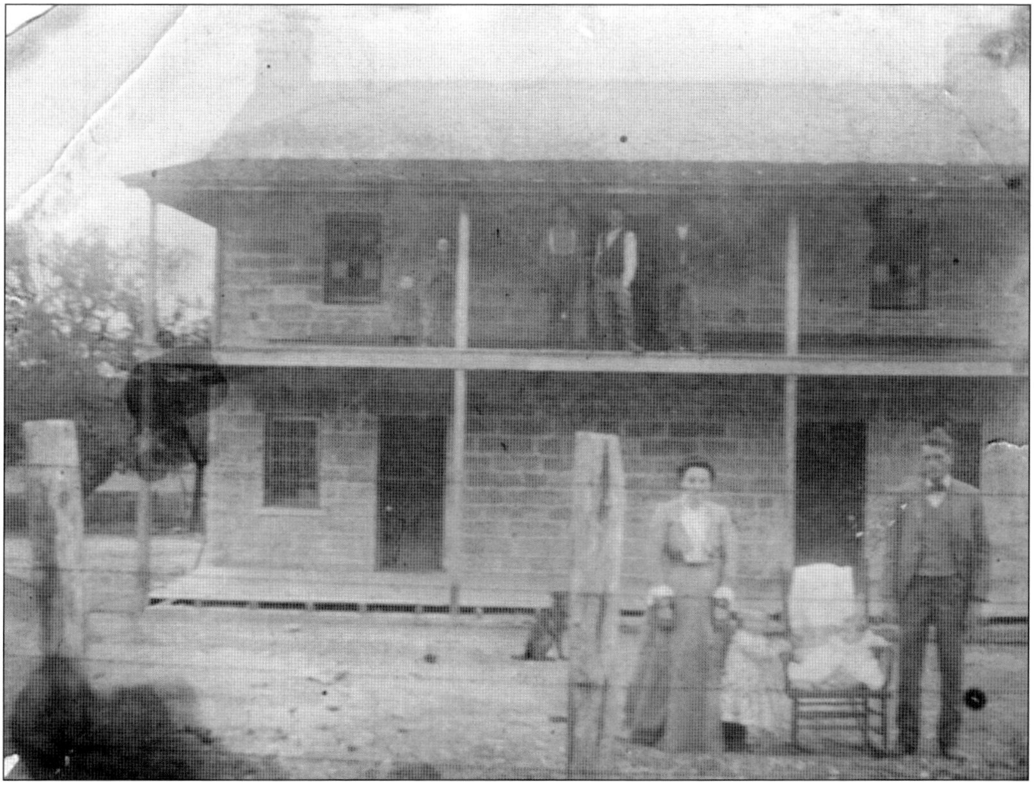

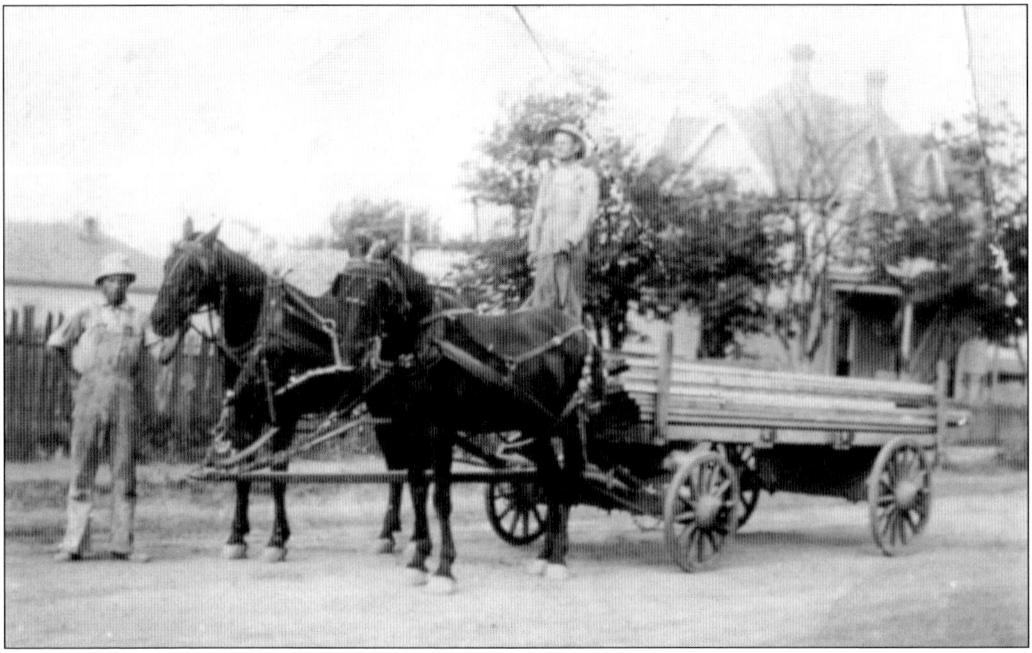

Although local blackjack and post oak rough lumber were occasionally used, quality lumber was preferred for building a store, church, or school. In this c. 1900 image, William Thomas "Tom" Coppedge stands in the wagon of materials that he bought in Waco to sell in Dublin. By 1910, Coppedge owned a grocery store. (Martha Hancock Starnes.)

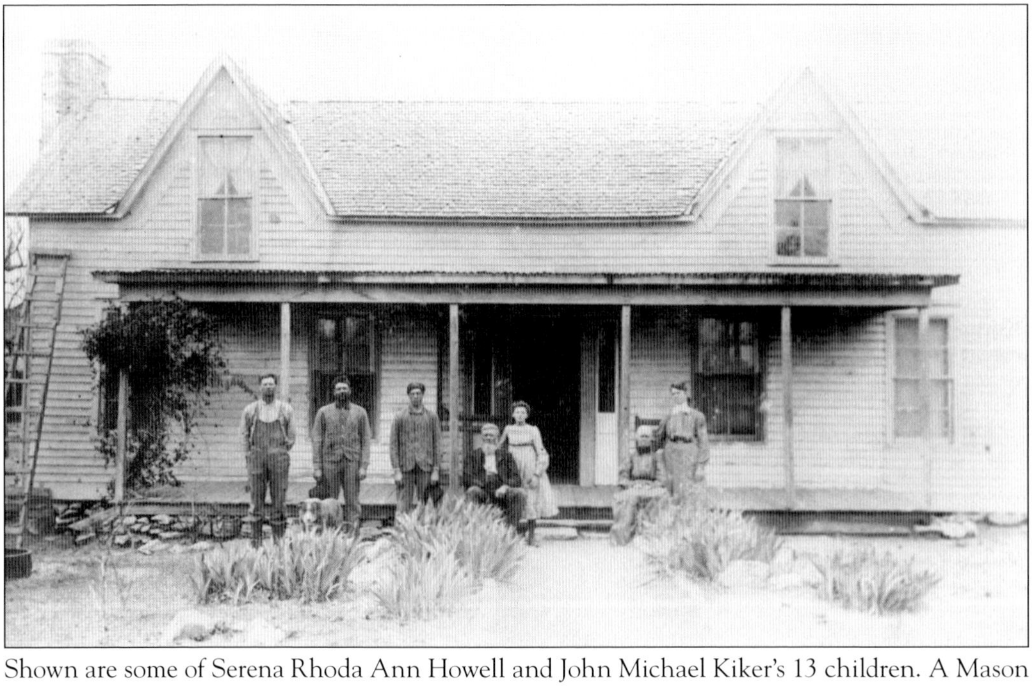

Shown are some of Serena Rhoda Ann Howell and John Michael Kiker's 13 children. A Mason and devout Christian, Kiker deeded 1.3 acres to Greens Creek Methodist Church in 1907. This photograph was taken around 1900, after Serena's death. Seated are John and second wife Catherine Noles Kiker.

Cotton ginner John Michael Kiker was promoted to second lieutenant while he and his brothers served with Company B of the Confederate 28th Alabama Infantry Regiment. Later, while serving as Erath County commissioner, Kiker employed convicts to work on county construction projects. Many a ginner lost fingers, a hand, or an arm trying to dislodge fibers that jammed in the cotton stand. Kiker lost his right hand and part of the left one.

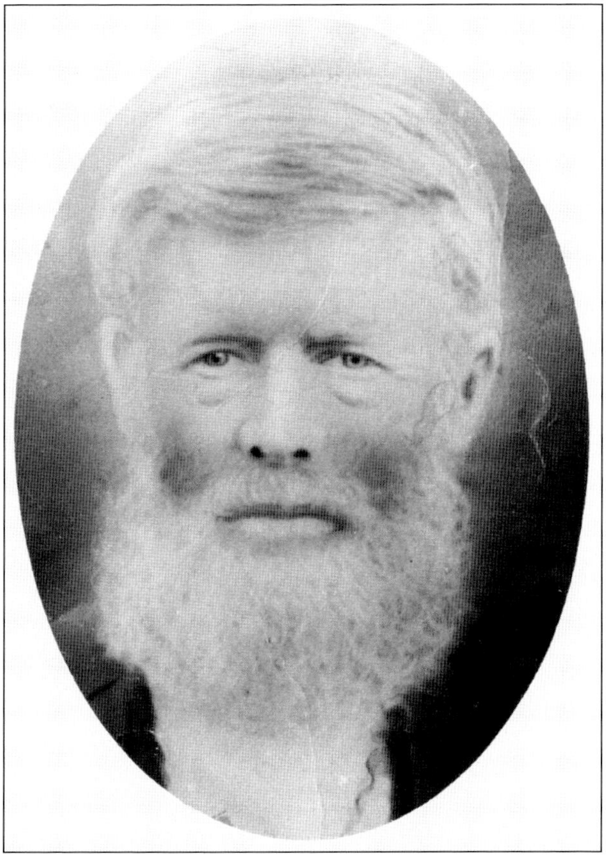

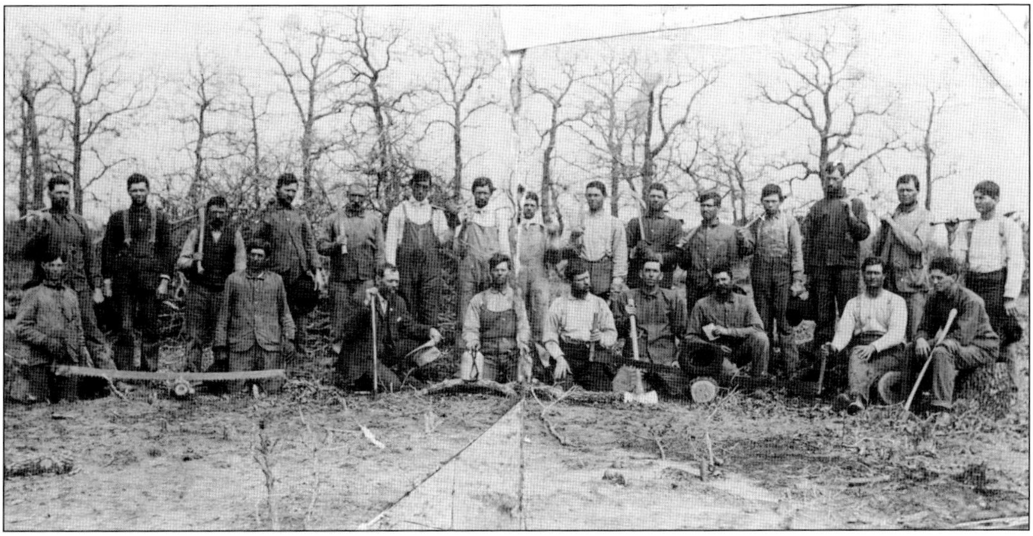

Descendants of Sarah Howell and Benjamin Kiker settled along Greens Creek in November 1873. In the fall of 1870, they journeyed from Georgia to Texas with a 13-family wagon train. Kiker brothers Newton Pickens, Eli Robinson, and John Michael, along with their brother-in-law Jim Holcomb, set up a cotton gin in 1878 that operated until Leander Kiker closed it in 1947. This photograph is labeled "Kiker Family Clearing Land 1896."

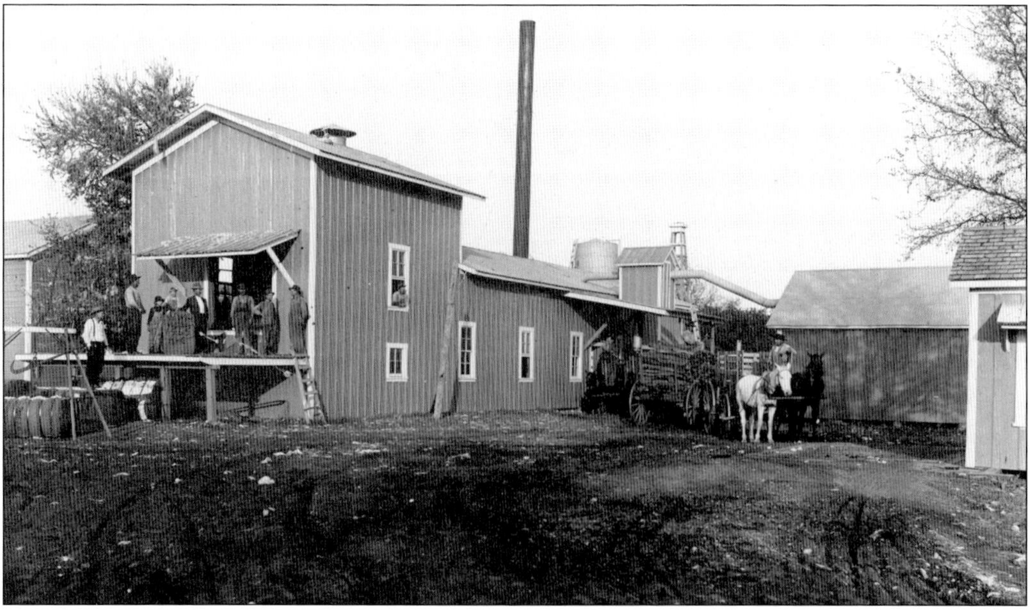

H.L. Kight of Dublin had gins in Bluff Dale, Desdemona, Hico, and Clairette. M.L. Blackmond became engineer at Kight's Clairette gin (shown), which was built in 1909. In October 1916, the boiler exploded, throwing shrapnel that damaged the church, the bank, and the homes of Blackmond, J.R. Cook, W.R. Hardon, and W.E. Salmon. Miraculously, no one was killed, and T.M. Lee suffered only minor injuries. (Suzanne Cook Taylor.)

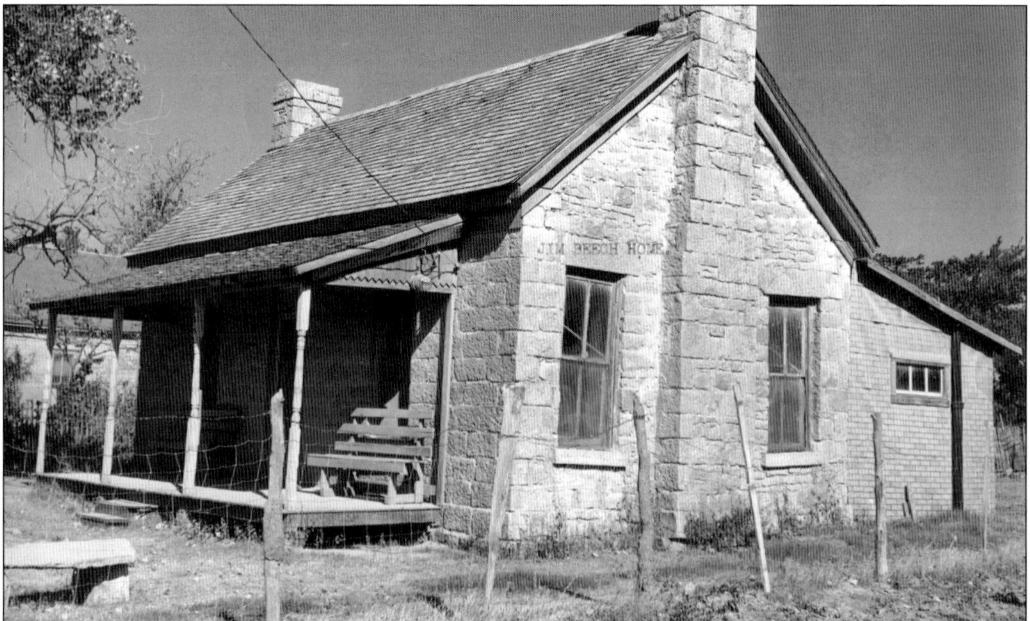

Possibly built as early as 1857, this hall-and-parlor style house made of native limestone bears a side gabled roof with a chimney at each end. James Beech, who purchased and ran Stephenville's first city flour mills and cotton gin, purchased the home sometime before 1878. Beech was also a liquor dealer who owned a blacksmith and wagon shop; he sold his property in 1899 when he moved to Oklahoma. (SHHM.)

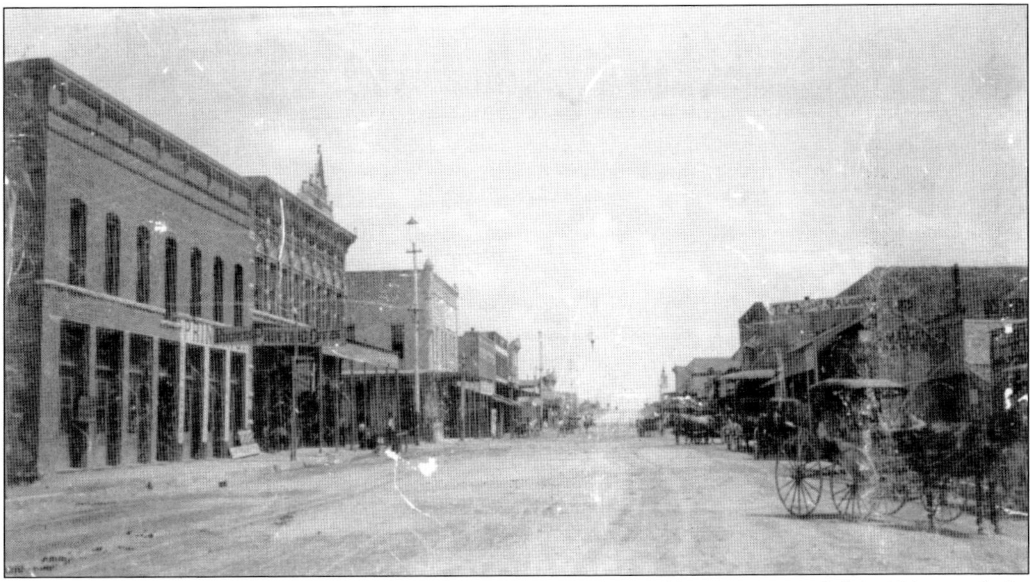

This photograph dates to sometime after the 1888 start of the *Dublin Progress* and the 1899 streetlight installation but sometime before the 1904 closure of the Palace Saloon due to prohibition in Dublin. The Dublin Bakery appears in *Dublin Progress* advertisements, with ownership periodically changing hands, from 1896 (when it was owned by T.J. Wood) to 1945 (when it was owned by the A.E. Davis family). The bakery began delivering bread to city customers in 1899. (Judith Robbins Lemons.)

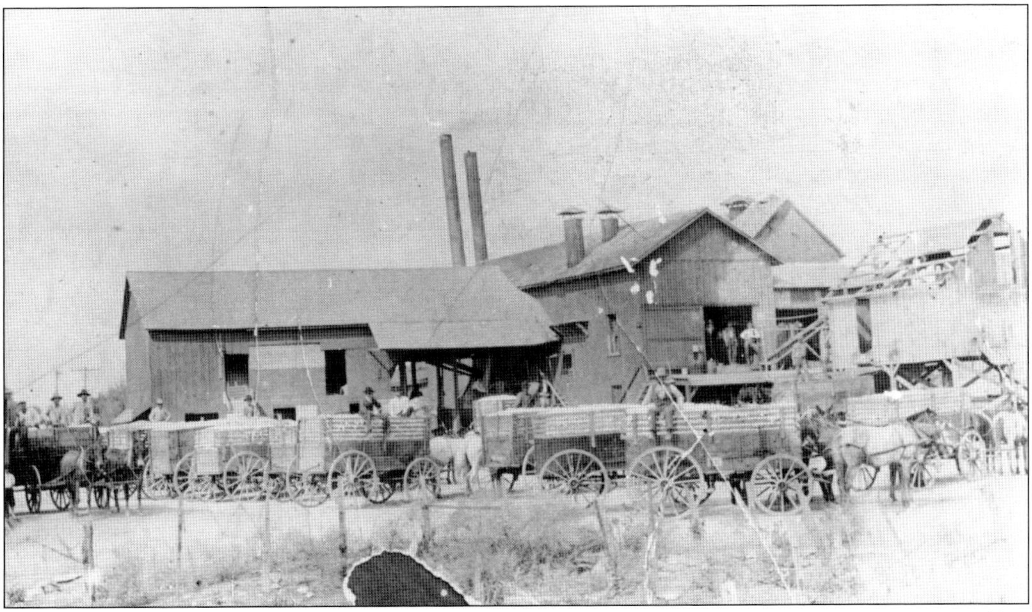

Three young ladies ginned a bale of cotton on New Year's Day at W.H. Armstrong's gin. Caddie, daughter of Will Whittenburg, ran the engine. Ethel Hilton managed the gin stands. Artie Armstrong operated the packer and press. As they worked, W.H. Armstrong hosted Dublin's popular bachelor R.L. Miller, introducing the women. The gin closed after the 1912 season. (Nelda Blankenship Keever.)

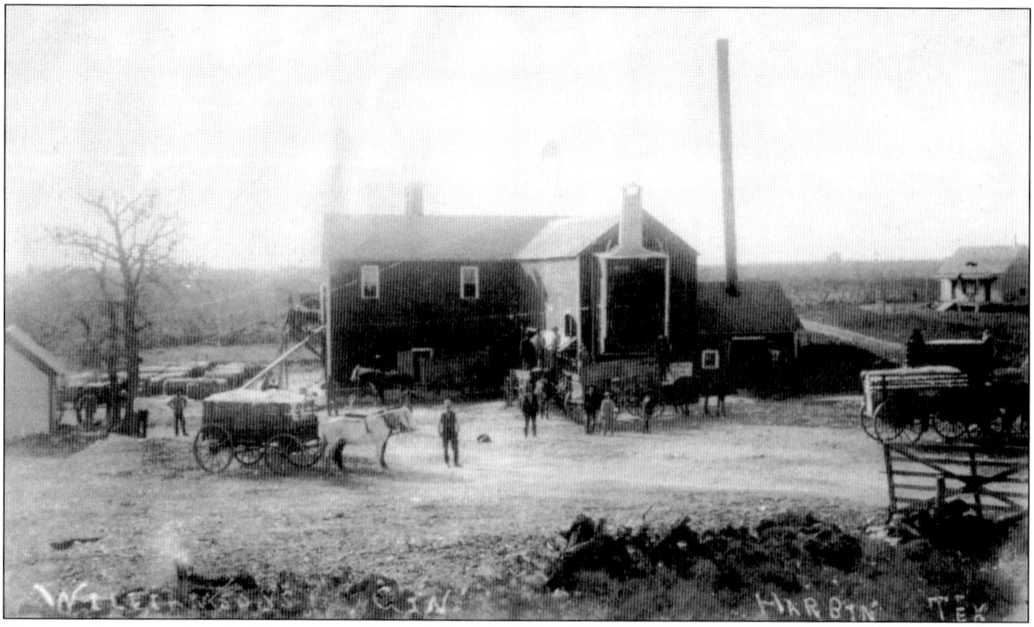

Benson Everrenthus Robbins purchased the Williamson gin in 1910, and lost his arm in the gin saws in 1911. In 1925, he built a state-of-the-art gin one block north of Dublin's Frisco depot. That gin was lost to fire in December 1932. The 1896 photograph below shows the multigenerational household of his parents, Nathaniel B. and Eliza Jane Durham Robbins. The portrait at far right is of their daughter Letitia Evergreen Robbins Clark, who died in childbirth in 1883. Standing from left to right are son-in-law David Clark, friend Bob ?, son John Clinton Robbins, daughter-in-law Ada Amanda Smith and son Emmett Lifus Robbins with their children (in front) Homer Robert and Claudia, son Everrenthus holding his daughter Velma, and daughter-in-law Mary Eldorado "Rado" McCleskey with their daughter Tressie standing before Nathaniel and Eliza Robbins. (Both, Judith Robbins Lemons.)

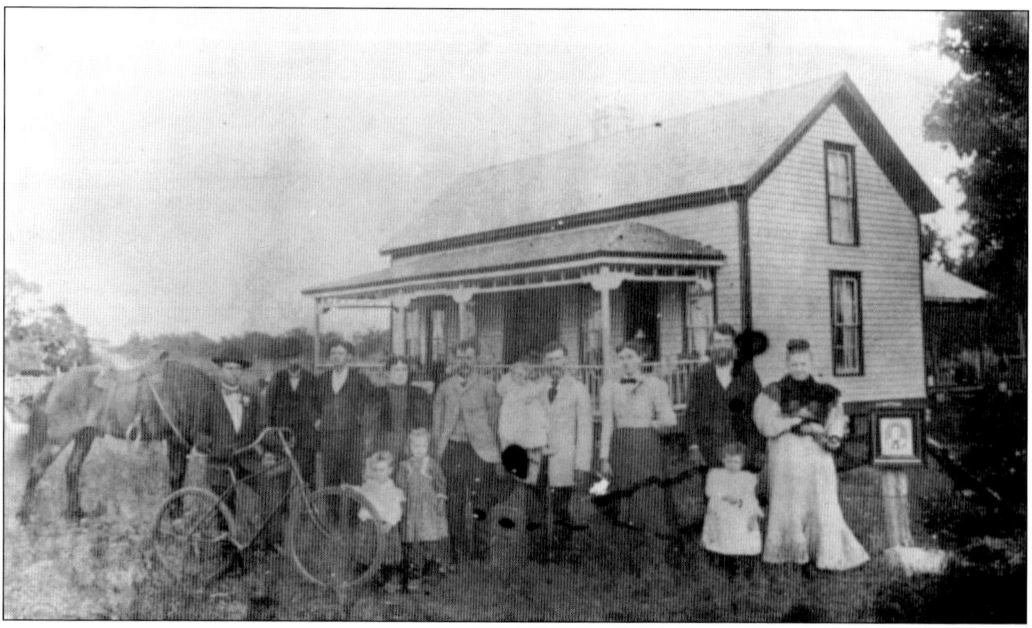

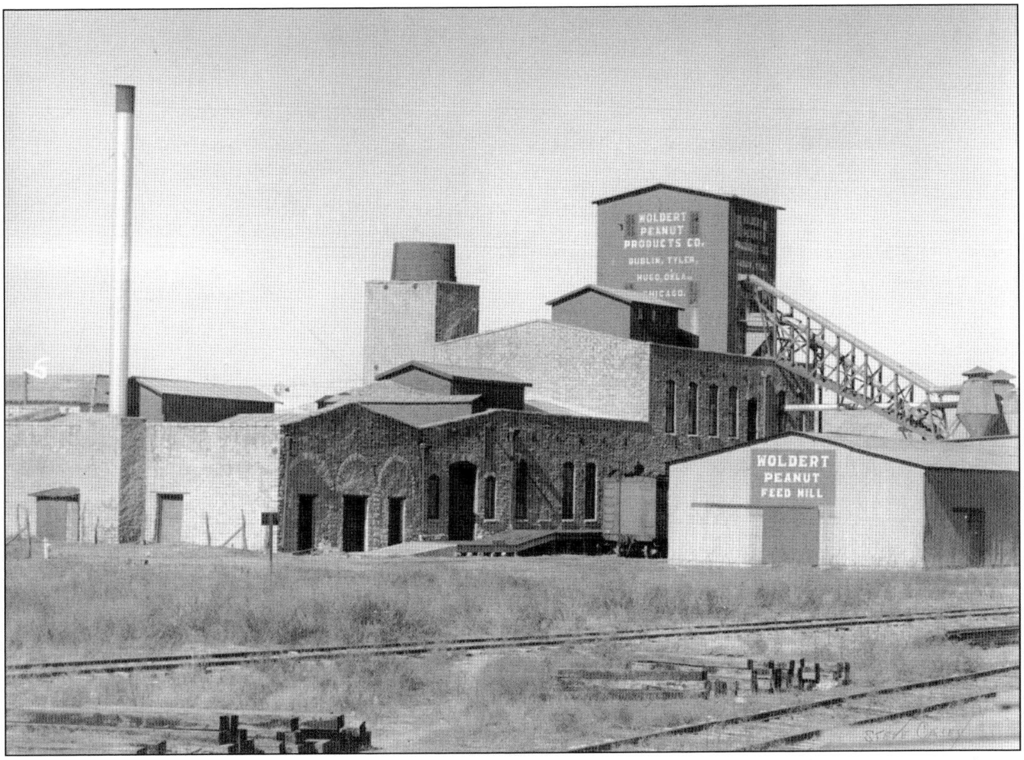

In September 1928, the Dublin Cotton Seed Oil Mill plant was sold to Woldert Peanut Products of Tyler. The existing network of railroad heads, warehousing, shipping facilities, and logistical support used in Dublin's cotton industry made it an ideal choice. This soon became the primary processing plant in central Texas. Peanuts arrived from across the state to be shelled or used to produce stock feed before being shipped across the country. (SHHM.)

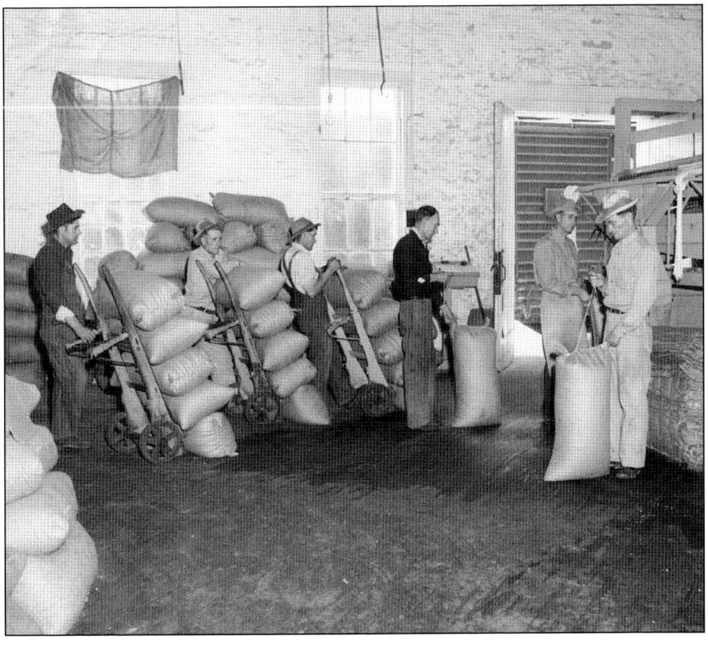

Although peanuts had been grown and sold locally for years, the introduction of the peanut mill generated economic growth that lasted for decades. Woldert Peanut Products sent Henry Lee White to establish the business. When the 1947 rich harvest filled the warehouse, peanuts in burlap sacks were stockpiled outside and protected from the weather with tarps. White made Dublin his home, operating the mill until his retirement in 1973. (SHHM.)

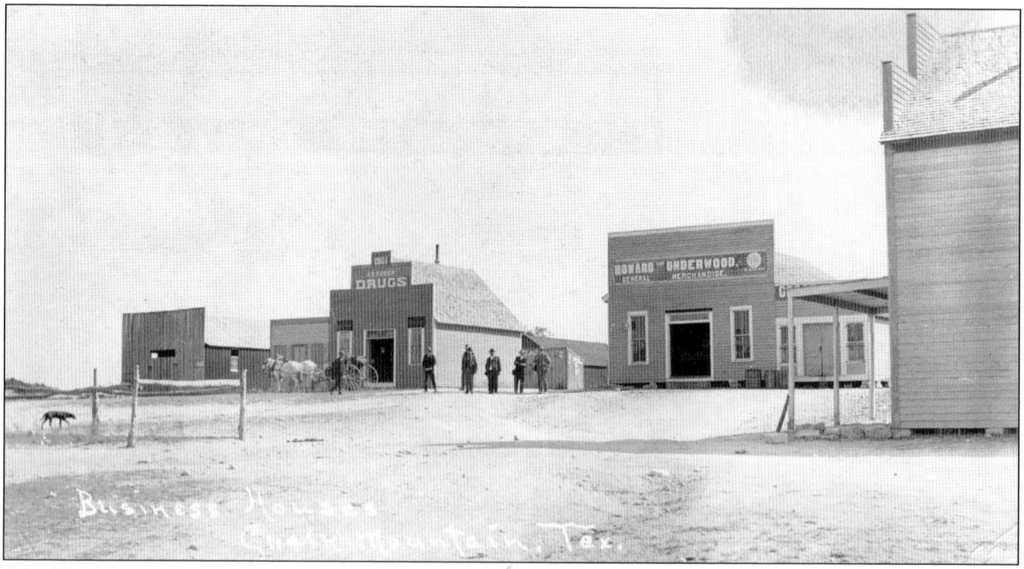

Chalk Mountain, which was a stage stop in 1859, had two churches, a school, and a gin by 1890. Local businesses that existed around the start of the 20th century included blacksmiths J.M. Cooper and Charlie Hamric, physicians Walter Allen and J.C. McDonald, and druggist A.H. Roden. Pictured in 1904, the storefront signage of merchants L.B. Howard and J.H. Underwood reads, "We Never Sleep." In 1915, Confederate veteran Hiram Berry Rogers deeded land in the area for a cemetery. (SHHM.)

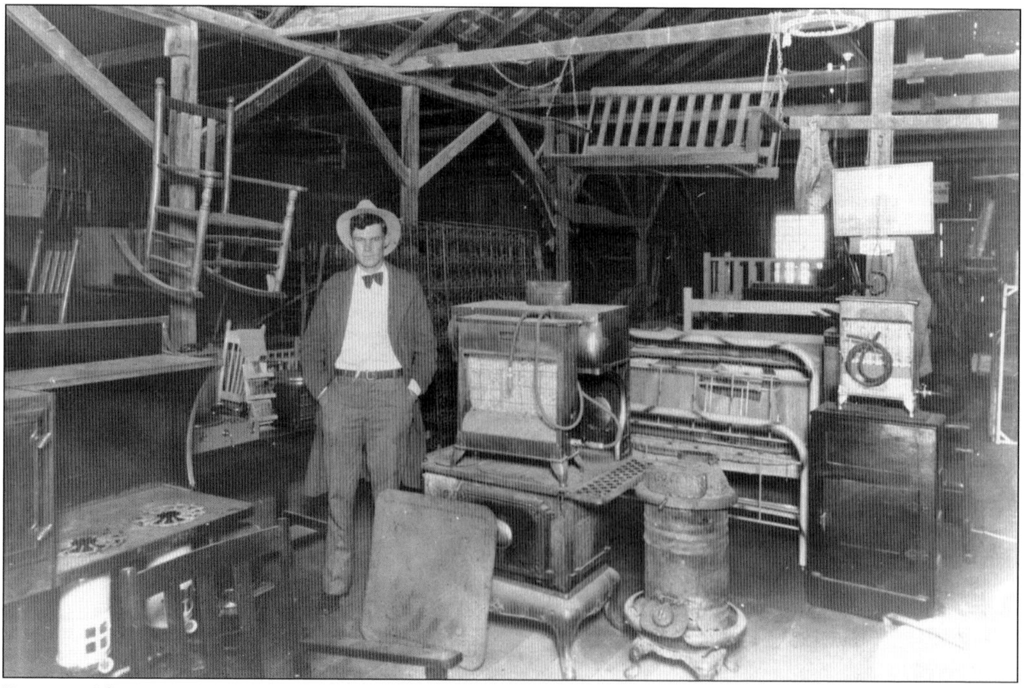

Born in Clairette in 1909 to Bessie Eleanor Barrow and Rufus Richard Alexander, Albert Cornelius Alexander (pictured) married Ida Mildred Hanshew in 1927. Albert supported his young family via his Hico furniture store. In 1940, he owned and operated a gas station. By 1949, the Alexanders had moved to Dublin, where Albert opened a furniture store that existed for over a decade. (SHHM.)

In 1900, Henry L. Minter of Stephenville ran a tenpin alley. By 1914, he owned a hotel, adding a café in the 1920s. He operated the Minter Grocery and Market on East Washington Street with his son George. This photograph is labeled: "Thurman Umburn, Edgar Perkins, Charlie Daisey, Mr. Hester (butcher), H.L. Minter, George Minter, Edgar Hubbard, Jack Hall." Henry Latimer was a deliveryman for Minter's grocery store. (SHHM.)

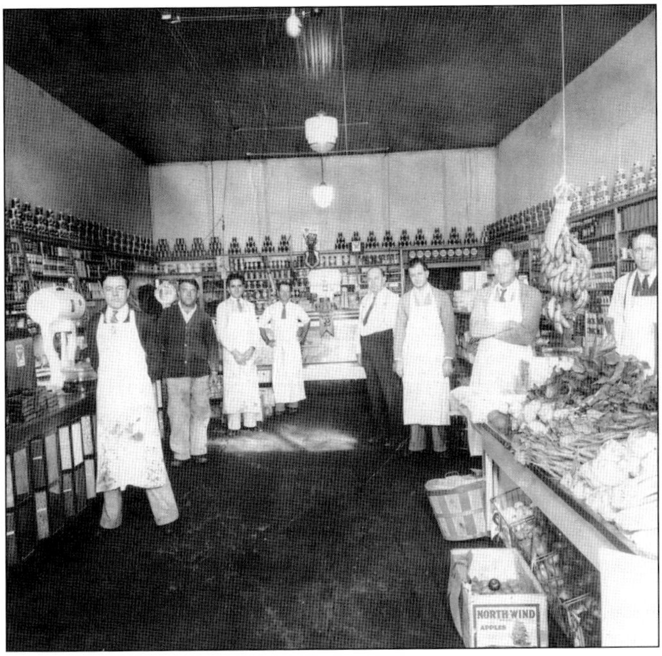

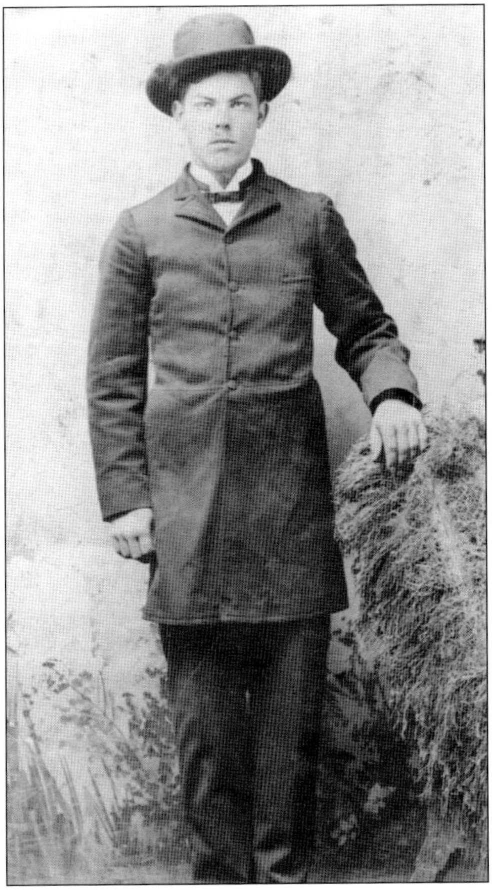

William "Will" Newton Hickey (1871–1950) grew up near Harbin and attended Brownwood's Howard Payne College. He and his wife, Annie Holt, had five children. Will was a teacher, Stephenville school trustee, proprietor of a racket store, and a Woodmen of the World officer. In 1911, he bought a Tolar gin. In the 1920s and 1930s, he owned and operated the Lingleville gas station. (Connie Conatser McSpadden.)

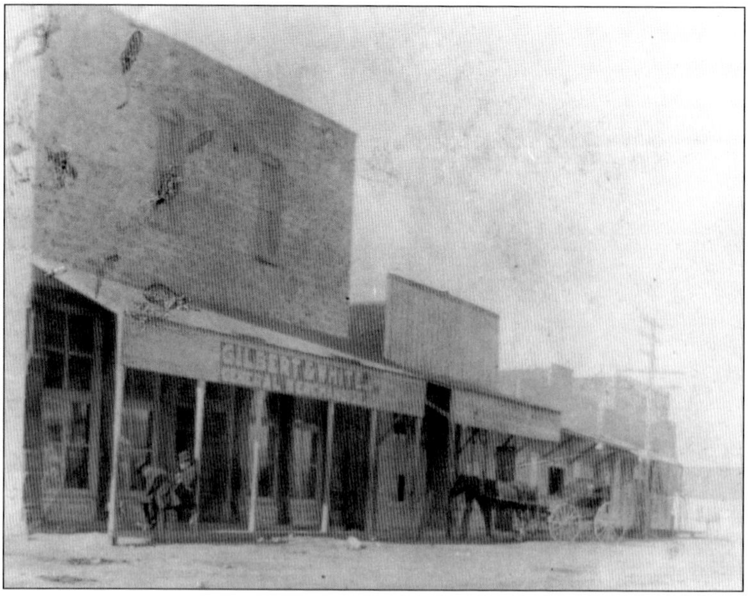

A Mr. Parker opened the first store in Purves, and H.P. Turney opened the second in 1896. When T.J. White purchased a half interest in the business of B.F. Gilbert in March 1906, it became Gilbert & White General Merchandise. They conducted business in this large stone building until October 1907, when they sold to Simmons and Son in exchange for 1,920 acres of West Texas farmland.

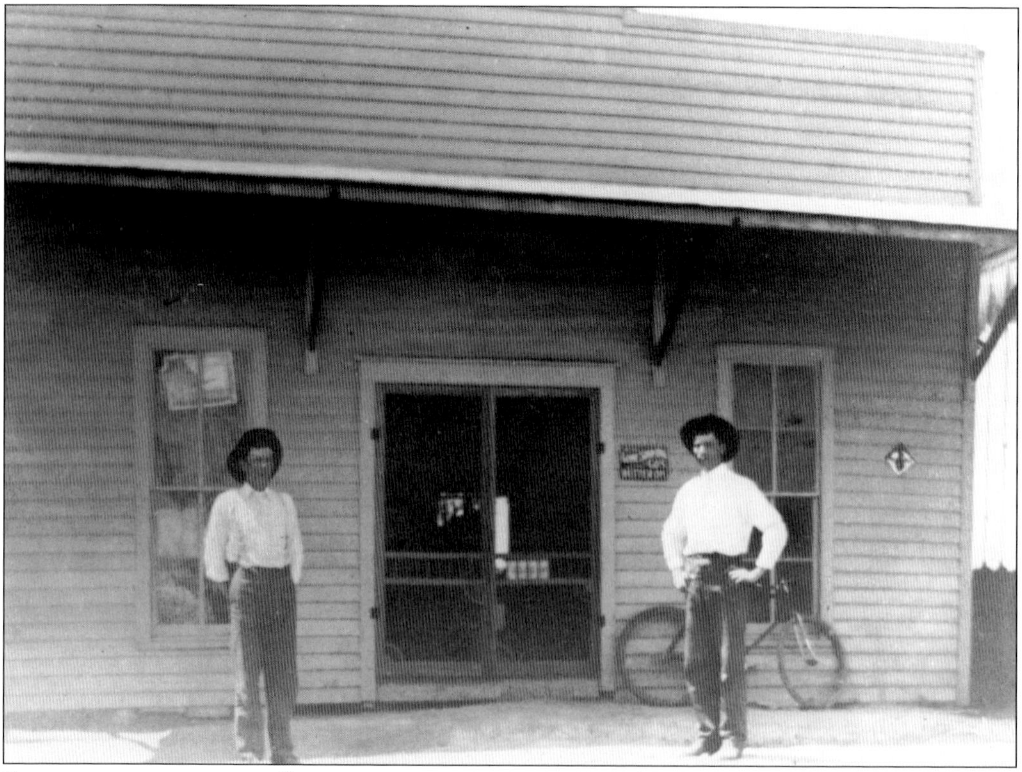

Even a community too small to support numerous commercial enterprises often had a local general store. In 1908, D. Miller of Dublin traded the Gilbert & White building to J.W. Onstott of Purves for another Purves structure called the Olinger store. The Lone Star Oil advertisement may date this photograph to the 1920s. (Linda Tolston.)

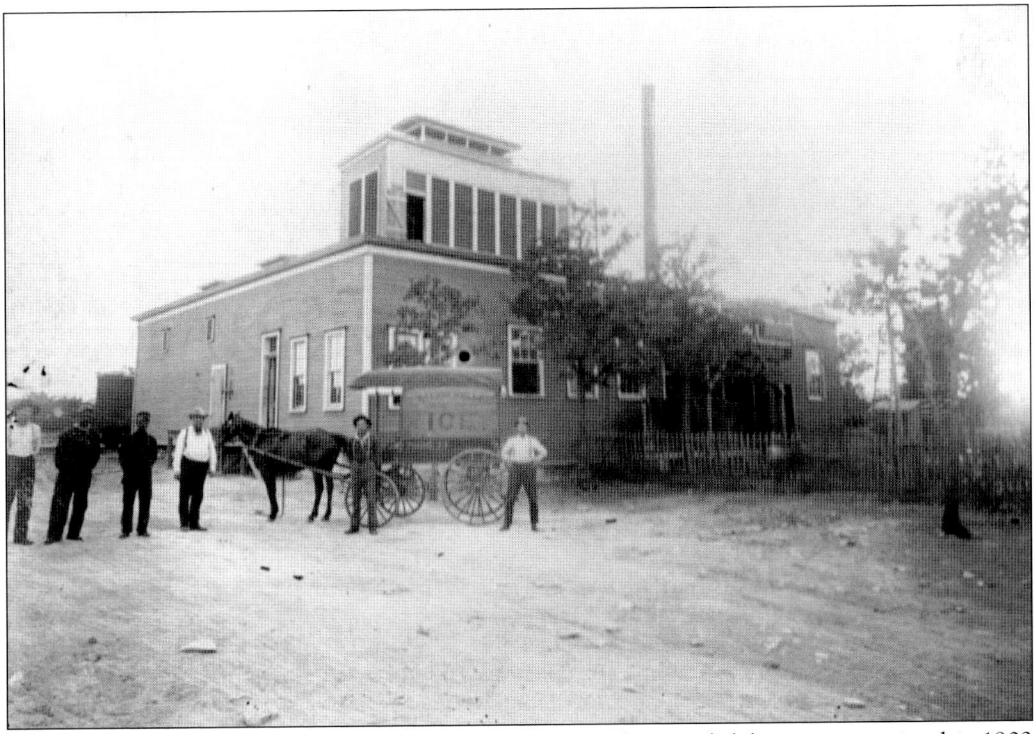

Six men stand before the Stephenville Ice Company plant and delivery wagon in this 1903 image. According to *People-Events and Erath County, Texas*, by Arden Jean Schuetz and Wilma Jean Schuetz, the first Stephenville ice plant was owned and operated by John Fooshe. Thurber had an ice plant by 1896, and Dublin had one by 1898. Each ice plant benefitted financially by shipping large orders via railway. (SHHM.)

W.H. Main opened Stephenville Bottling Works next to W.A. Dawson's saloon in 1900. Main acquired water from Mineral Wells to carbonate it. George Henry "Bud" Ramsey of Lingleville was a farmer, Populist Central Club member, musician, and song leader. Before 1910, he was manufacturing soda water at Stephenville's bottling plant. A wire "U"-type cork was pushed down on the glass bottle to open it. (SHHM.)

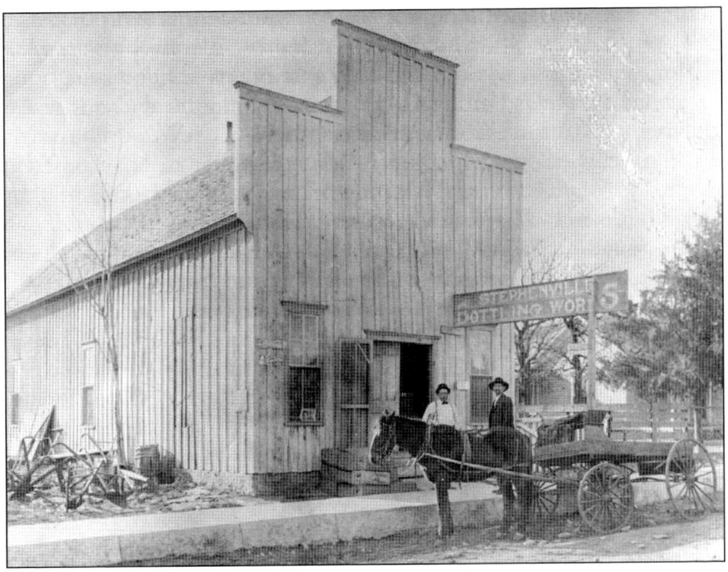

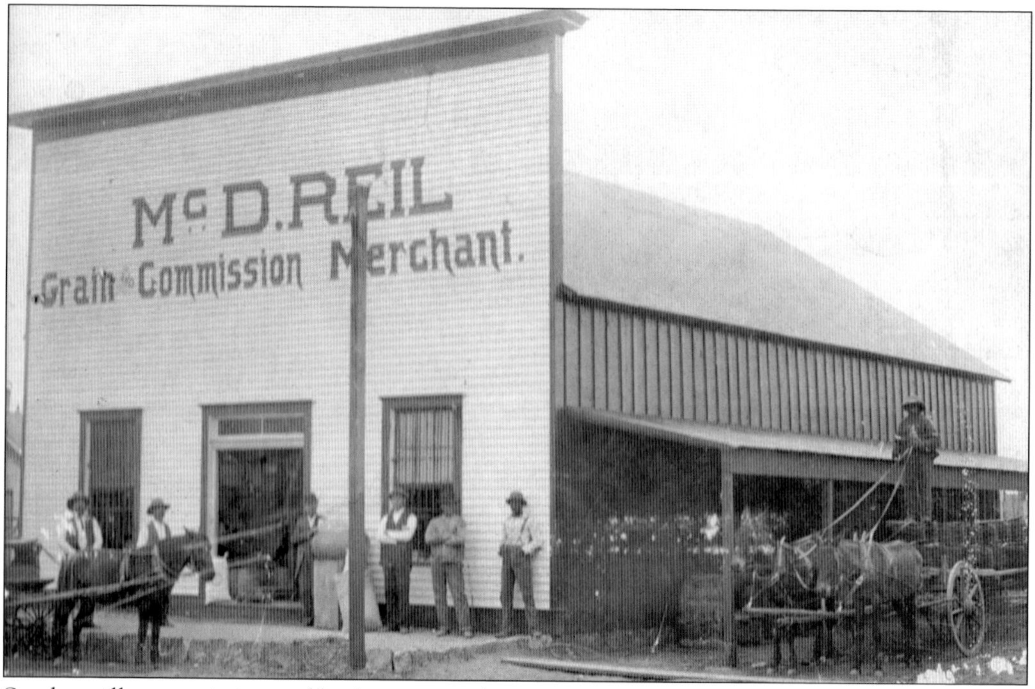

Stephenville commission and brokerage merchant George McDuffie Reil, or "McD. Reil," bought and sold all manner of goods. He was a First National Bank director, an IOOF officer, and a charter member of Stephenville's Knights of Pythias lodge. He served with W.J. Wilson and Lee Young on the first board of trustees for the Stephenville Presbyterian Church.

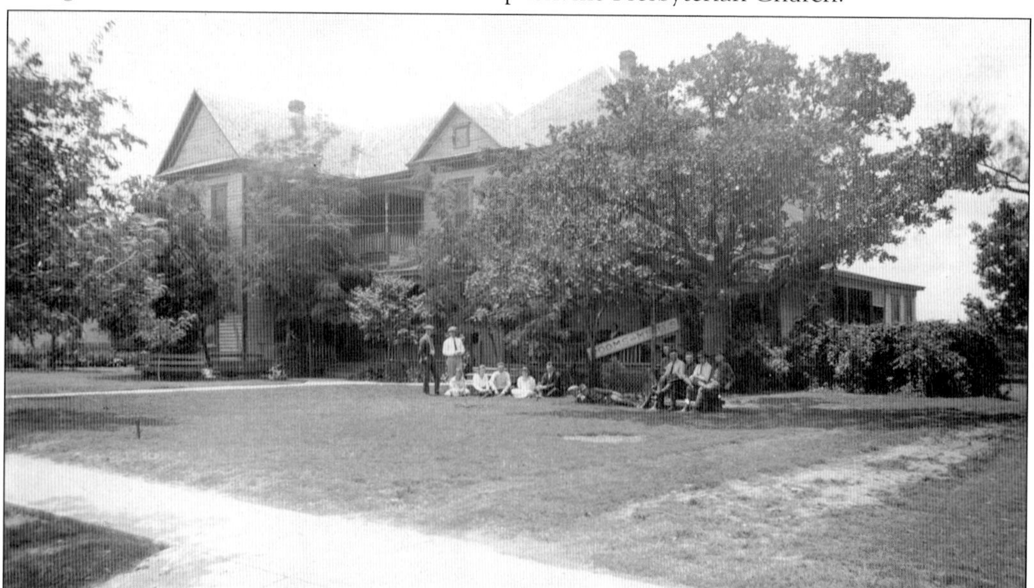

Mothershead Cottage is pictured here in 1908. After the death of her grocer husband, Henry, Sallie McCleskey Mothershead opened her home as a boardinghouse. A charter member of the Stephenville Twentieth Century Club, Sallie served as its 12th president. She was a leader in the creation of the library, the first museum, and the local chamber of commerce. Sallie McCleskey closed Mothershead Cottage in 1952 due to her declining health, and she died in 1959. (SHHM.)

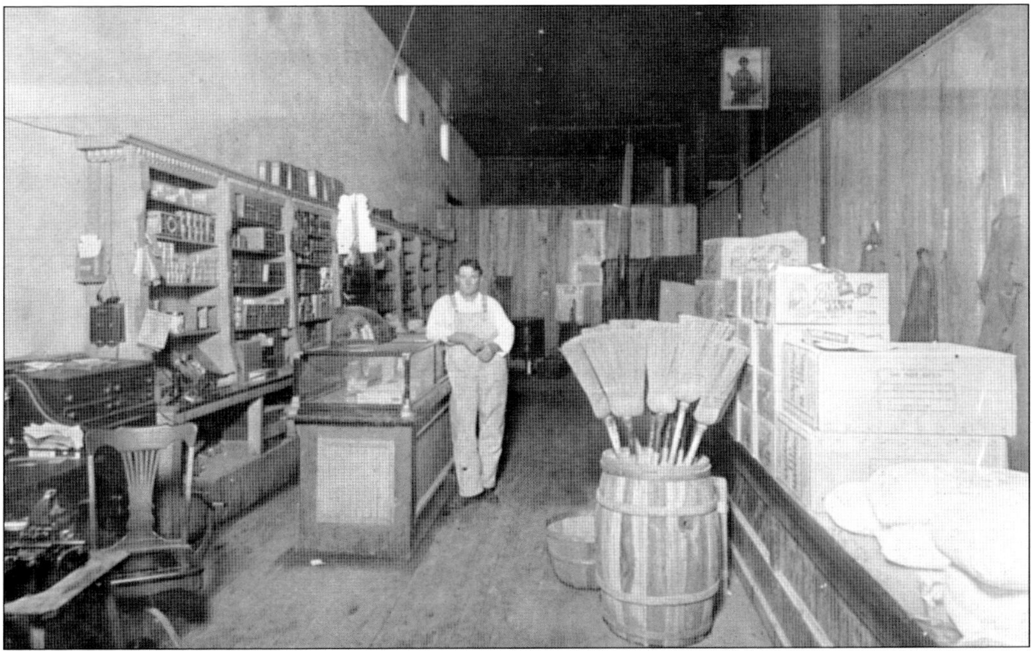

In the 1910s, William Thomas "Will" Pyeatt (pictured) advertised paying the highest prices for country produce while providing delivery of "Staple and Fancy Groceries" from his Dublin store. In the 1920s, he added confections, colas, and tobaccos. By 1930, he and his wife, Willie Belle, operated a store and café. While running his Dublin café, philatelist "Uncle Bill" chatted with patrons about his coin and stamp collections. (Catherine Rampley.)

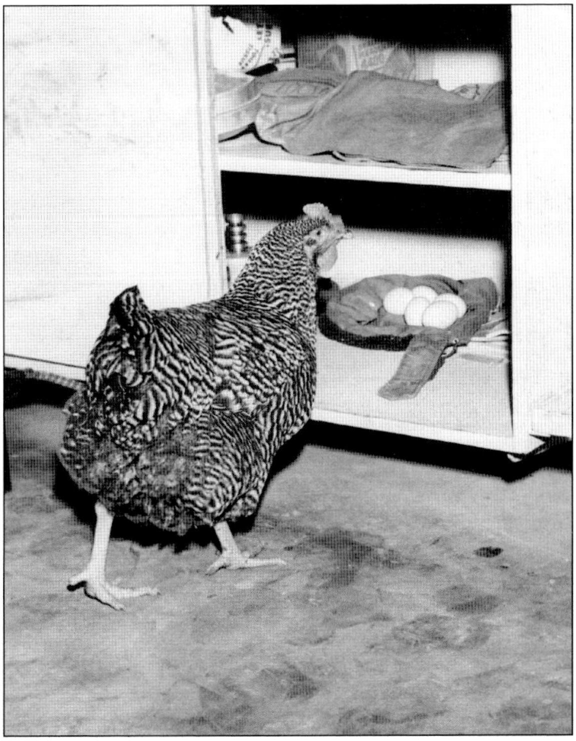

When John A. Rampley owned Stephenville's Sinclair Service Center across the street from Jake and Dorothy's Café, he had a regular morning visitor. Big Bertha, a Plymouth Rock hen, visited the business at 403 East Washington Street daily, laying an egg during each visit. If the cabinet was closed, she patiently waited until someone opened it. Big Bertha was a pet of Kay Neely, who lived nearby. (Catherine Rampley.)

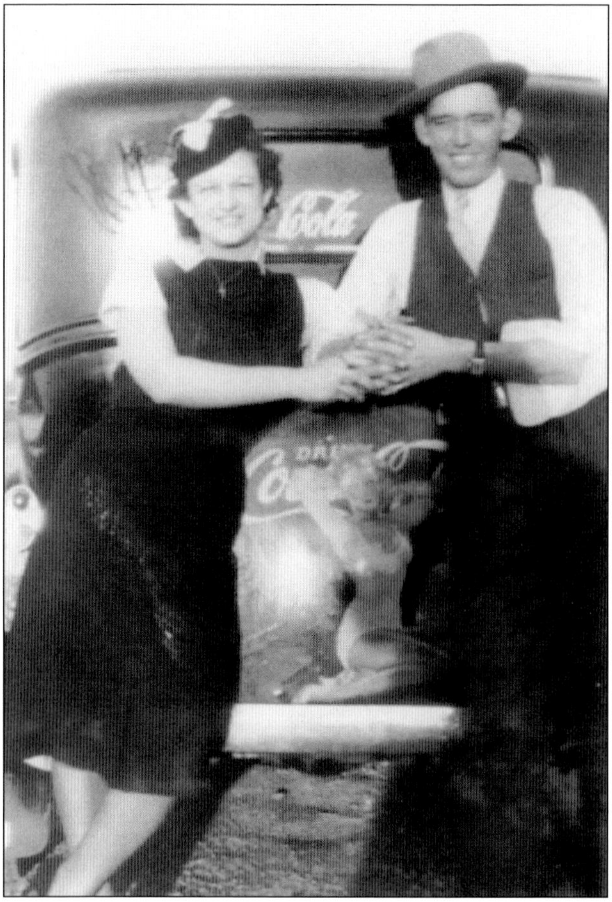

Woodrow Francis "Woodie" Howell (right) was born to Amanda Pearl Reed and Abraham Gideon Howell of Dublin. In 1939, Woodie married Lela Maudean Dendy (left), daughter of Mary Idora Thomas and Joseph Wallace Dendy. The couple moved to Abilene in 1950, where Woodie became a co-owner of Abilene Air Conditioning Company. Woodie was active in the South Abilene Kiwanis Club, where he served as president. (Barbara Dalton Jones.)

Twenty-year-old Woodie Howell (left) of Dublin was a driver for Coca-Cola in 1937. His good buddy and coworker Len Wells Dalton was a Coca-Cola salesman. A few years later, both men served in World War II—Howell with the Army and Dalton with the Navy. (Barbara Dalton Jones.)

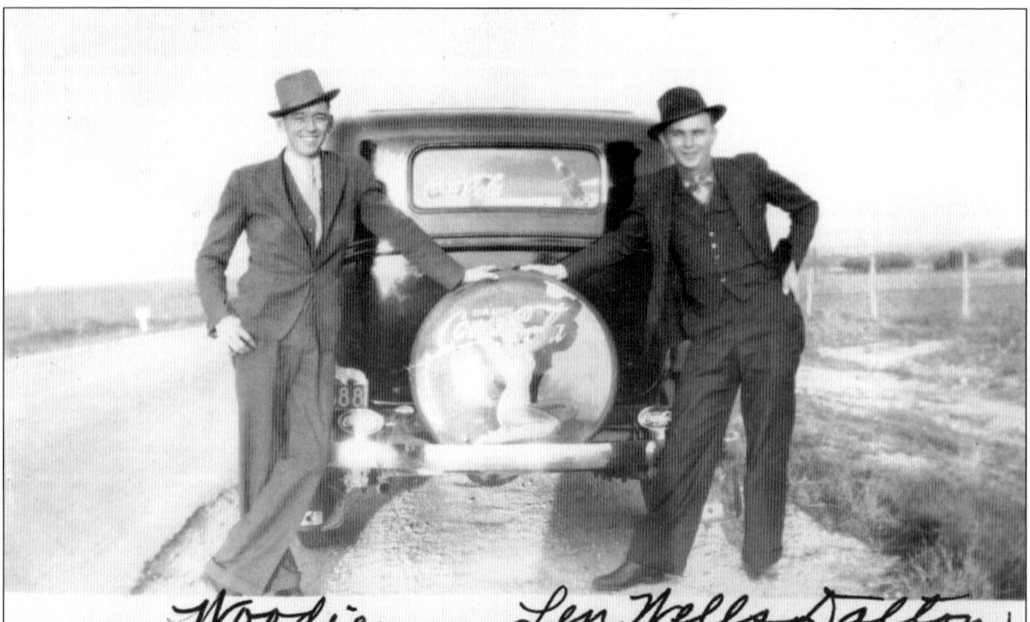

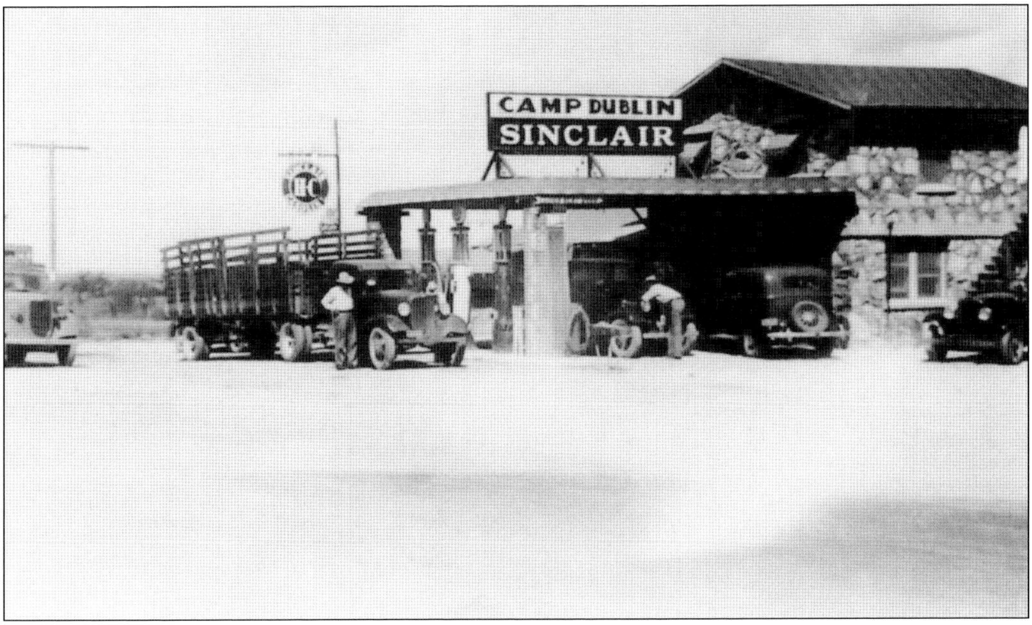

Civil War veteran organizations Grand Army of the Republic and United Confederate Veterans Association promoted comradeship, pension rights, widow and orphan relief, and homes for old soldiers. For years, men attended a regional multiday reunion camp held just outside of Dublin. In 1930, the Dalton family acquired the Camp Dublin property, building a service station, store, and café there. A 1937 Camp Dublin lunchroom advertised a "Sunday Dinner of Baked Chicken with Dressing, English Peas, Green Beans, Corn, Fruit Salad, Hot Rolls, Pineapple Up-side-Down Cake, Drink, and Dessert for 30 cents." A 1938 remodel led to the stuccoing of the bus stop's rock exterior and the addition of four motel cottages with hot and cold running water. The Dalton family managed the travel center in the 1930s and 1940s, offering Sinclair gas and Goodyear tires.

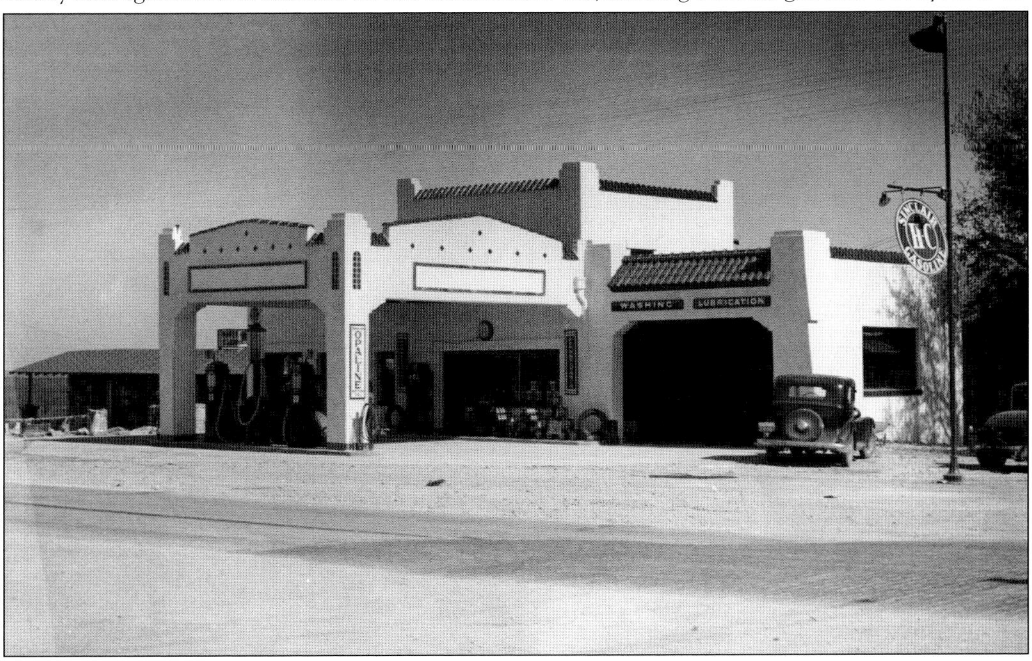

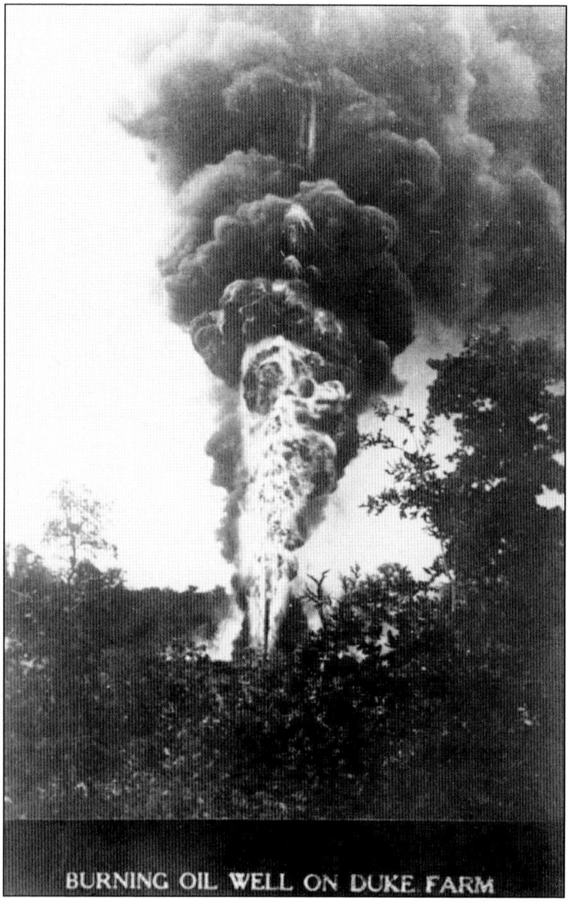

In September 1918, a Desdemona wildcat oil well on Duke Farm hit gas, caught fire, burned out after several days, and then became a great oil producer. Drilling and its many support businesses greatly influenced the region for about three years. Farmers rented rooms, leased land and mineral rights, and hauled freight using wagon teams. Livery and transfer businesses, rooming houses, and eateries opened and closed during this time. (SHHM.)

By 1930, half of the population had moved west. Orchards, nurseries, peanuts, feed crops, and dairy emerged. Poultry became a leading crop from the 1930s into the 1950s. Here, a Railway Express Agency truck is pulling a series of flatbed trailers of turkeys from Tarleton State University's poultry husbandry department. From left to right are an unidentified student; T.A. Hensarling, department head from 1939 to 1946; and Prof. E.C. Johnson. (SHHM.)

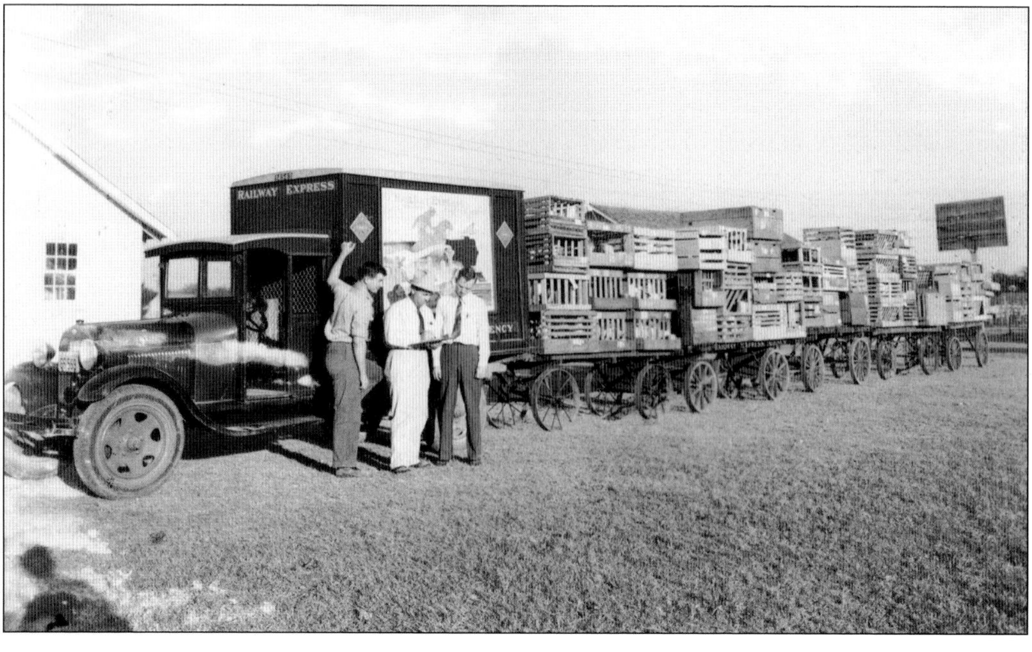

Four

Thoroughfares and Connections

Surveyor, soldier, and legislator George B. Erath, for whom the county was named, remembered the area from an earlier trip through the region. While the Bosque and Paluxy Rivers were not particularly navigable, fresh water served as a conduit for movement, and movement created thoroughfares.

As early as 1860, a stagecoach carried freight, mail, and passengers through Erath County as it traveled west. One route traversed from Waco to Hico and on to Duffau Springs. Spent horses were relieved with stops at Armstrong and Chalk Mountain. The operation of the stagecoach was erratic during the Civil War. In the 1870s, the Chidester Stage Line traveled from Fort Worth to Bluff Dale, Stephenville, Dublin, Comanche, and westward.

By 1874, the coach heading from Fort Worth to Fort Yuma passed Dublin daily each way. Called the "big route," this was the longest line in the country at that time. Baptist minister Alexander Henry Dobkins provided replenishment and respite at his Double Inn. This continued until the arrival of coal-burning locomotives.

In 1876, no Texas railway existed west of Fort Worth. Buggies and hacks made regular runs from Stephenville to outlying towns such as Harpers Mill and Thurber. Cattle drives in the 1870s rambled across Big Pasture Crossing to and from the Leon River. Until the Texas Central Railroad entered the county in 1881, all groceries, lumber, and freight were hauled from the nearest railhead at Waco by ox- or mule-drawn wagon.

The arrival of the railroad reshaped the Cross Timbers and West Texas. A portal to the outside world was opened as the rails provided a means for the transportation of goods to and from market. Railway lines were built by pick and shovel with dirt and rock moved by wagon teams. Railroads crept onward, fostering evolution along their path. Depots seeded towns such as Alexander and Harbin. "Out near the Mayfield place" became Clairette. Trains also carried the mail. In 1889, the Fort Worth & Rio Grande Railway reached Stephenville via Bluff Dale. Travel and transportation gave life to small villages. Later, improved road conditions and gasoline-powered vehicles sealed the fate of those same locations.

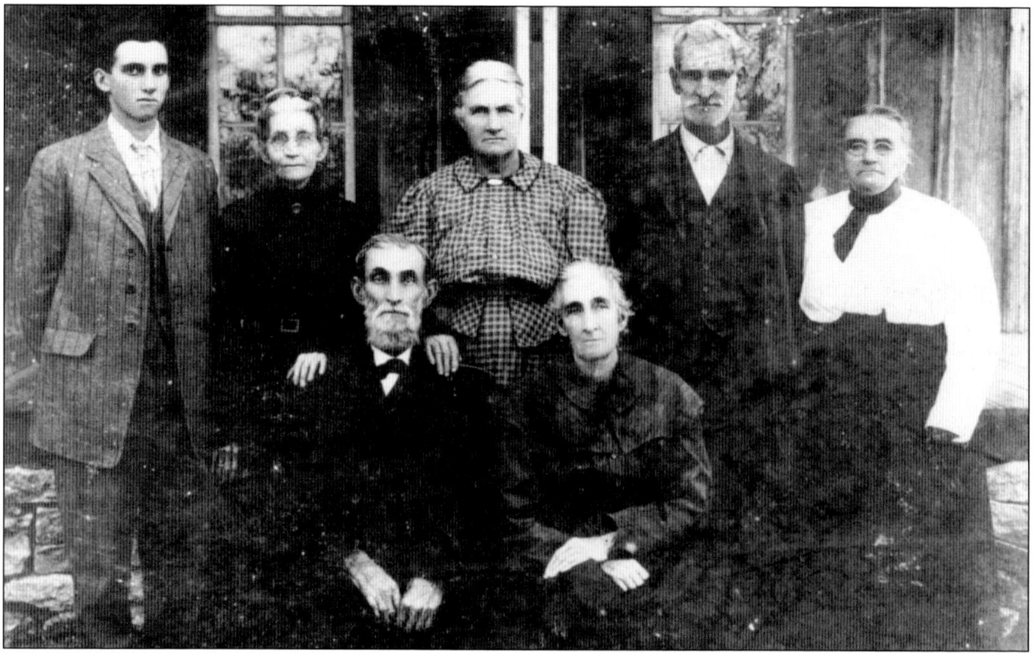

One by one, the children of Abraham Leverett journeyed from Alabama to Texas, making Greens Creek their home. Pictured here are, from left to right, (first row, seated) Nicholas T. Leverett and his daughter Elizabeth Leverett Strickland; (second row, standing) James, son of Eli Kennedy Howell; Abraham's children Matilda Leverett Howell and her twin Malitta Leverett Bradfield; Gideon Leverett; and Gideon's wife, Sarah Armstrong Leverett. (Barbara Dalton Jones.)

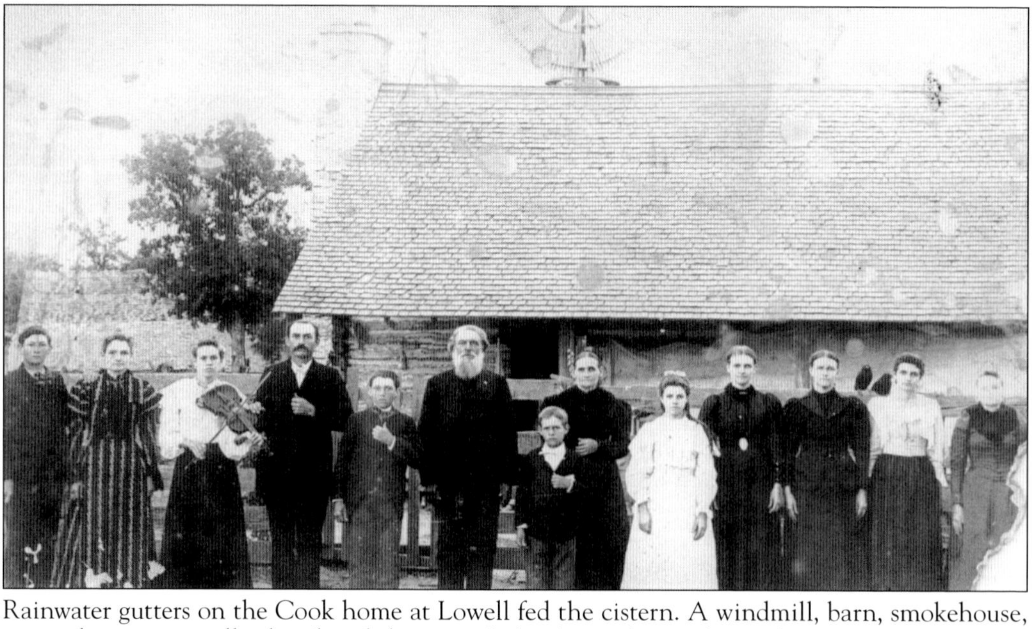

Rainwater gutters on the Cook home at Lowell fed the cistern. A windmill, barn, smokehouse, corncrib, granary, cellar lined with homemade bricks, and roses lay within a fenced yard. The Cook family members pictured here around 1900 are, from left to right, Joe Dudley, Amanda "Mandy," Oda, Walter, Lee, Lum, John Thomas, George Finley, Malescia Almeda Graham, Delmar Pearl, Lizabeth Rosalie, Cynthia Paralee, Ira Dell, and Alice Jane. (Nelda Blankenship Keever.)

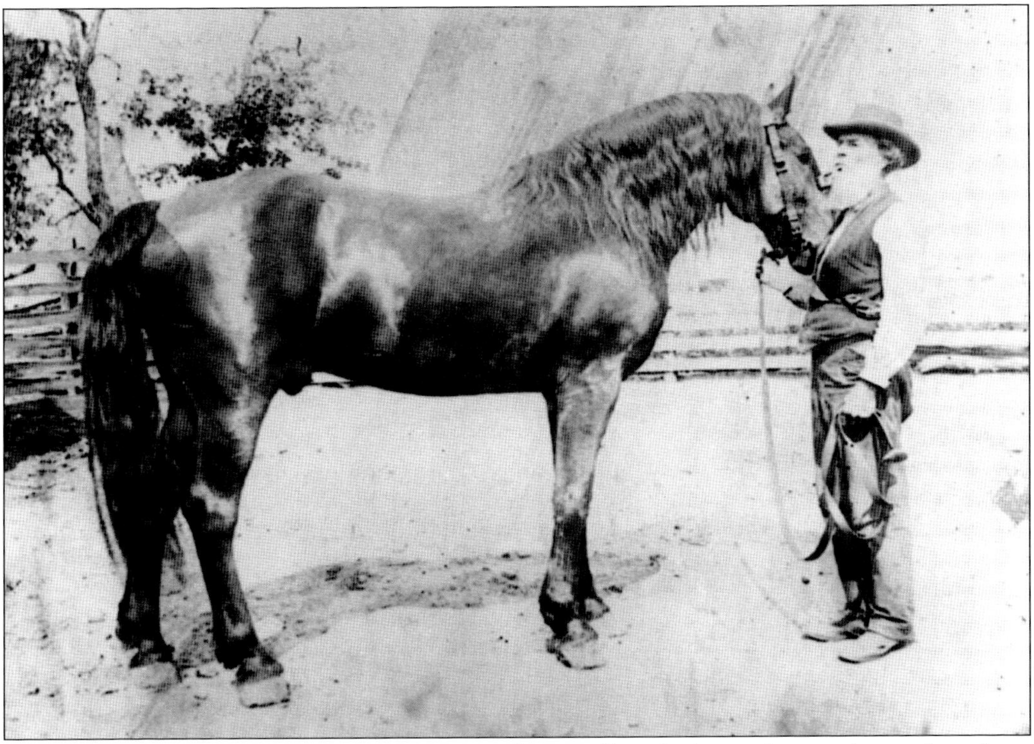

John Thomas Cook returned to Georgia to purchase Dallas, the horse that was his pride and joy. The Cook place on Armstrong Creek was a Butterfield Stage stop. A stop might exist every 16 to 20 miles for fresh horses. After driving all day, a driver would stay overnight in the bunkhouse before heading out on a returning stage the following day. A racetrack was located north of the stagecoach run. (Nelda Blankenship Keever.)

These unidentified Edna Hill men formed a line at the cotton gin with their wagons loaded with as much cotton as the team could pull. Prior to railroad tracks being laid around 1880, cotton was not a cash crop in the area due to the difficulty and expense of moving freight to market. With the change in transportation options, some 50 gins opened around the county. Wagon teams remained essential.

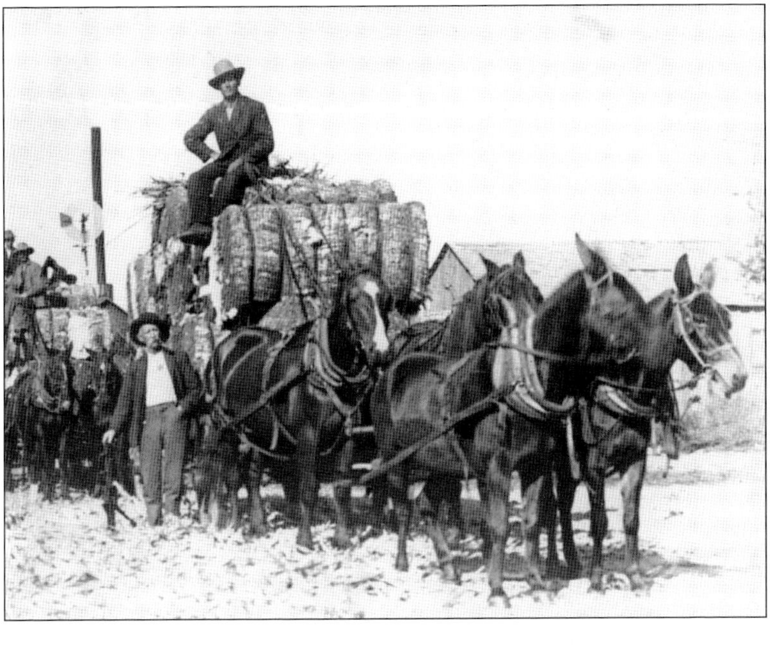

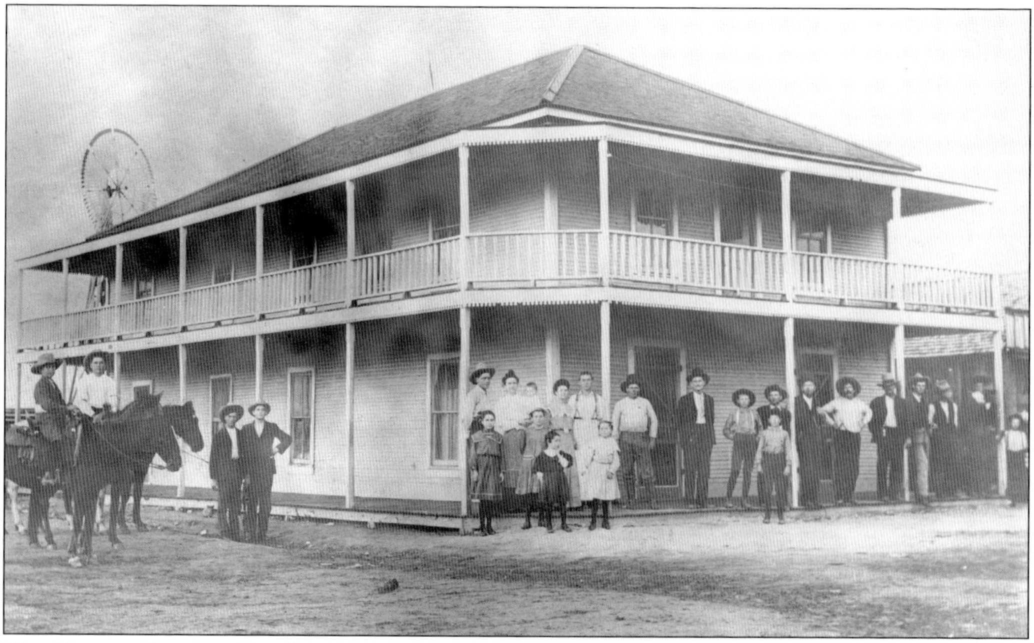

The 22-room Stephen Hotel at Purves, one of the largest in the region, was owned and operated by Mattie Case Stephen from 1900 until it burned down in 1914. The hotel hosted boarding travelers and permanent occupants, and the lobby was used for community gatherings. In this image, the Jim and Leathia Whisenant family is standing at center, with baby Wayland in Leatha's arms. The man in the suit standing to the right of the door is Leathia's father, J.J. Knox.

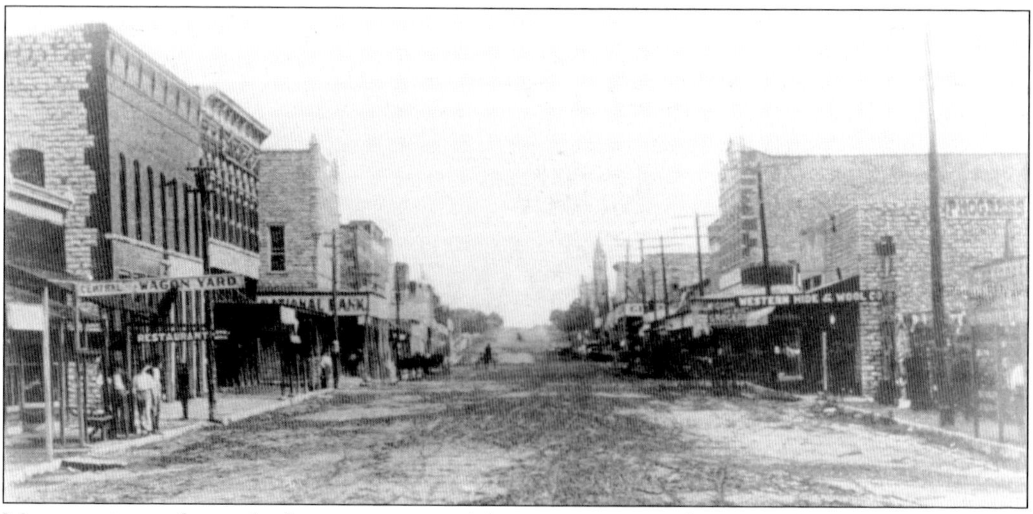

Men are pictured outside the restaurant and front entrance to the Central Wagon Yard. Utility poles and the distant First Methodist Church steeple date this image to around 1901. Horse and buggies or wagons and teams were the norm on the busy, sandy dirt roads. In this image looking north on Patrick Street, McCormick Grocer is north of Western Hide and Wool Company and the *Dublin Progress* newspaper office.

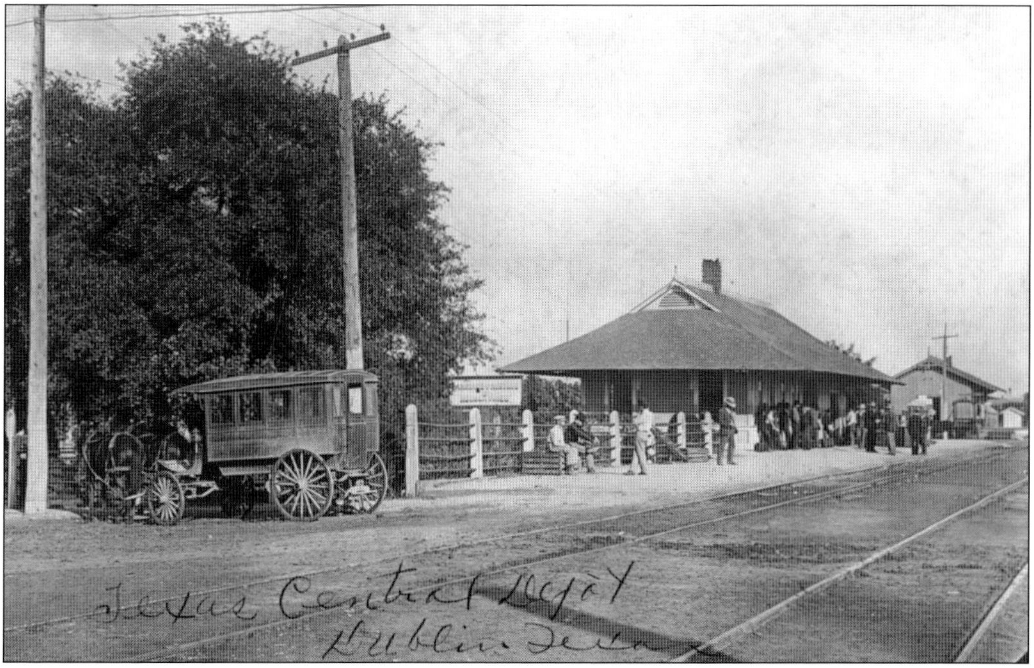

A crowd awaits the next arrival at the Texas Central Railroad depot in Dublin. In the 19th century, the railroads often provided rides for patrons to and from depots and hotels. The imprint in the metal above the windows of the passenger van reads: "Always on Time." A team of horses waits, ready to deliver customers aboard the metal-rimmed, wooden-wheeled transport.

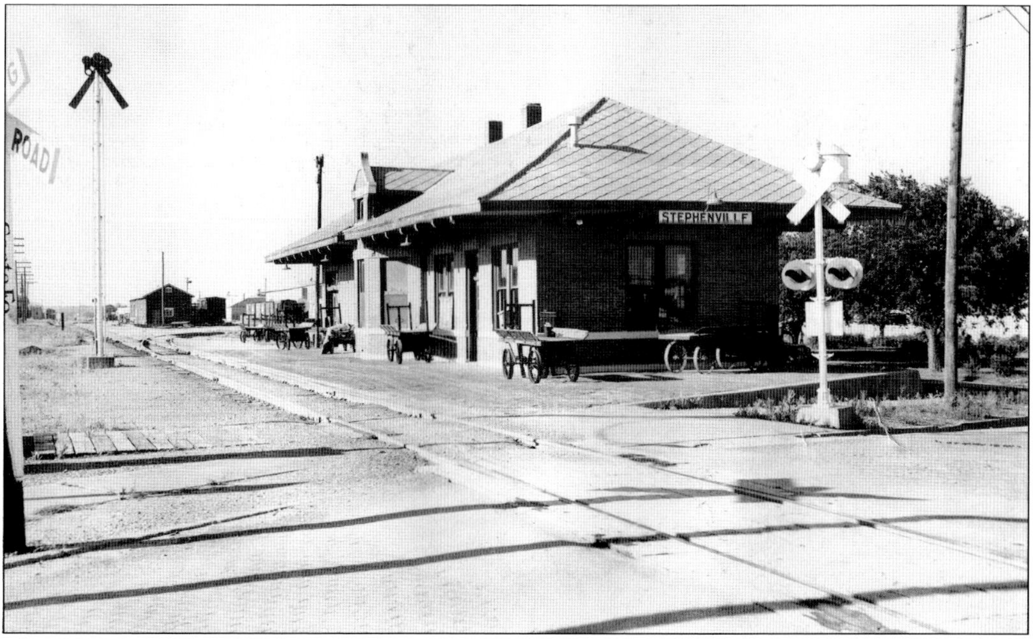

Flooding of the Bosque River to the south of the courthouse influenced commercial growth to the north and west of the square. When railroad tracks were laid in the 1890s, Stephenville's Santa Fe Railway depot was constructed on West Tarleton Street near Washington Street. Shown surrounded by baggage trolleys and freight wagons, the structure was demolished in 1958.

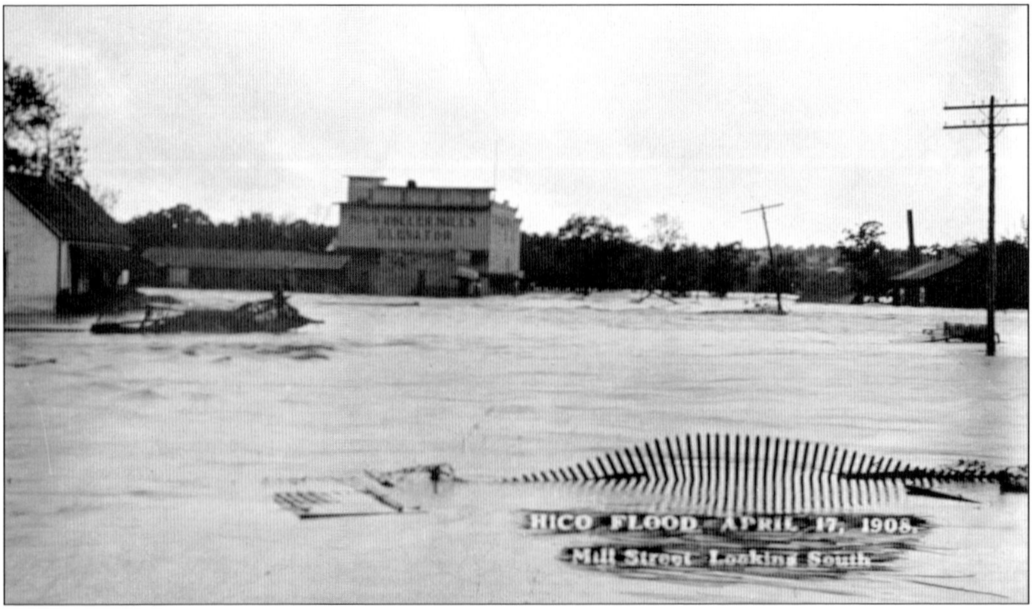

Torrential rainfall on April 16 and 17 in 1908 impacted much of Texas. Damage throughout the state was estimated to be in the millions. Erath County suffered thousands of dollars in property loss. The oil mill in Hico lost 200 bales of cotton, 12 oil tanks, and the cotton and seed hull house. Bosque River floodwaters at Stephenville's Arendell gin met markings from an 1892 flood. Pony Creek experienced a rise of 20 feet. An Alarm Creek sandbar piled "as high as a house." At Selden, three children were struck by lightning. High winds and hail beat fruit from the trees. Knee-high corn was replaced by logs and debris. Livestock disappeared or drowned. Some lost food stores, cooking utensils, clothing, and livestock feed. Many were left homeless as rushing waters damaged or washed away houses, barns, and fences.

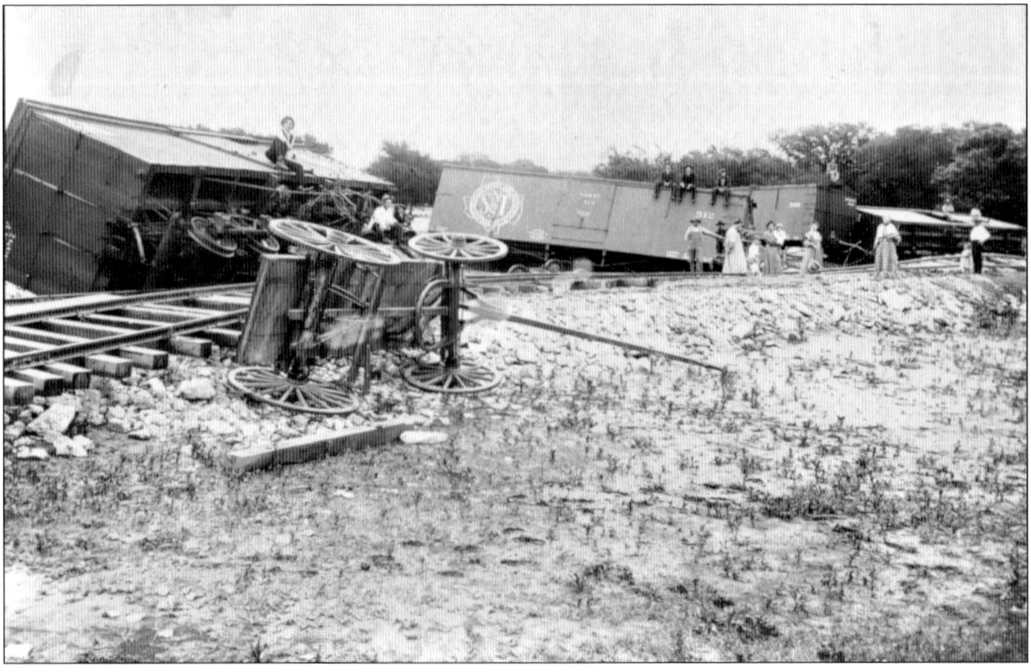

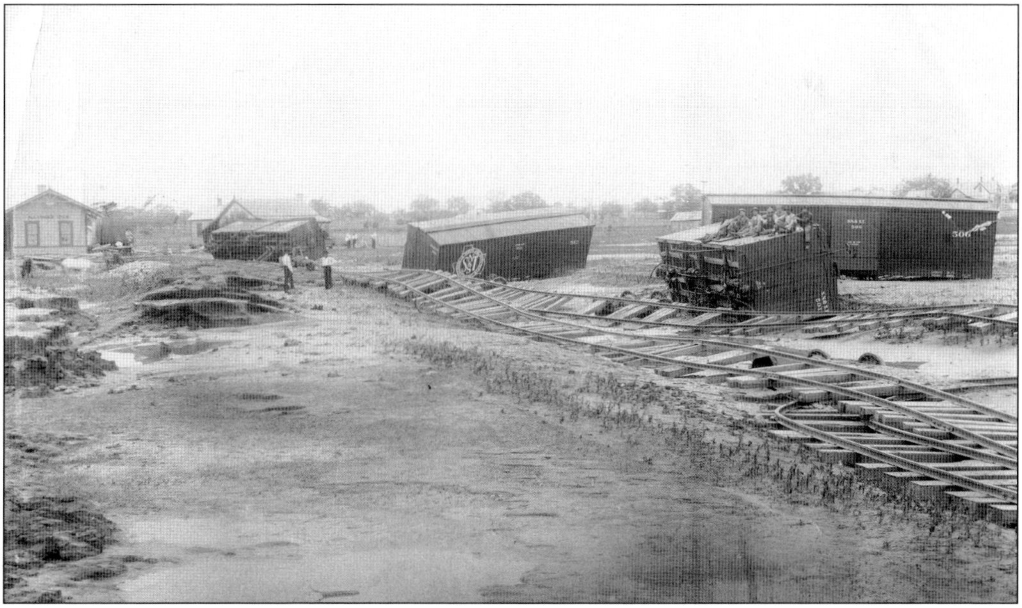

The Stephenville North & South Texas Railway made Hamilton no longer dependent on wagon freight from Hico and Gatesville. The venture was promoted by Cage and Crow Bank, whose directors included John L. Spurlui, Bruce Crow Cage, James McGonigal Cage, James Day Cage, James House Cage, William Samuel Watson, Marshall Ferguson, and Mary Jane Crow. Claud Webster was the Texas Central Railway conductor when the washout occurred. The Leon River crossing was destroyed. One length of rails was carried away a quarter mile. The Fort Worth & Rio Grande Railroad sustained damage near Harbin. Flooding paralyzed travel and commerce, because repairs could not be made until the waters receded. Many sightseers came to see the toppled cars and mangled rails. (Both, Catherine Rampley.)

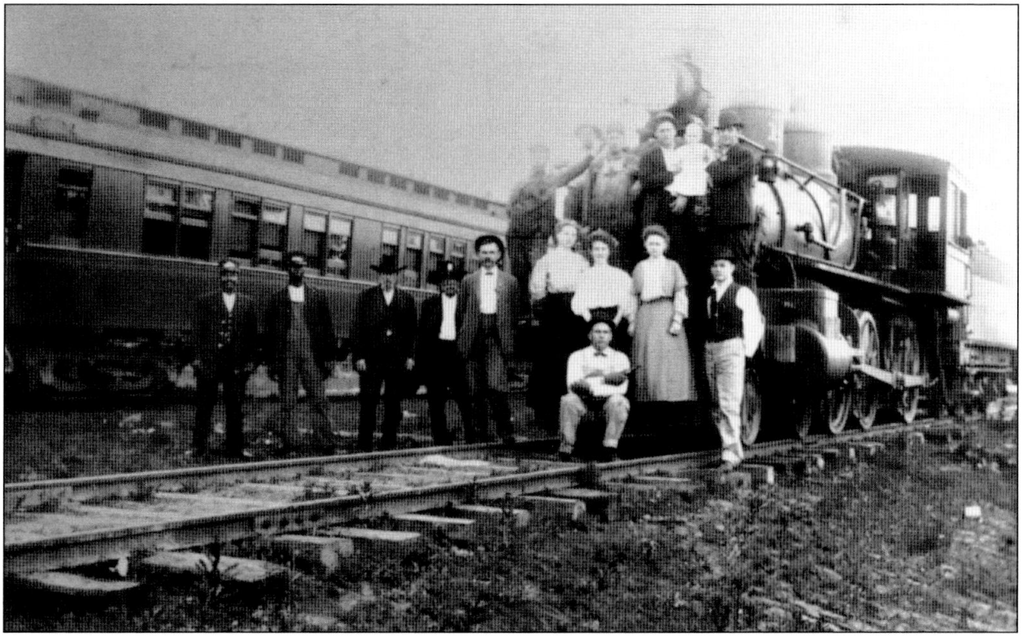

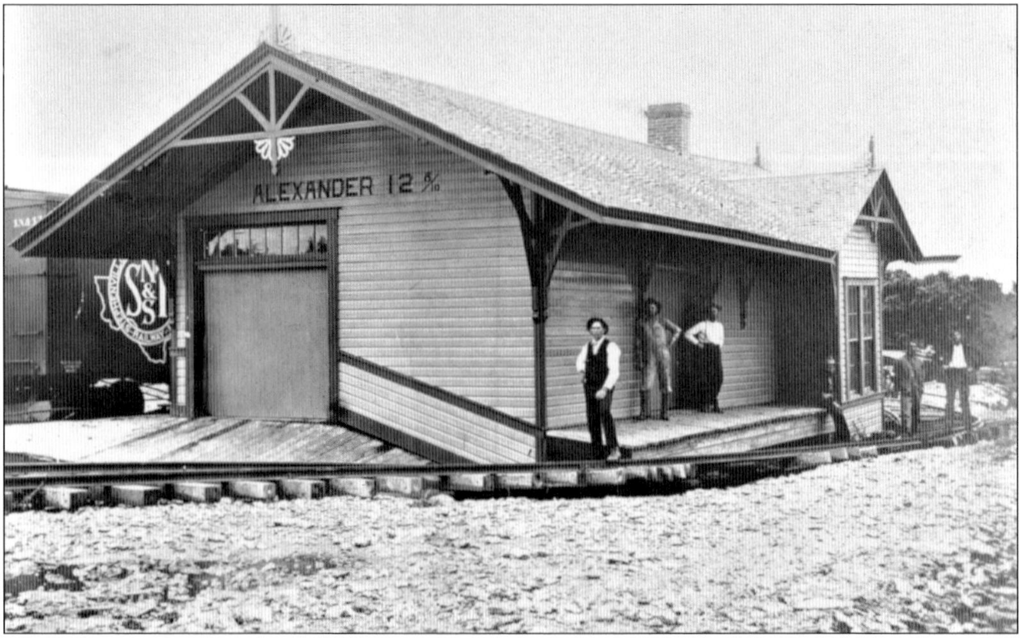

The Stephenville North & South Texas Railway laid 43 miles of track between Stephenville and Hamilton. The railroad shared a station with Stephenville's Fort Worth & Rio Grande Railroad (Frisco). It had two locomotives, a roundhouse, and depots at Hamilton, Carlton, Spurlin, and Alexander. Rails crossed the Texas Central Railway, which journeyed from Waco to Hico, Duffau, Clairette, Alexander, Harbin, and Dublin close to today's Texas Highway 6. (Catherine Rampley.)

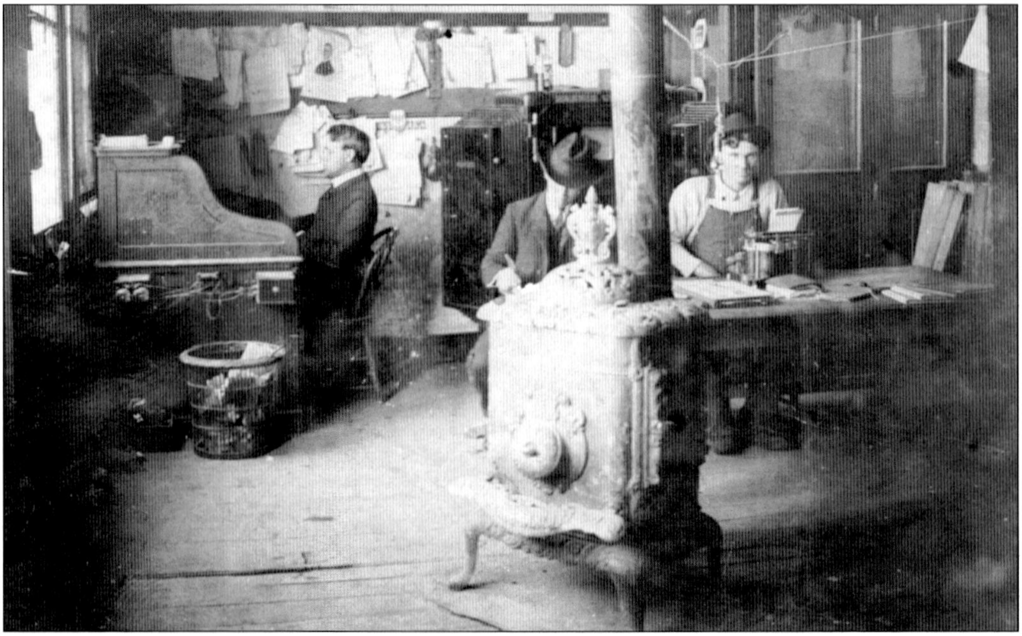

Born in 1878, William "Bill" Thomas Pyeatt (right) married Willie Bell Watson in 1902. In 1909, he left his position as cashier at Dublin's Texas Central Railway depot for a similar assignment in Oklahoma. Not finding it to their liking, they returned to Dublin and became business owners. Over the years, they had stores or cafes in De Leon, Stephenville, and Dublin. (Catherine Rampley.)

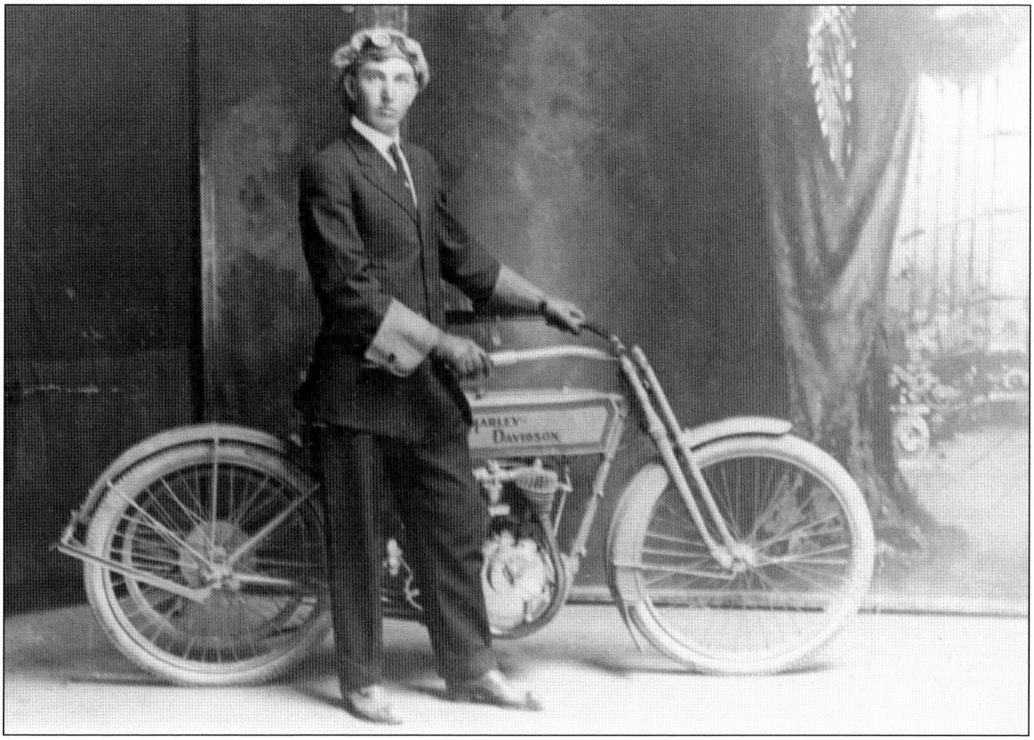

Shown with an early Harley-Davidson motorcycle, Oscar Lee Bristow was 1 of 10 children of Emily Dulcinia Beshears and Samuel Houston Bristow. Horace and Oscar played basketball at Purves, and Horace taught from 1912 to 1916. Oscar married Myrtle Jefferson Olinger of Alexander. They relocated to Fort Worth for employment but remained active in Purves with annual homecoming celebrations and their family and friends. They are buried at Pecan Cemetery.

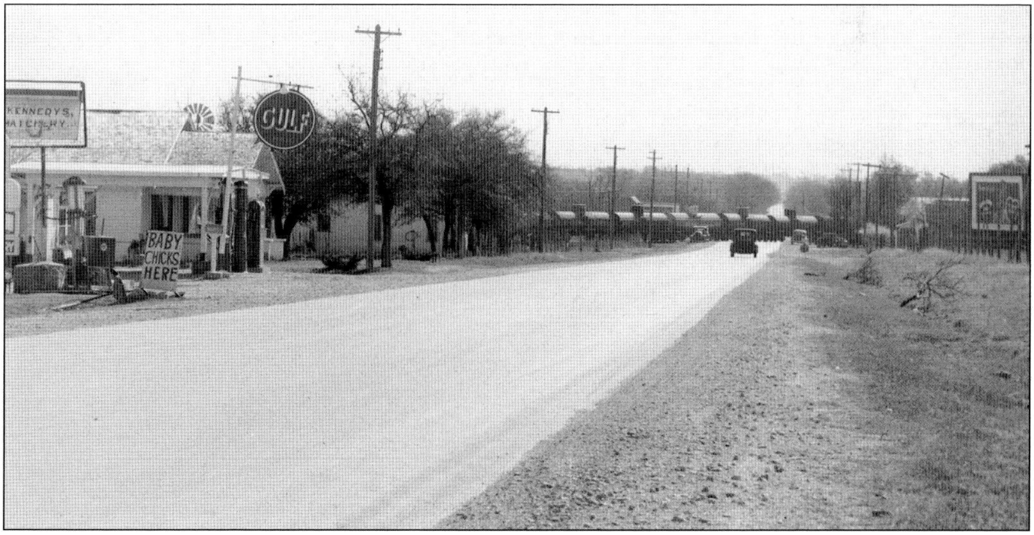

Vehicular traffic stops as the Texas Central Railway at Dublin crosses the road to De Leon. After several years at the De Leon Gulf station, Raymond Butler contracted with Gulf to manage the station in Dublin in 1925. In 1940, Kennedy's Hatchery advertised two-week-old baby chicks for a sale price of $6 per 100, and $8 per 100 for three- and four-week-old chicks.

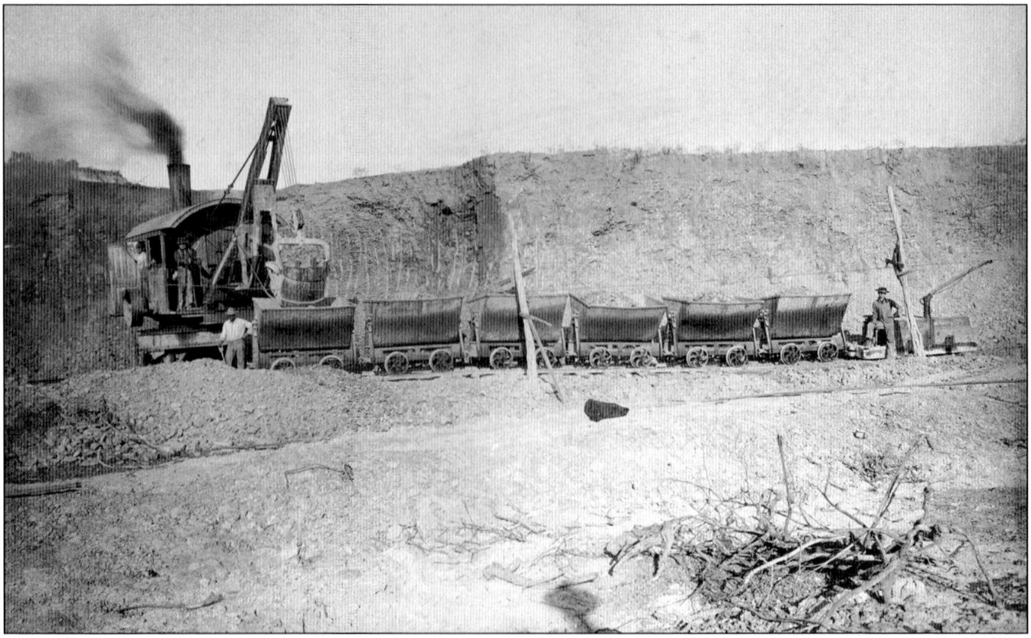

From 1888 to 1921, the Texas Pacific Coal Company mined coal in the northwest corner of the county near Thurber. In 1918, the Thurber Brick Company was established in the same area to manufacture tile, sewer pipes, paving bricks, and stoneware. Small amounts of oil and natural gas were also mined. The mining of Thurber coal deposits and manufacturing of paving brick brought European immigrants to the area.

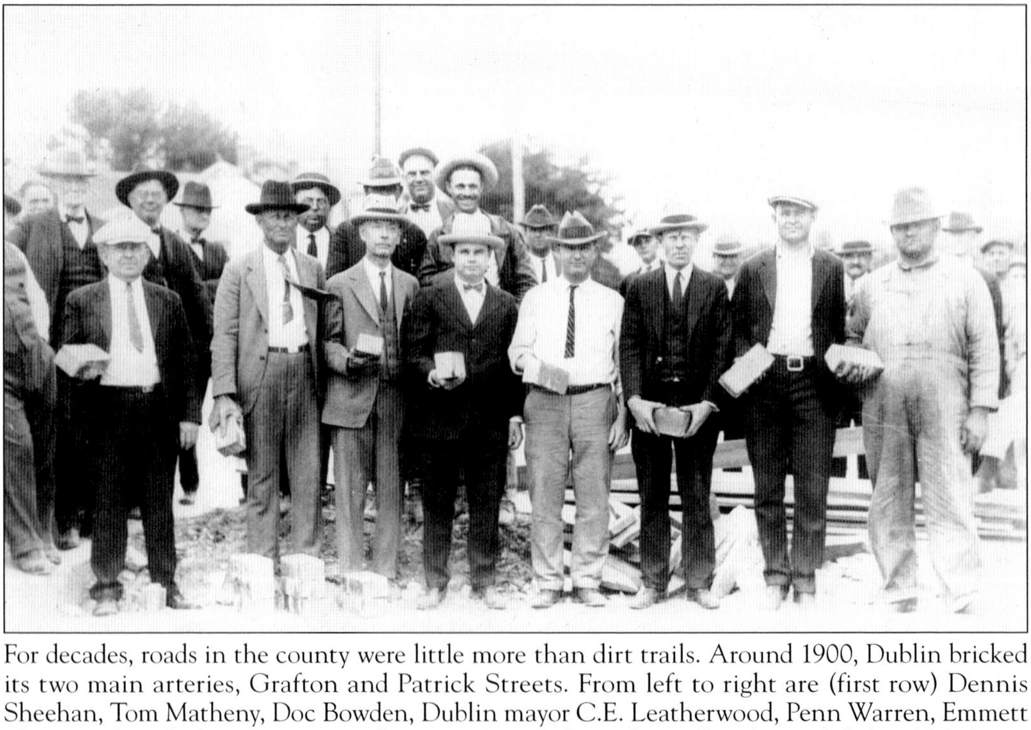

For decades, roads in the county were little more than dirt trails. Around 1900, Dublin bricked its two main arteries, Grafton and Patrick Streets. From left to right are (first row) Dennis Sheehan, Tom Matheny, Doc Bowden, Dublin mayor C.E. Leatherwood, Penn Warren, Emmett Blain, unidentified, and Harry Bradberry; W.P. "Uncle Buck" Hallmark stands behind Matheny.

The first dirigible in Erath County arrived at Thurber in October 1924. Those with vehicles drove to get a closer look. Built in 1923, ZR-1, or the USS *Shenandoah*, completed the first crossing of North America by airship. The first of four US Navy rigid airships, it was the first fueled by helium rather than hydrogen.

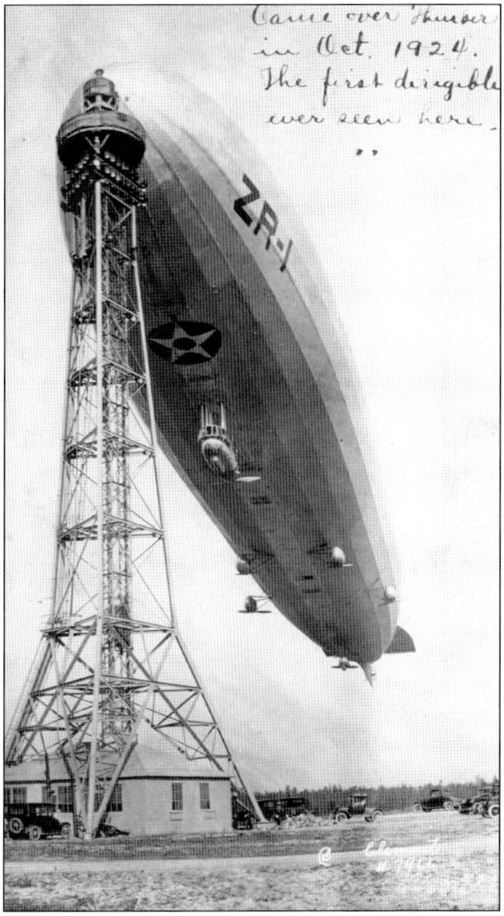

Labeled as "Railroad Bridge on Bosque River," this postcard features 13 men pausing from work to pose for the photograph. The reverse side identifies the card as printed by Wiseman Studios of Hico. Signs of pick and shovel work are reminders of the many bridges dug and built by hand before the availability of gasoline-powered construction equipment.

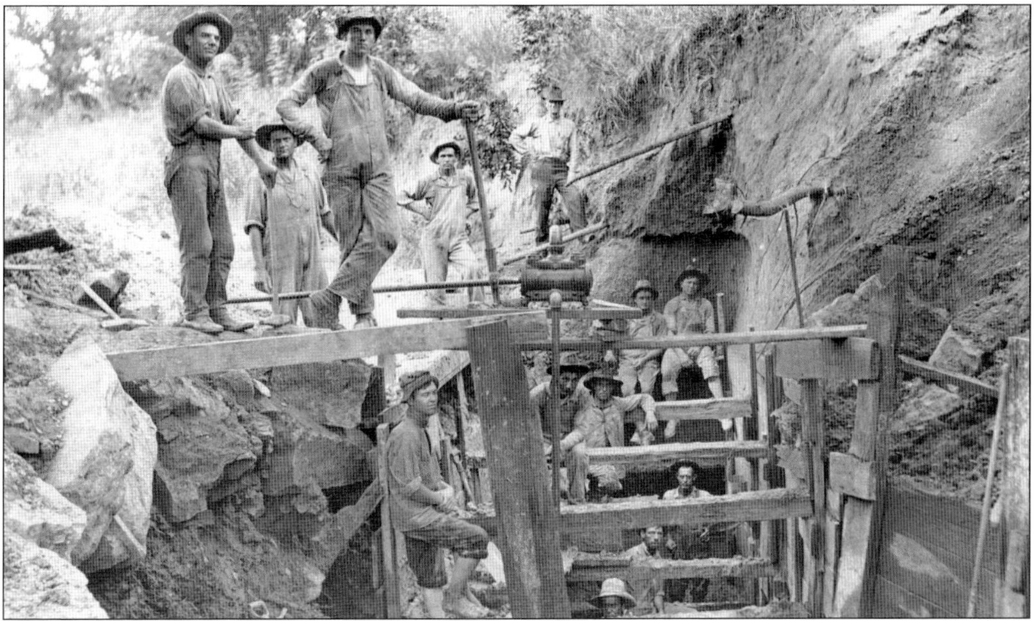

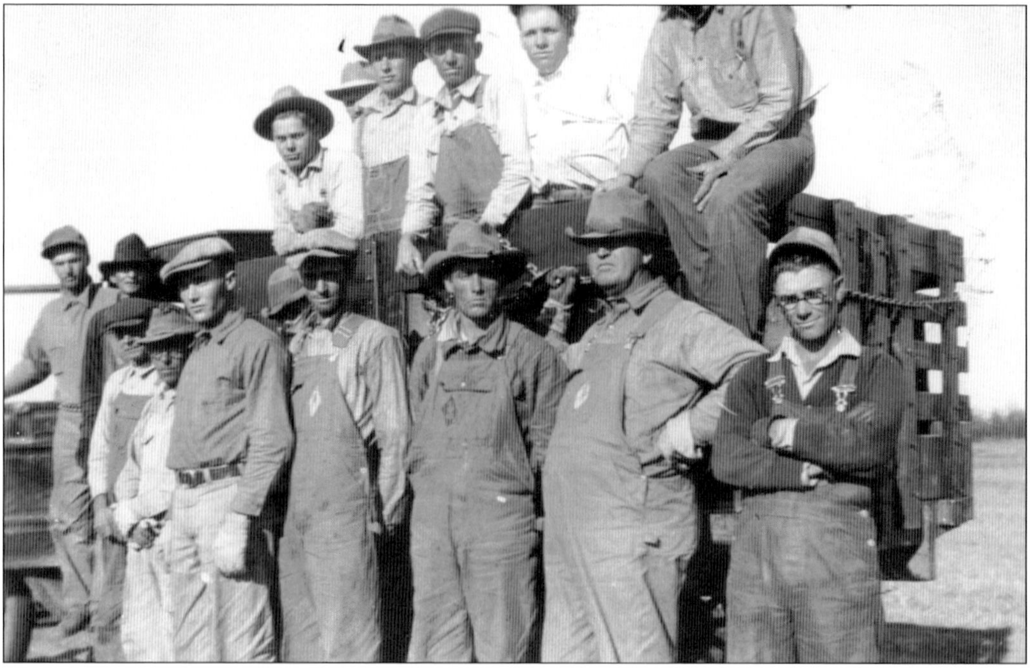

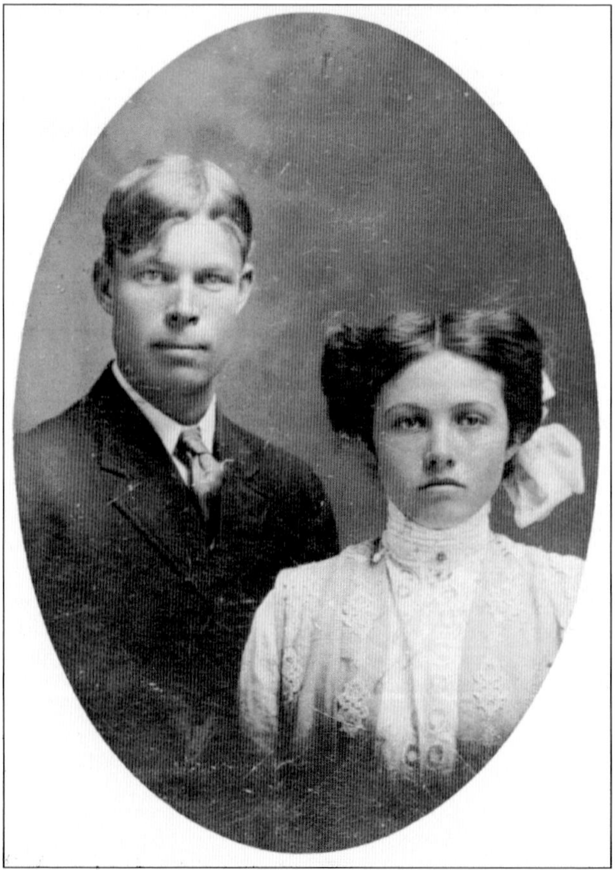

These 16 Edna Hill and Purves men were part of a federally funded Works Progress Administration (WPA) project for the building and improvement of roads. Government programs such as the WPA and Civilian Conservation Corps were established to provide jobs for those struggling during the Great Depression. Lingleville, Morgan Mill, and Stephenville had schools with gymnasiums and indoor restrooms built by WPA workers.

Goldie Ethel "Codie" Nixon and Lon Washington Randolph rode from Shiloh to the Dublin home of Rev. Lee Jones to be married on October 3, 1909. The ceremony was performed while the couple and their witness, Carra M. Bruner, remained in the buggy. The blue-eyed, red-haired Lon was a lifelong farmer, and on his 1942 World War II draft registration, he reported that he was employed by the Works Progress Administration.

Five

Law, Justice, and Order

By 1860, members of the peaceful Anadarko and Caddo tribes, who may have deterred Comanche raids, were removed to reservations in Indian Territory. The Erath County government had been in place for only five years when the Civil War began in 1861. Some men returned to their native states to enlist, while others joined Texas units. With the exodus of federal troops from frontier forts, Confederate Texas state troopers had hundreds of miles to protect and defend. The lack of law and order attracted a lawless contingent. Seniors, women, and children were confronted by deserters and dodgers, fugitives from justice, disorderly settlers, and marauding Comanches. Some temporarily fled eastward; others never returned. Minimal relief came during Reconstruction.

No district court was held in 1868 or 1870. In 1871, Erath lacked a county attorney, clerk, judge, and tax assessor. Sheriff W.G. Waller was also the tax collector. Four justices of the peace—Borroughs, Dobkins, Belcher, and Ramsey—conducted county affairs. An 1875 Texas State Constitutional Convention followed the 1874 election of Gov. Richard Coke and a Democratic legislature. A new constitution brought change, including established county roles of an animal and hide inspector, an attorney, constables, a clerk, four commissioners, a judge, justices of the peace, a sheriff, a surveyor, a tax assessor, and a treasurer. The three-day period for voting at the courthouse was changed to a single election day with voting boxes throughout the county.

A number of reputable citizens and Confederate veterans felt that lawbreakers were not being brought to justice and that worthy trial judgements were unlikely. More than one powerful vigilante group was formed. A juror's fear of retribution favored both the rustler and the vigilante. Law enforcement was tough on men. In 1877, Sheriff James Mastin was killed by a horse thief he was trying to arrest. In 1879, deputies John Ross and Marion Robertson were gunned down while serving a warrant for unlawfully carrying a pistol. Men and women often crossed from one side of the law to the other. Gilbreath and Turnbow men were known to ride with the mob but later worked as sheriffs, squashed illegal activity, and brought many to justice.

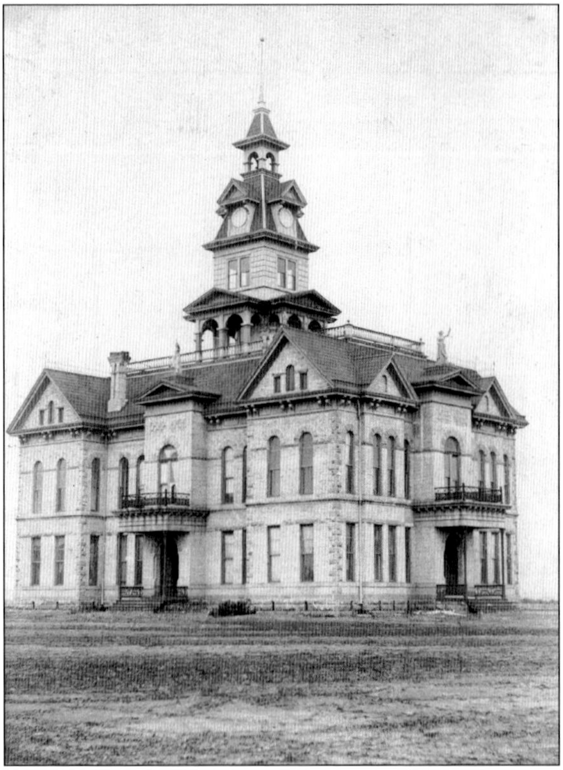

Erath's first courthouse doubled as a fort during Comanche raids. County documents were lost when the wooden structure burned down in 1866. A two-story stone successor was completed in 1876 and razed in 1891. Its replacement (shown here) has a three-story Victorian design by architect James Riely Gordon and was erected by contractor S.A. Tomlinson. Native white limestone and red Pecos sandstone provide its striking appearance. A 1993 remodel provided additional modernization.

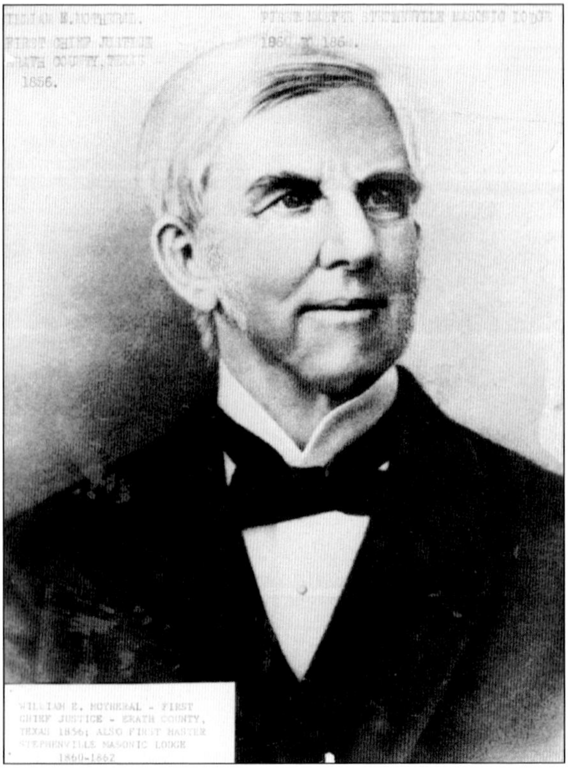

In the first county election of August 1856, William E. Motheral was elected chief justice—a role that corresponds to what is now county judge. Motheral was a charter member of the 1860 Stephenville Masonic lodge, and in 1861 and 1862, he rode with Erath County minutemen led by Capt. John E. Keith and 1st Lieut. John Salmon. He was Company A captain of the Frontier Protection Rangers called up by the Texas governor. (SHHM.)

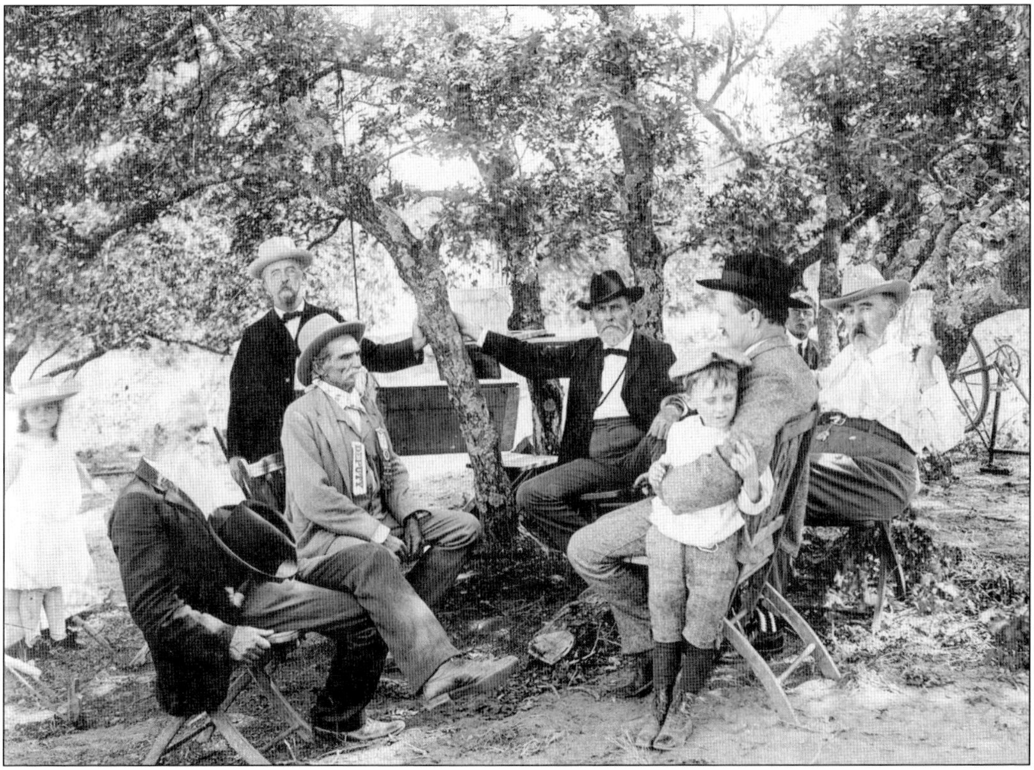

Confederate and Union veterans and the public attended annual Erath and Comanche Ex-Confederate Association reunions at Dublin. The F.M. Marrs family donated this 1900s image that includes, from left to right, (first row) Ezekiel Dunagan McCleskey, unidentified (the deputy ribbon indicates an organizer), and an unidentified man holding an unidentified boy; (second row) George McDuffie Reil ("McD. Reil"), F.M. Marrs or William Columbus McCleskey (center), and W.P. Orr. (SHHM.)

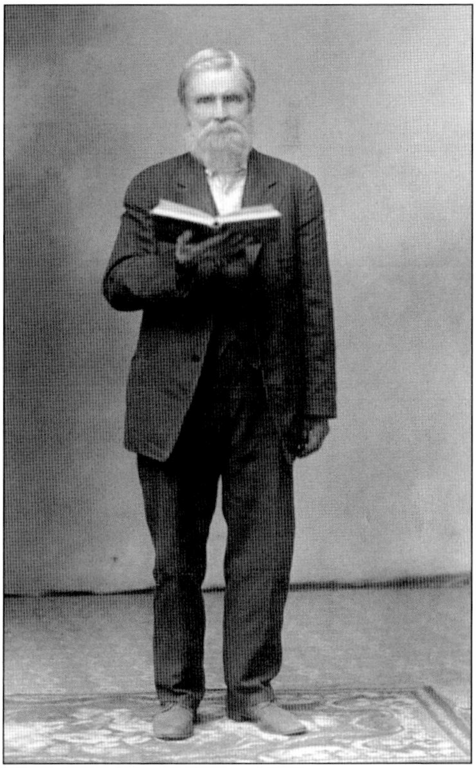

Tennessee-born William Baldridge Hicks served the Union in Missouri's 46th Volunteer Infantry. He and his wife, Sarah Adeline Johnston, moved to Texas in 1866 and bought land in Erath in 1875. They had 13 children. A Cumberland Presbyterian Church elder, William was remembered as one of the most beloved men in the Shelby community. The Hicks family farmed near the Belchers. (Jan Jennings.)

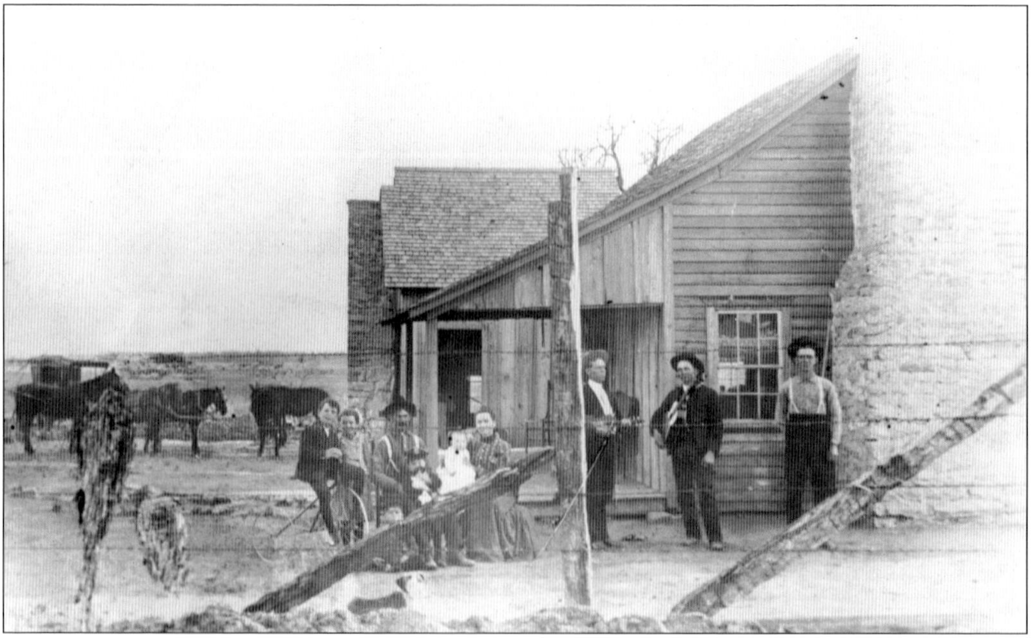

Columbus Price "Lum" Burnett arrived in the area in 1858 with his siblings and widowed mother, Elizabeth Ann Oaks Burnett. His older brother James came earlier to build the house. In 1862, the 30th Texas Cavalry, Company G, recruited John and Lum along with Dublin men Joshua Elkins, Charles D. Ely, William Howell, Elisha and Nicodemus Keith, James M. Martin, Cornelius and George R. O'Neal, Andrew and Lafayette Tucker, and Sgt. Robert Lesley.

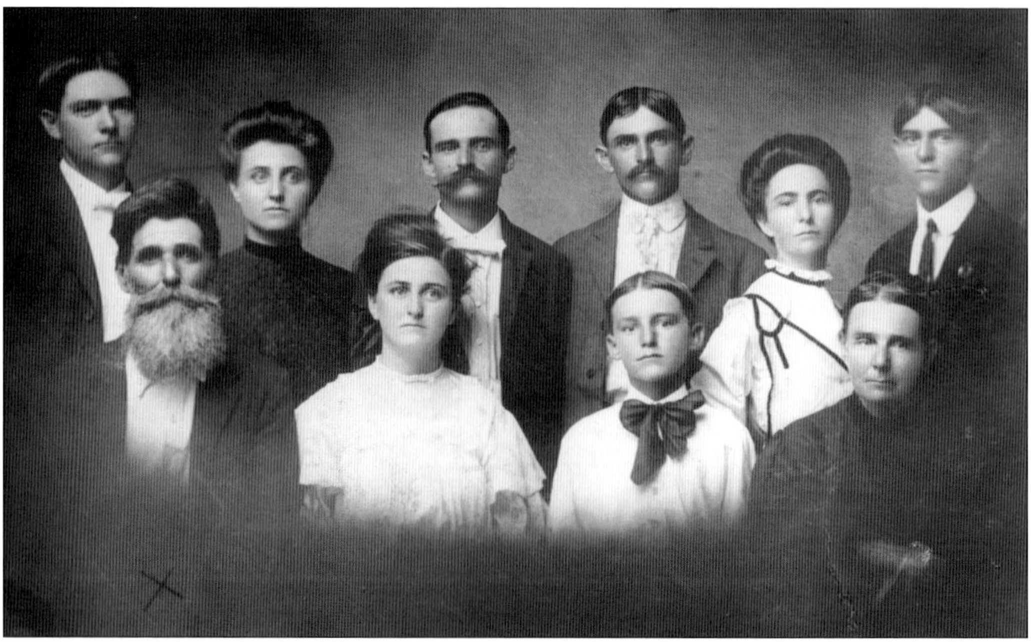

Lum Burnett was an officer of Erath's Pomona Grange and a frequent court juror. He is pictured here with his family (from left to right), (first row) Columbus Price, Alice Getrude, Charlie Price, and Sarah Frances White; (second row) William Calvin, Elizabeth Ann, Andrew Herman, James Rufus, Eda Frances, and Asbury Lee Burnett.

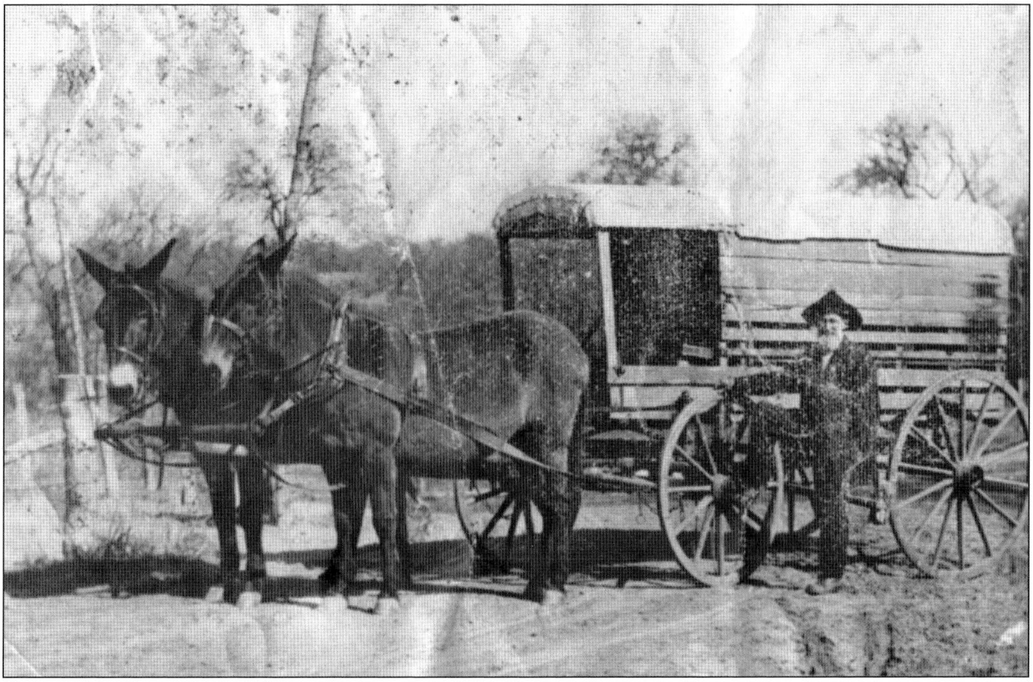

Prior to the arrival of the railroad, William Marion Case hauled lumber from Fort Worth with his ox team. Because cattlemen, farmers, and hunters only made it to town twice a year, peddlers carried wares to their customers. Frontiersman and mobile merchant Case trekked throughout Comanche, Erath, and Hamilton Counties. His mule-drawn wagon was loaded with clothing, drugs, household goods, and miscellaneous items to sell or trade. (SHHM.)

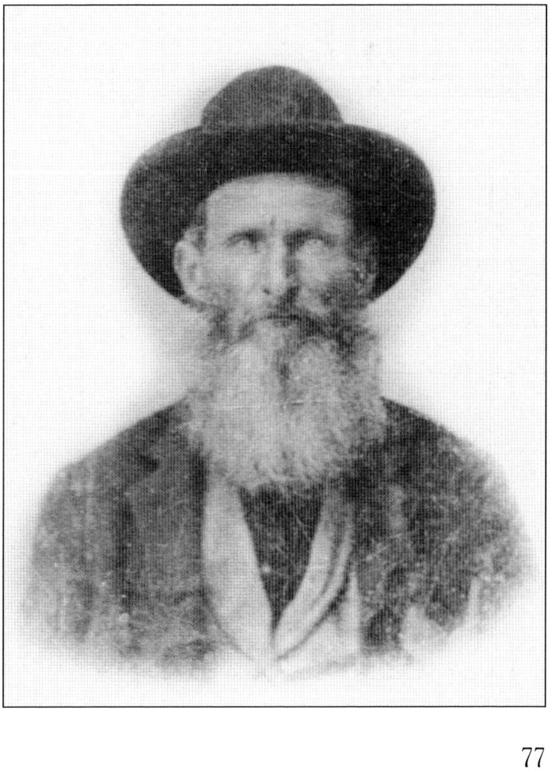

William Case served in the Confederate mounted Parson's Brigade, a cavalry unit providing outposts and scouts. After he married Nancy Ann Stalcup in 1868, they farmed 10 miles south of Dublin near Purves. Their daughter Cynthia Allie married Richard Gainer Jeffreys, and other daughter Mattie Martha married Madison Leander Stephen. Nancy and William braved the hardships of frontier life until his death in 1915. (SHHM.)

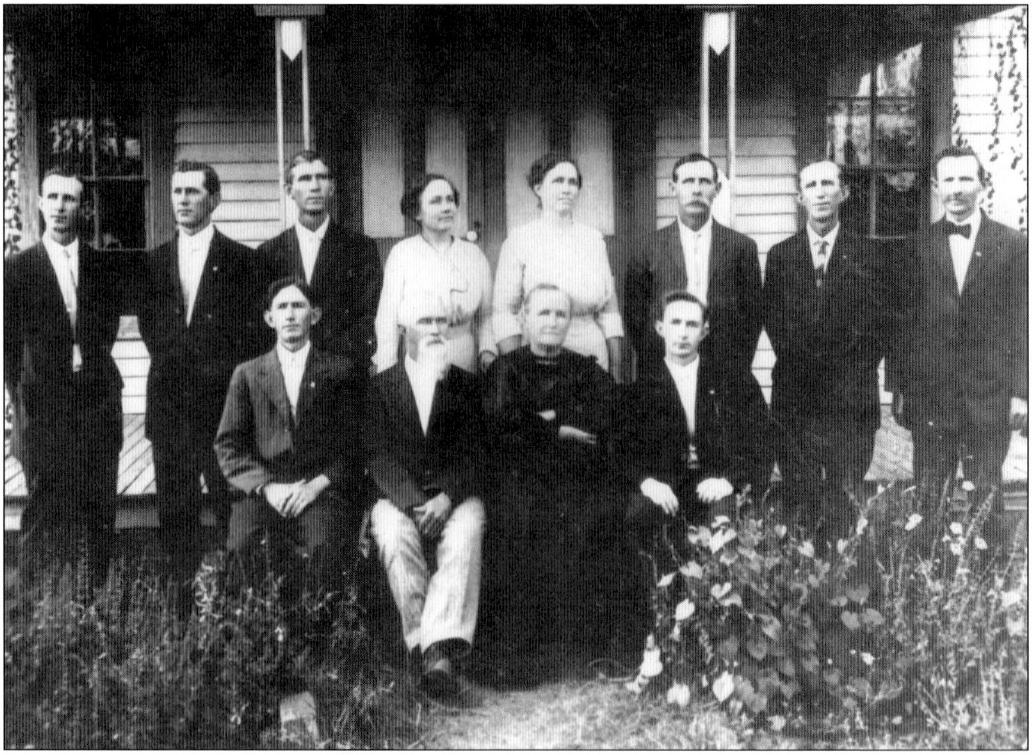

Rock Island POW camp survivor John Bell Moring married Catherine Barbara "Cate" Jenkins, daughter of Mary Ann Freshour and Michael Oliver Jenkins. The Jenkins and Moring families settled in the Barton Creek communities of Hannibal and Liberty. The Moring family members pictured here are, from left to right, (first row) Maurice, John Bell, Cate, and Tait; (second row) Silas, Clyde, Perry, Alice, Fanny, Ben, Will, and Joe. (Ruth Graves Fletcher and Evelynn Hill Kelly.)

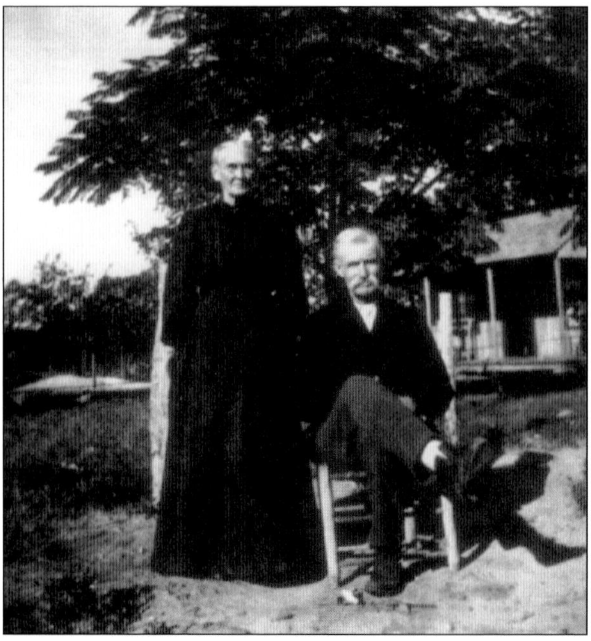

In opposition to his grandfather and brother, James William Guthrie joined the Confederates. Captured in Kentucky in 1862, he was sent to Chicago's Camp Douglas. After losing his only brother in the war, Guthrie wandered until he married Margaret "Maggie" Rhea. In 1874, they farmed near Huckabay. They had an orchard and raised honey and children. Maggie gathered and spun wool to make their clothes. James and Maggie are buried at Shelby Cemetery. (Jan Jennings.)

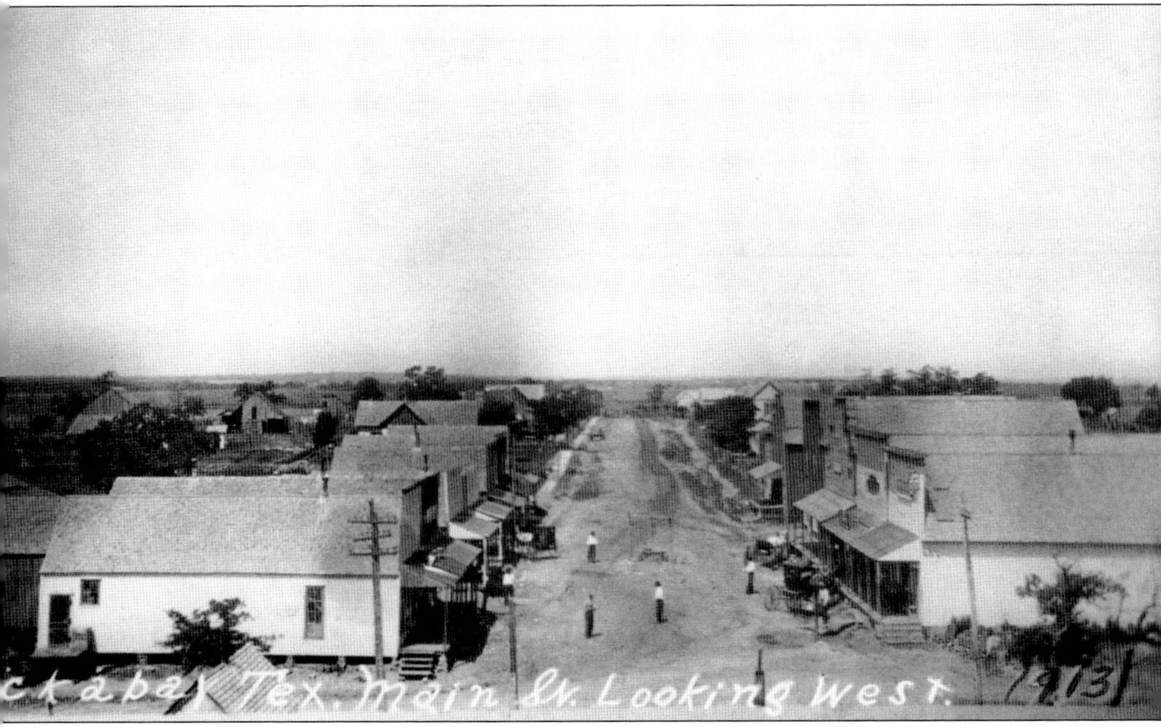

An 1875 wagon train of 10 Arkansas and Tennessee families stopped on the Bosque headwaters. Lige Barnhill, John Copeland, W.C. Copeland, Ben Fincher, John Gentry, George Gresham, John Huckabay, John W. Jones, Abe Metsgar, and "Dad" Wylie claimed 160 acres. They built homes and dug wells and called the area Flatwood. John Copeland taught at the first school and donated land for a cemetery and school. G.W. Glenn opened the first store in 1878. William "Bill" C. Rigsby opened a mill and gin. Church of Christ, Baptists, and Methodists established churches by 1881. Farmer and storekeeper John Huckabay made a weekly mail run to Stephenville. Flatwood became Huckabay when it received its own post office in 1888. By 1890, Huckabay had drug, general, grocery, and mercantile stores, two blacksmiths and two barbers, and an undertaker. West Texas State Bank existed for a short time. In 1902, C.H. Hale founded Huckabay Academy, a high school that also offered college courses before it closed in 1914. The men pictured are enjoying a game of marbles in the main street of Huckabay in 1913. (SHHM.)

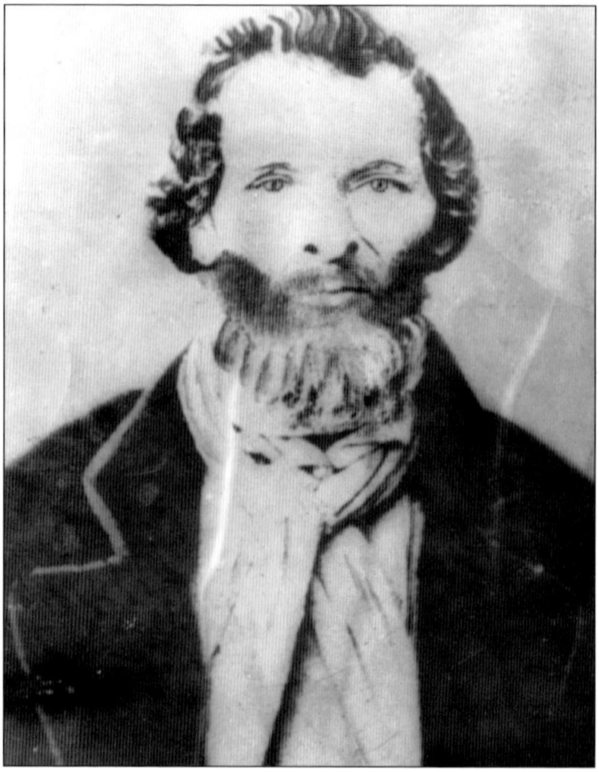

Chesley Turnbow had kin on both sides of the law. Several were accused vigilantes. His son Andy was arrested for murder. Three of his four grandsons were arrested for train robbery and convicted. His son-in-law sheriff John R. Maloney was gunned down in 1867. Three of his grandsons were elected sheriff—John Gilbreath, Jim Turnbow, and Carl Turnbow. One grandson was jailed for rowdy behavior when two other grandsons were serving as sheriff and deputy.

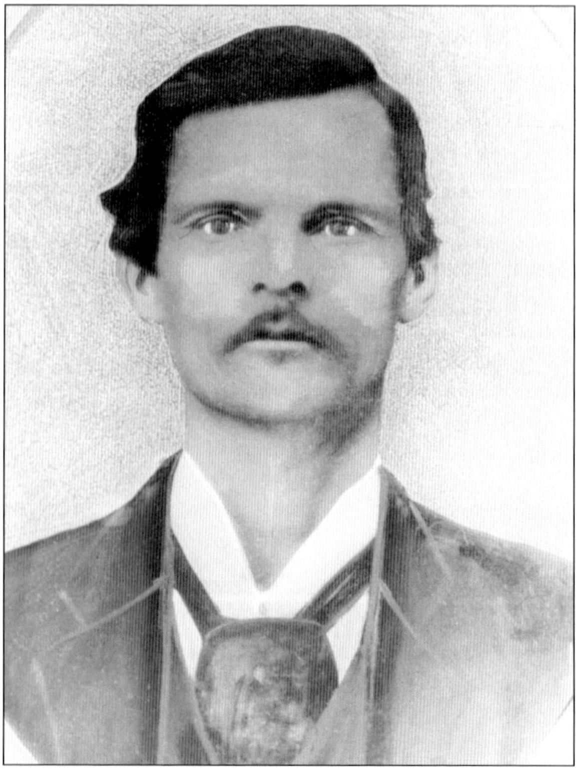

Accused vigilante John Chesley Gilbreath was elected the county animal and hide inspector in 1876. In 1882, although threatened, he ran for and was elected sheriff, serving from 1882 to 1885. He set about apprehending lawbreakers regardless of kinship or community stature. He and his deputies filled the jail with accused cattle and horse thieves, killers, rapists, and robbers. He was successful in breaking up the dangerous Thurber-based John Glenn crime syndicate.

A September 1883 raid on a camp of horse thieves was just another day at work for sheriff John Chesley Gilbreath (left), deputy John Caudle, and jailer Bill Chaney (right). Gilbreath came to Resley Creek with his extended family in 1855. While serving as sheriff from 1882 to 1886, he was credited with breaking up the 1880s "mob rule" and ending Erath's era of organized crime. (SHHM.)

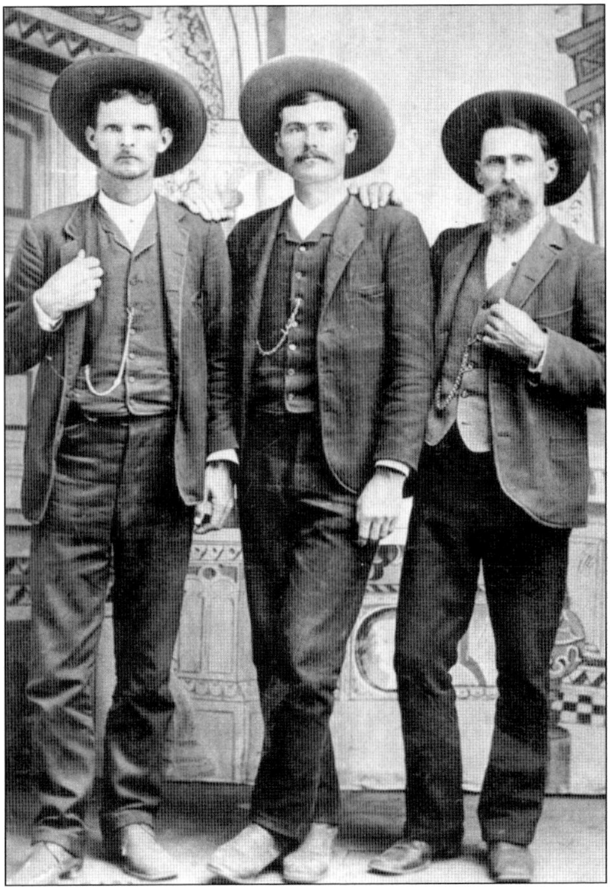

Judge T.L. Nugent's 1886 grand jury indicted two horse thieves and two attempted murderers. They reported that county books were in order, but jail and public road improvements were needed. From left to right are (first row) foreman George McDuffie Reil, unidentified, Jack Ready, Bob Loflin, and Leonard Franklin Roberts; (second row) Bill Wyly, Isaac Alexander "Eck" Bell, Andrew Jackson "Jack" Wells, John J. Ray, Alex Walker, and Patrick Marion Larner. (SHHM.)

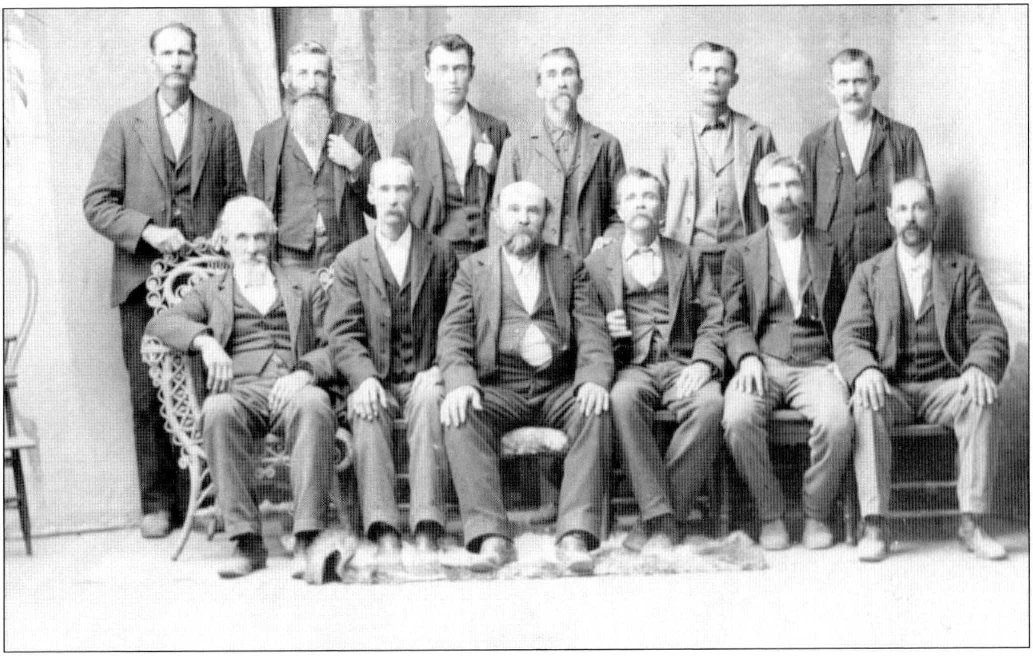

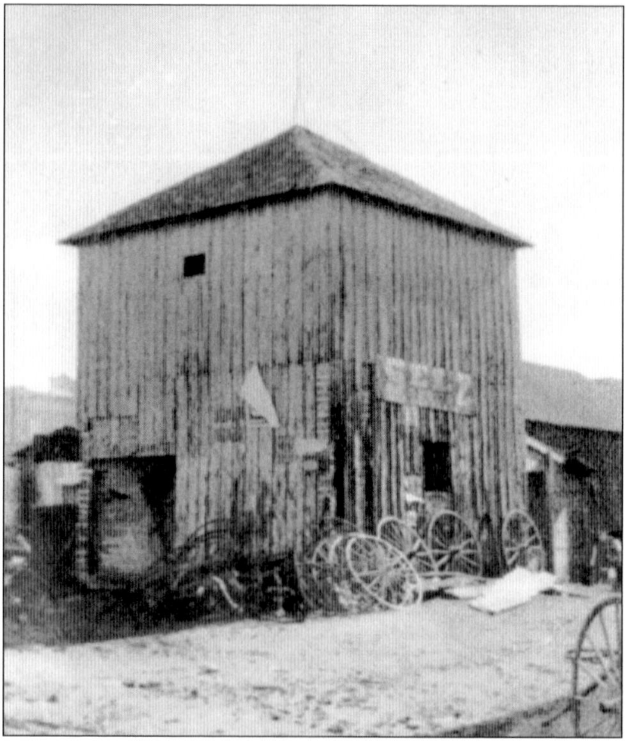

An outside ladder was used to incarcerate a prisoner on the upper floor of the Erath County jailhouse. Note the one small window for air and light. Serious criminals were often taken to Comanche, Hood, McLennan, or Tarrant County jails. A stone jail was built by 1879. Around 1898, sheriff Nathan J. Shands allowed visiting farmers to sleep on the third floor and experience the malodorous jail below. A new jail was finished in 1905. (SHHM.)

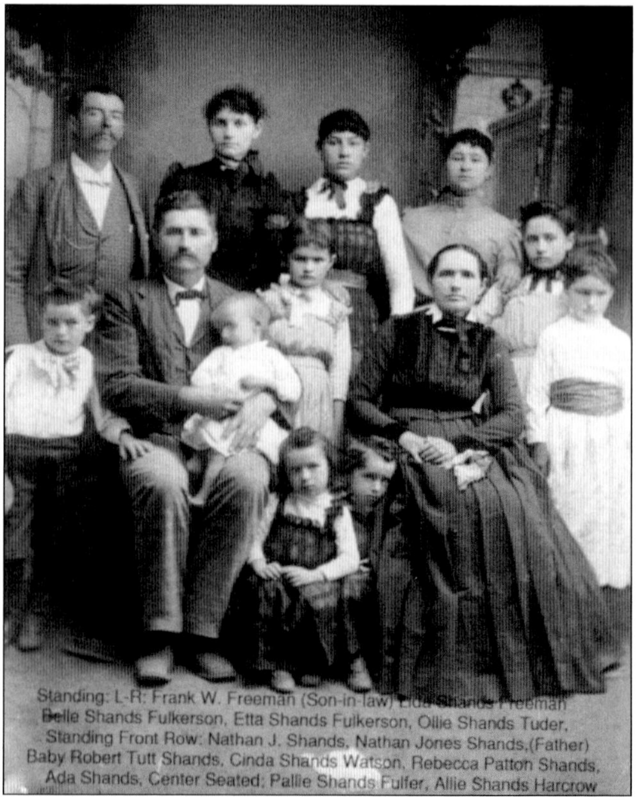

Deputy Nathan J. Shands followed John Chesley Gilbreath as sheriff, serving five terms. A sheriff's family typically lived at the jailhouse. An armed Rebecca Shands once subverted an escape when serving meals. From left to right are (seated in the center foreground) Pallie and Allie; (first row) Nathan Jr., Nathan Sr. (holding Robert Tutt), Cinda, Rebecca Patton, and Ada; (second row) sheriff Frank Freeman, Lida, Belle, Etta, and Ollie Shands. (Ruth Graves Fletcher.)

Robert Tutt Hume, who served as sheriff from 1899 to 1902, carried out the first of two legal Erath County hangings. This photograph was taken on November 10, 1899, the day Tom Wright, who had been convicted of murdering Dublin constable John Adams, was hanged. Because public hangings were illegal, Hume built a walled-off two-story scaffold with a window for speeches. Still, many buggies, wagons, and hacks gathered at the execution site. (Jan Jennings.)

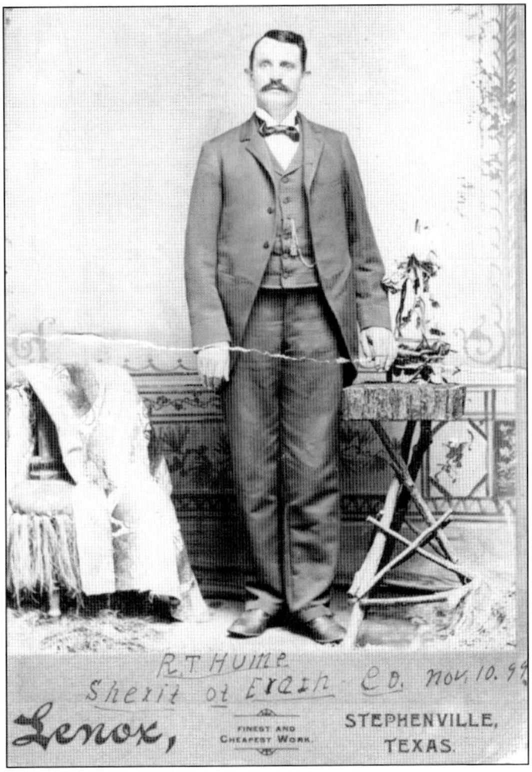

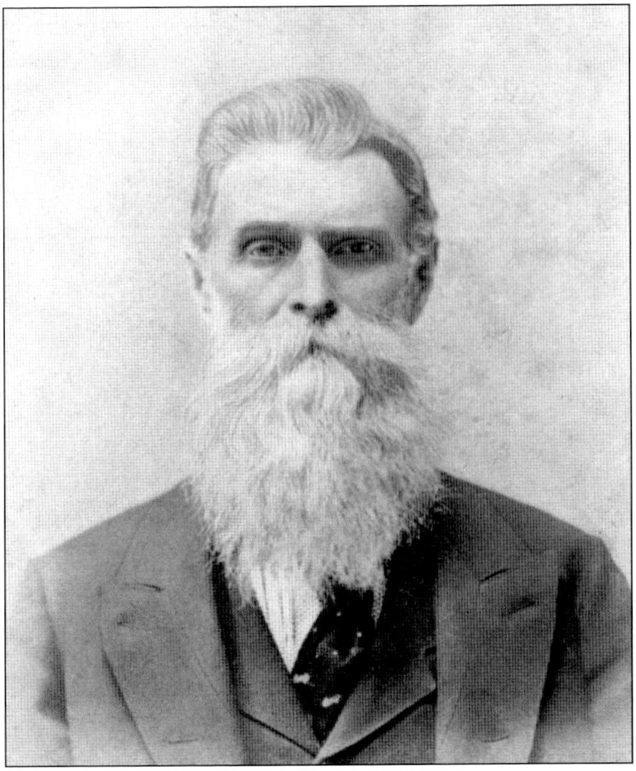

Matilda Ferrell Roberts and William Bye Whitacre settled at Keyser in 1860. Until 1865, he was a first lieutenant in the state militia defending the Texas frontier. In 1866, William served as justice of the peace and district clerk and blacksmithed in Stephenville. In 1870, he bought land near Lingleville. In 1894, he was elected to the state legislature. (SHHM.)

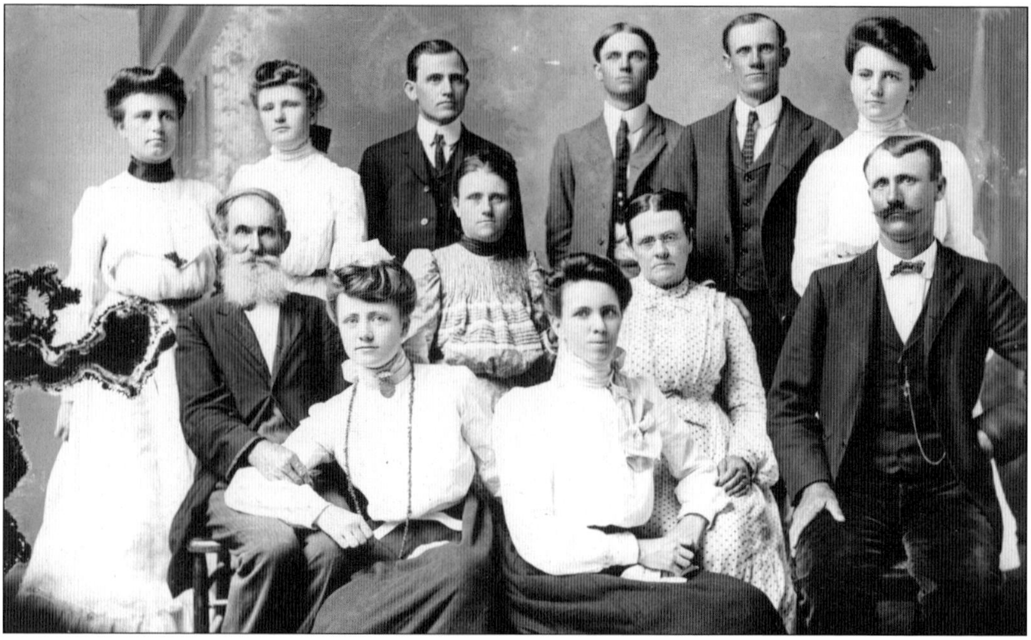

Representing Erath County in the 25th Texas legislature for 1897 and 1898, Rev. Uriah Jackson "Uncle Jack" Morton also preached local Methodist circuits between 1871 and 1894. His family members pictured here are, from left to right, (first row) Abbie Atlee and Sallie Garrett; (second row) Uriah, Alva Frasier, Malvina Kiker, and Elbert; (third row) Julia Ann Pounds, Mary Ellen Greenwalt, Rev. Charles A., Lester Burton, Rufus Alston, and Vian Morgan.

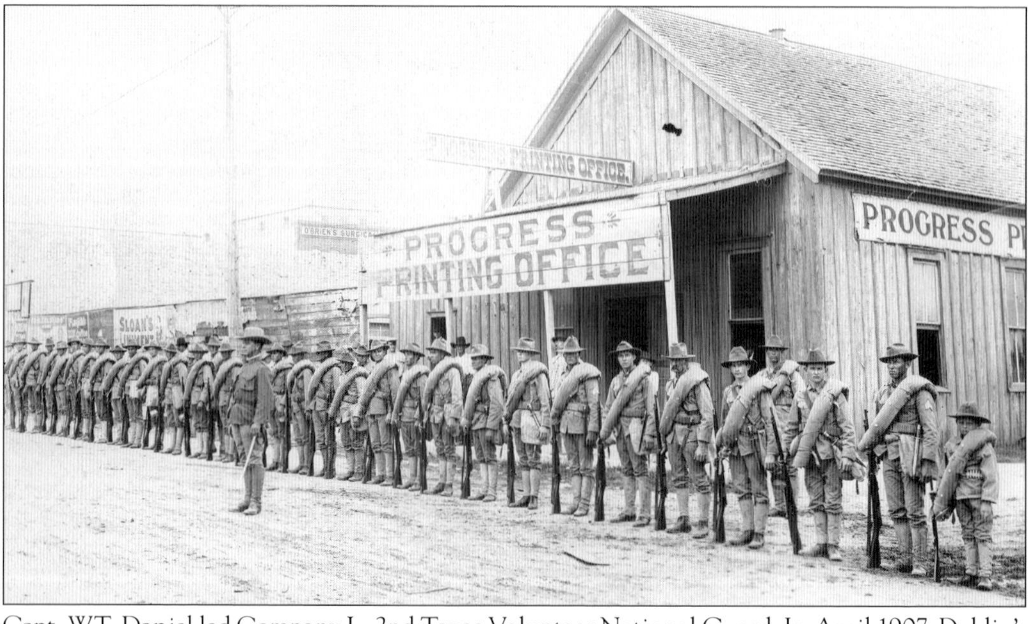

Capt. W.T. Daniel led Company L, 2nd Texas Volunteer National Guard. In April 1907, Dublin's Mayfield Rifles of the Texas National Guard received new blue uniforms and guns. They began weekly evening drills in preparation for July's weeklong camp in Austin. The following month, they demonstrated drills during Dublin's Great Annual Celebration, which included Woodmen Day (August 6) followed by Ex-Confederate Days (August 7 through August 9).

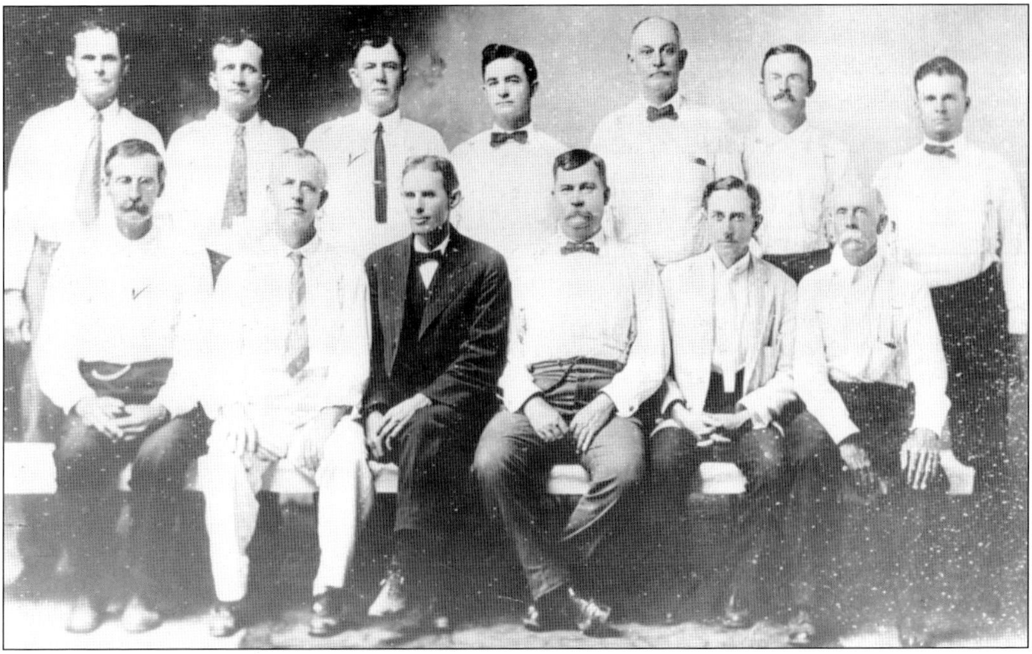

The members of the 1911 grand jury pictured here are, from left to right, (first row) S.J. Webb, W.J. Clay, district judge W.J. Oxford Sr., sheriff Dave Deaton, district attorney Will Pannell, and Jim Snapp; (second row) Lingleville County commissioner Jim Leatherwood, Dublin Co-op store manager W.H. Young, unidentified, Penn Warren, two-term county clerk George B. Maloney, W.R. Strong, and Ed Arnold; two members of the jury are not pictured. (SHHM.)

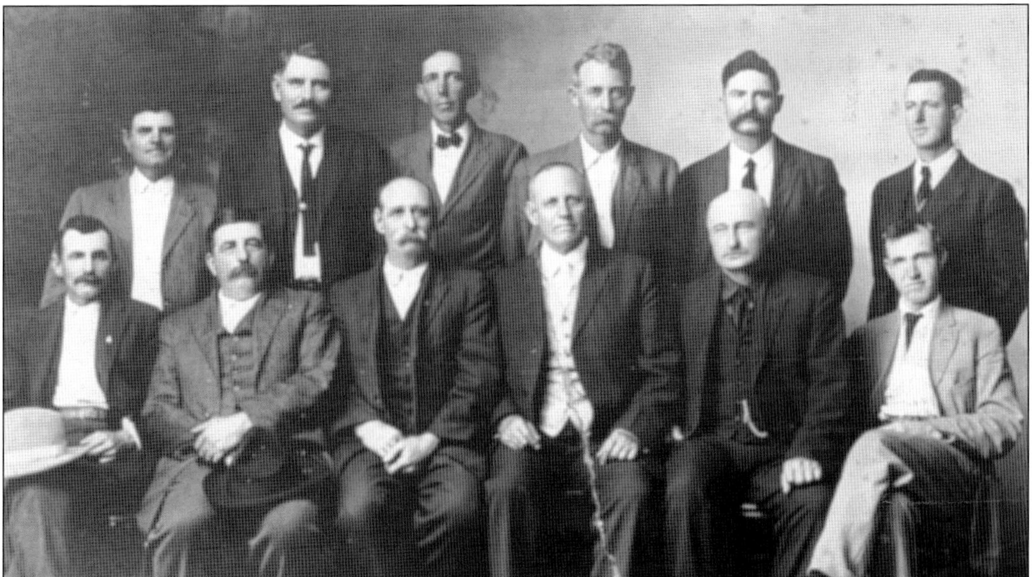

The second week of the November 1916 Erath County grand jury convened with judge W.E. Bower. The jurors were J.S. Freeman and Oscar Apple from Huckabay; Luke Barrett from Dublin; Cleve McAllister from Route Five; J.H. Bramlette from Bluff Dale; N.A. Hill from Gordon; W.T. Dowdy from Huckabay; D.N. Kiker from Dublin; J.N. Davis from Huckabay; Lewis Fields from Stephenville; and J.E. Carter and J.S. Carr. (SHHM.)

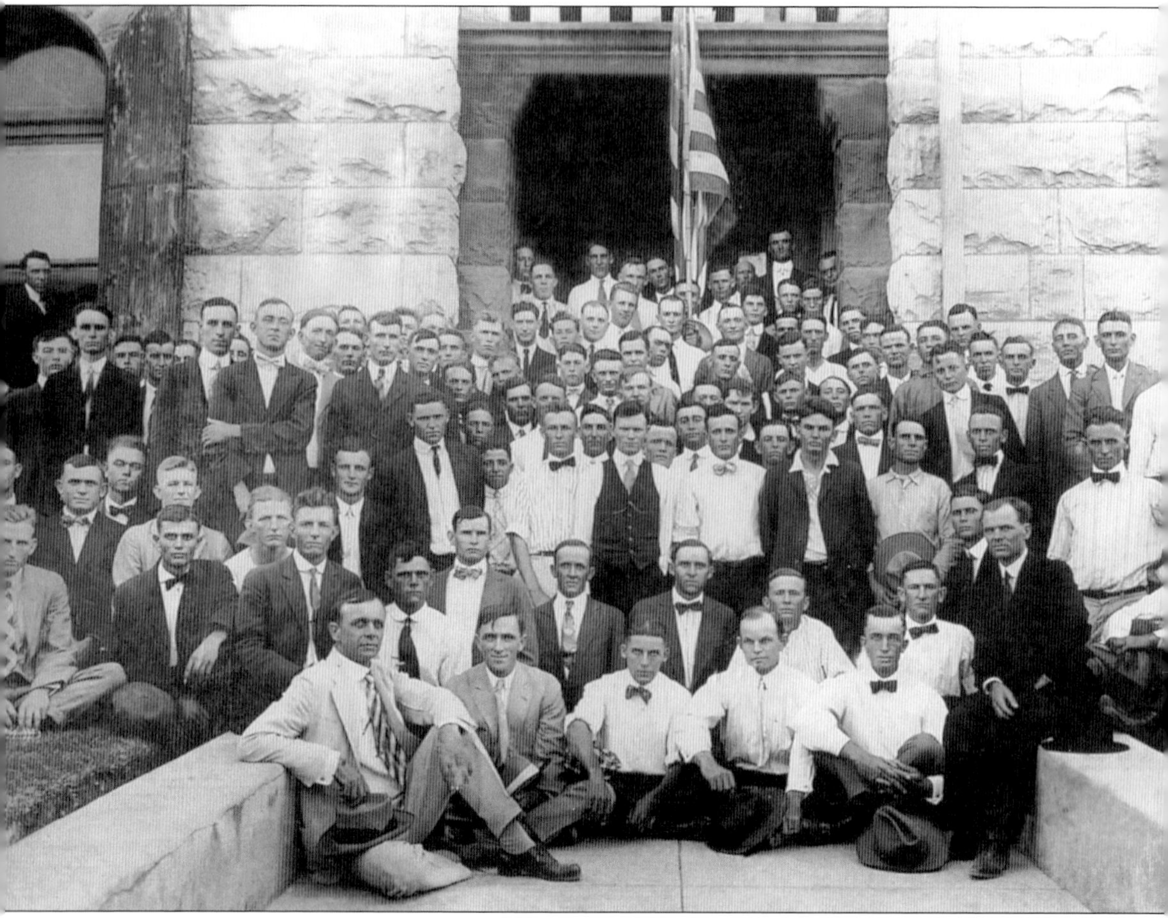

This K.N. Baxley photograph of "Erath Boys Who Left to Join the Colors, September 19, 1917," is from the front page of the September 28, 1917, issue of the *Dublin Progress and Telephone*; this was only one of multiple gatherings at the courthouse steps for group departures by bus. The paper named the men and their respective hometowns. The communities represented on that day included Alexander, Bluff Dale, Carlton, Chalk Mountain, Dublin, Duffau, Exray, Gordon, Hico, Huckabay, Iredell, Johnsville, Lingleville, Lipan, Morgan Mill, Selden, Sisk, Stephenville, and Thurber. About 1,300 Erath County men and women served during World War I. The Great War ended on the 11th hour of the 11th day of the 11th month of 1918. More than 600 World War I veterans are buried in Erath County cemeteries. Although it is incomplete, a World War I Honor Roll monument on the courthouse square names 33 men who gave their lives during the war. Some are buried at sea. Some rest in American military cemeteries on foreign soil. Many are buried locally. (SHHM.)

Six

Civic Duties

Redrawn lines and new counties redistricted some communities. Established in Erath, Paluxy and Rock Church are now in Hood County. Chalk Mountain remains in Erath, while its cemetery lies in Somervell. Edna Hill, Hico, and Little Mexico are similar examples. Patrons of businesses and school students easily commute across county lines. Thurber's coal mines and brickyards drew workers from Eastland, Erath, and Palo Pinto. Birth certificates, marriage licenses, and registries of marks and brands might be filed at the nearest courthouse rather than by legislative lines. Wooden courthouses frequently burned down, particularly during Reconstruction. There were periods in the late 19th century when Erath court filings were directed to Comanche or Palo Pinto Counties.

By 1870, cotton dominated Erath's agrarian economy. As prices fell, poverty increased among farmers. The Farmers' Alliance, formed in nearby Lampasas County to promote cooperative practices, spread throughout the area. Dublin's Evan Jones was Erath's chapter president from 1884 to 1888. Jones and others lectured throughout the Midwest and South, growing the organization across the country. Jones was elected president at the state and national levels when the group was renamed the Farmers' and Laborers' Union of America.

Before Rural Free Delivery and automobiles, the village post office was a central spot in the community. The mail made its way to people after being transported by horseback, stage, railcar, or vehicle. The earliest route came by rail from Waco to Meridian, then on horseback to Stephenville. In 1857, addressees picked up letters at John Stephen's store. Paluxy got a post office in 1858, Squaw Creek in 1859, and Duffau in 1860. Dublin, Rock Falls, and Wenona got their post offices in 1875, with Bluff Dale and Morgan Mill following in 1877. Mail was delivered by horse and buggy in 1914, although a resident might walk two miles to the mailbox. Jim Wheat's *Postmasters and Post Offices of Texas, 1846–1930*, is one of few records commemorating discontinued offices—and thus communities—such as Acrey, Bishop, Dillard, Eshman, Horseshoe, Immermere, Millerville, Ogan, Pizarro, Sap Oak, Skippers Gap, and Tempest.

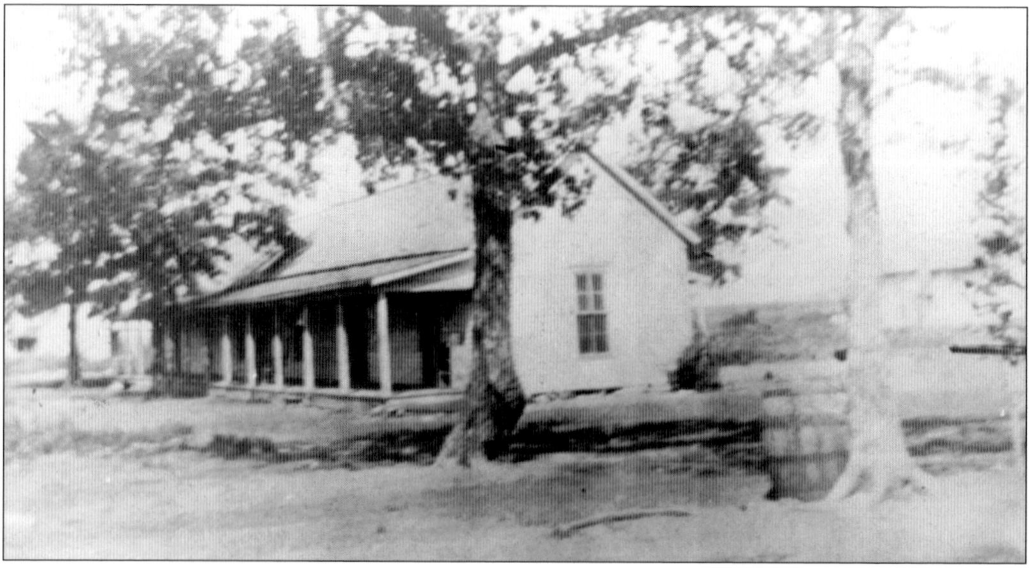

From 1881 to the 1930s, Erath County operated a poor farm to care for indigent, pauper, and criminal inhabitants at public expense. The residents were often elderly or disabled, but local criminals were sent to work on the farm as well. Some charges they faced included adultery, assault, gambling, lunacy, theft, or vagrancy. The poor farm cemetery includes marked and unmarked graves. (SHHM.)

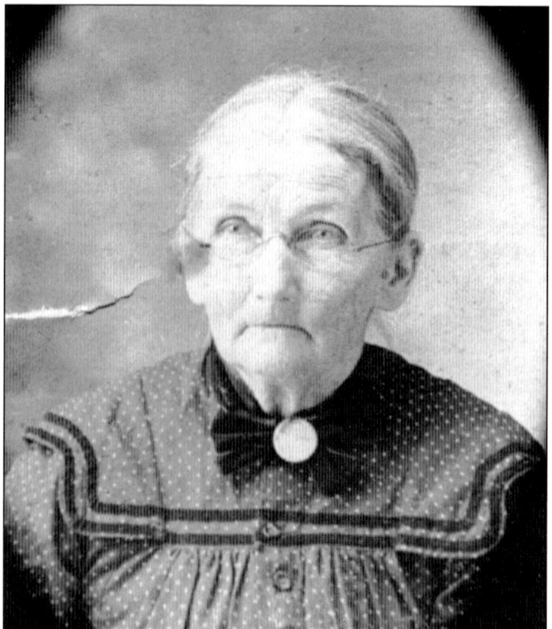

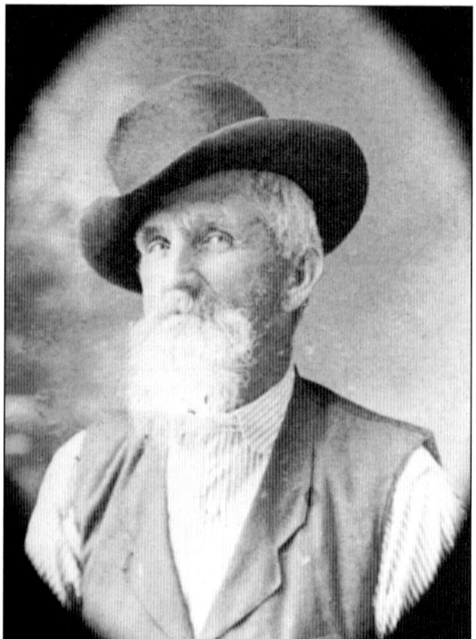

The Harriet Albritton and Terrell Bryan family lived at the poor farm in the 1880s while Terrell was the superintendent. Terrell later had a feed and wagon yard and was elected justice of the peace. He served on the Masonic committee, setting the new courthouse cornerstone, and was active with Woodmen of the World. The Bryans attended Stephenville's Methodist Episcopal Church. (Diana Bryan Quinn.)

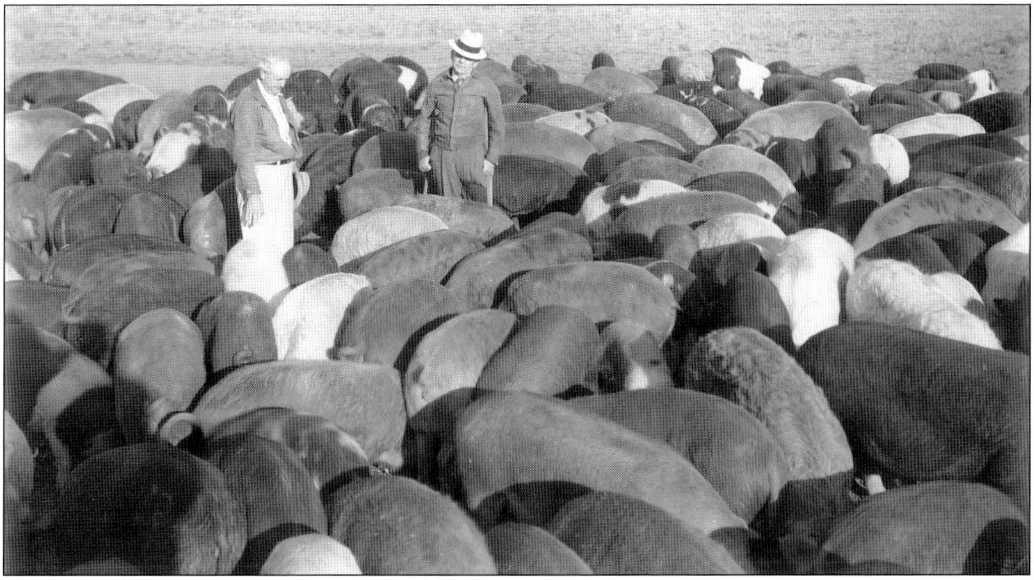

Stephenville's Clark Field airport is named to honor former county clerk and longtime mayor Henry Clark (left). In 1917, Texas state representative Clark and senator Scott Woodward introduced a successful bill to merge John Tarleton Agricultural College with Agriculture and Mechanical College of College Station. (SHHM.)

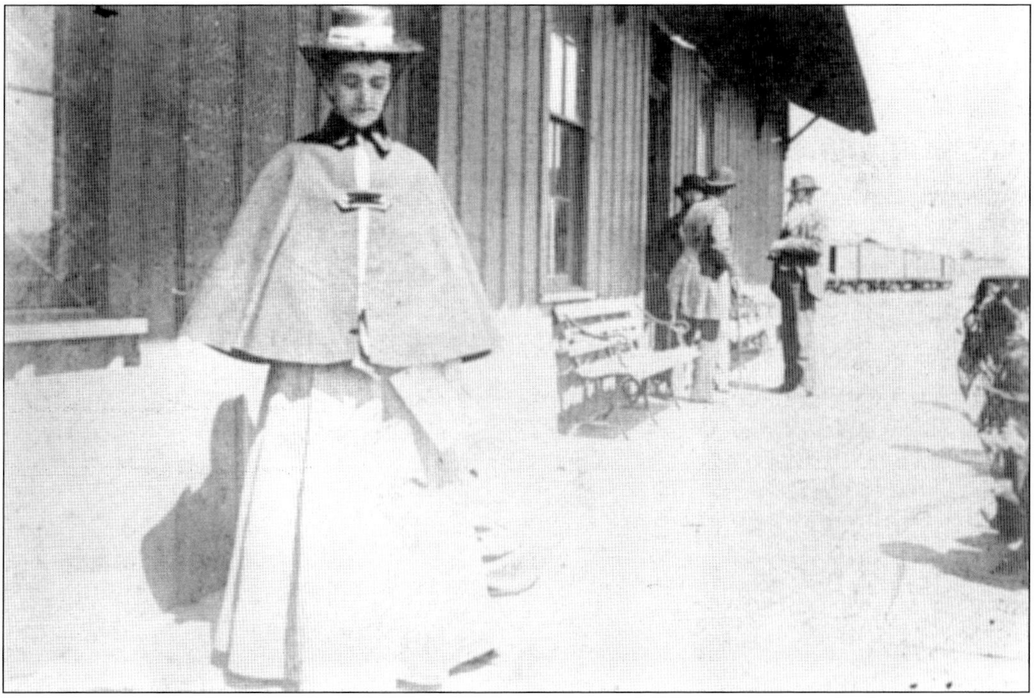

In this 1893 photograph at the Stephenville train station, Stephenville postmaster Susie Hyman is preparing to travel to a Washington, DC, conference with the postmaster general. Hyman was a teacher in Stephenville's early free public school. In February 1885, she attended the World's Industrial and Cotton Centennial Exposition in New Orleans, representing the *Stephenville Empire*. (SSHM.)

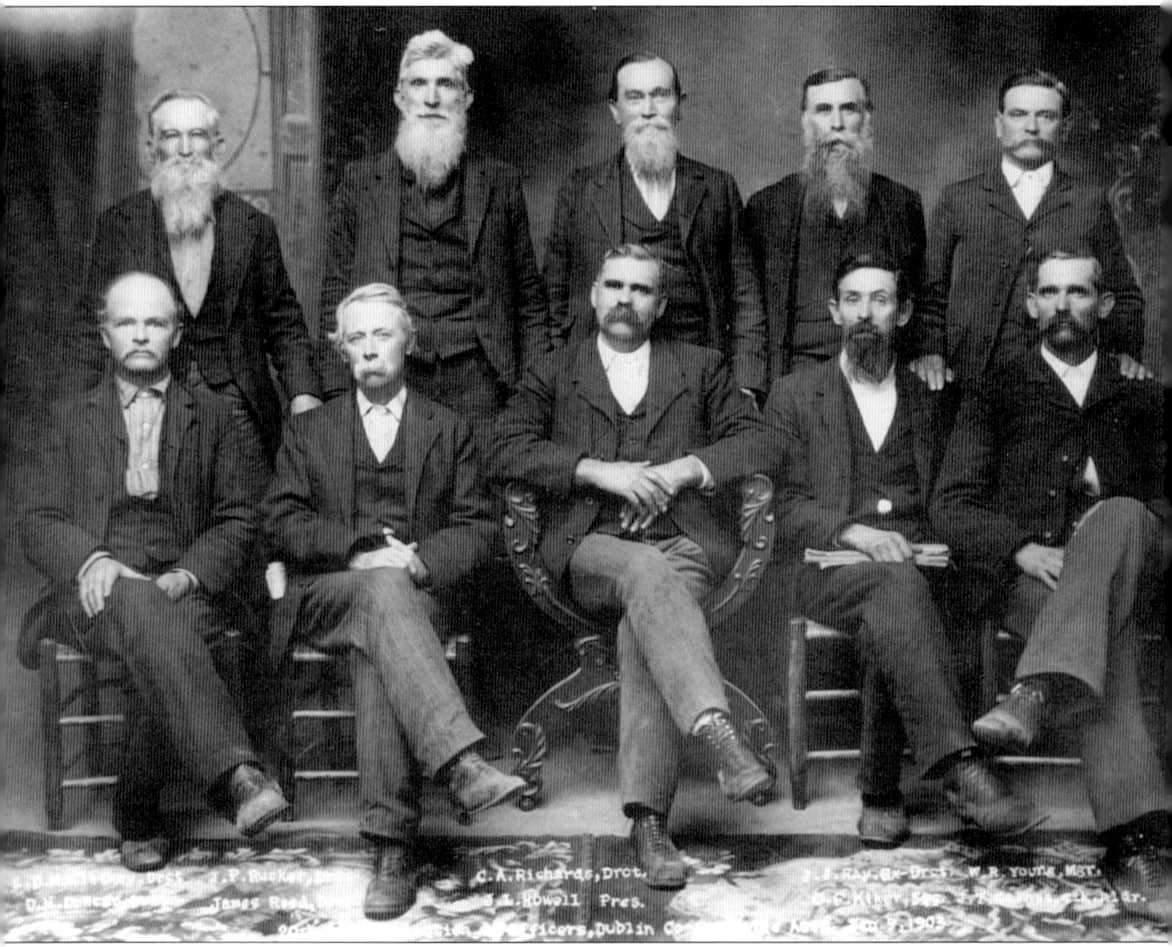

After Reconstruction, organizations like Patrons of Husbandry or the Grange addressed economic, educational, and social hardships of farmers. Their efforts included cooperative buying and selling, schools, and socials. The Dublin Co-operative Association officers pictured here in January 1903 are, from left to right, (first row) D.H. Duncan, James Reed, James Love Howell (president), Charles "Charlie" Franklin Kiker (secretary), and J.T. Barnes; (second row) Ezekiel Dunagan "Uncle Zeke" McCleskey, J.P. Rucker, C.A. Richards, John J. Ray (former director), and William Roberson Young (manager). All agriculturalists, these men served the county in multiple ways. Howell, a salesman for the co-op mercantile business, also served as justice of the peace and a county commissioner. Kiker preached in Stephenville. Carpenter and stonemason McCleskey guided the building of many structures, including Greens Creek Tabernacle, and was said to have never missed church or an ex-Confederate reunion. Postmaster Ray was a Dublin Masonic lodge charter member. One of the co-op organizers, Young, a Mason, was manager of the Dublin Mercantile, generally called the grange store. (Barbara Dalton Jones.)

In 1891, the Erath County Farmers' Alliance sought to build an advanced level school. Also known as Alliance College, the Alliance High School of Lingleville opened in 1893 with about 100 students. The school remained open until 1897, when the alliance experienced financial challenges. The building later housed a public school.

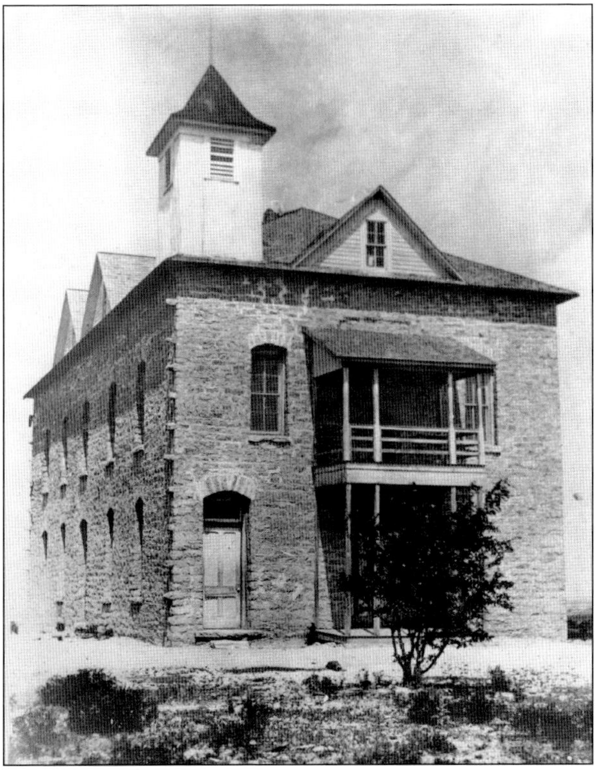

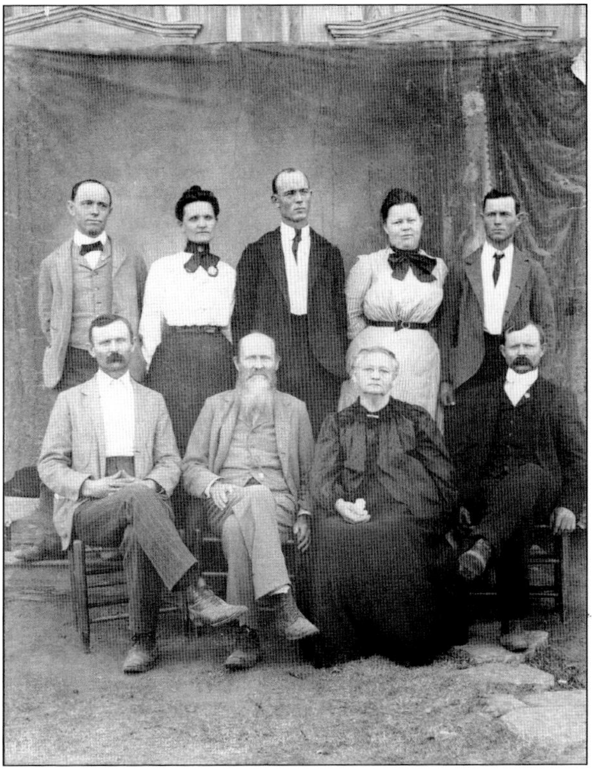

Daniel Roberts Thornton fought with the Texas Confederates. He served as county commissioner from 1876 to 1878 and donated land for local schools. He is pictured here in 1905 with his family; from left to right are (first row) Thomas Peter, Daniel R. Sr., Mary Anna, and Henry Clayton; (second row) William Luther, Lucinda Elizabeth Faith, Arthur E., Anna Clark, and Daniel R. Thornton Jr. Daniel's son Columbus Erastus was not present.

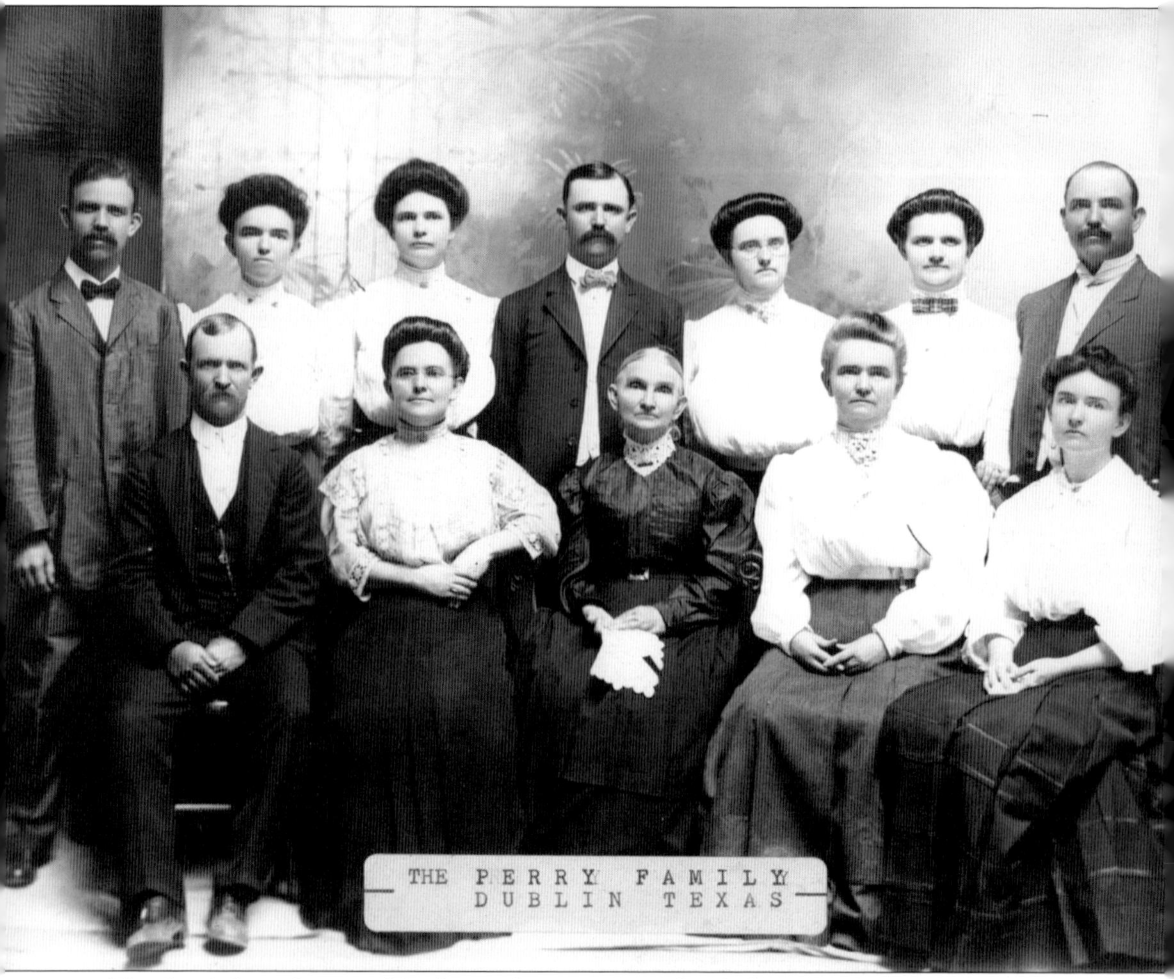

The Sarah Jane Story and Wilbur Fisk "Doc" Perry family became charter members of Dublin Methodist Church in 1881. From left to right are (first row) Raleigh Colquitt, Fannie Lula, Sarah Jane, Emma Beaufort, and Llerena Collingsworth "Collie"; (second row) Ernest Early, Fraulein Isla, Patricia "Pattye," Turner Hunt, Mabel Anna, Tabitha Tilman, and Leroy Hill Perry. Sarah, daughter of a circuit-riding Methodist preacher, and Doc, a Civil War nurse, reared industrious offspring. Their son Raleigh was a successful Dublin farmer and father of Henry Grady and grandfather of Wilbur Wright, who each represented the region in the Texas state legislature. Fannie and her husband owned the E.E. Powell Livery. Mabel and Emma were teachers. Emma was the first female county school superintendent in the United States. Collie was the mother of Dr. Llerena B. Friend, director of Barker Historical Library at the University of Texas at Austin. Ernest and Hunt were pharmacists at Stephenville's Perry Brothers Drug. Isla married J.D. Brock, Pattye married A.W. Whitfield, and Tabitha married John Lacy. Hill owned hardware stores at Spur, Menard, and Gorman.

Henry Tilden Belcher and his future wife, Addie Wells, attended Union community school. On his parents' Shelby farm, Henry could hear the whistles of eight gins—in Exray, Huckabay, Topaz, North Bosque, South Bosque, Pigeon, Lingleville, and Burklow. From 1917 to 1920, he was a tax assessor who traversed the county on horseback. He owned the first Model T Ford in Stephenville and served on city council in 1929 and 1930. (Jan Jennings.)

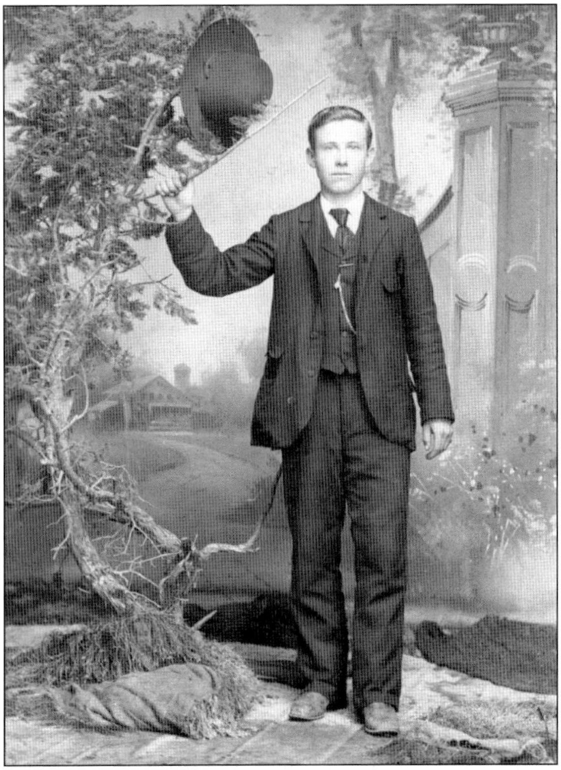

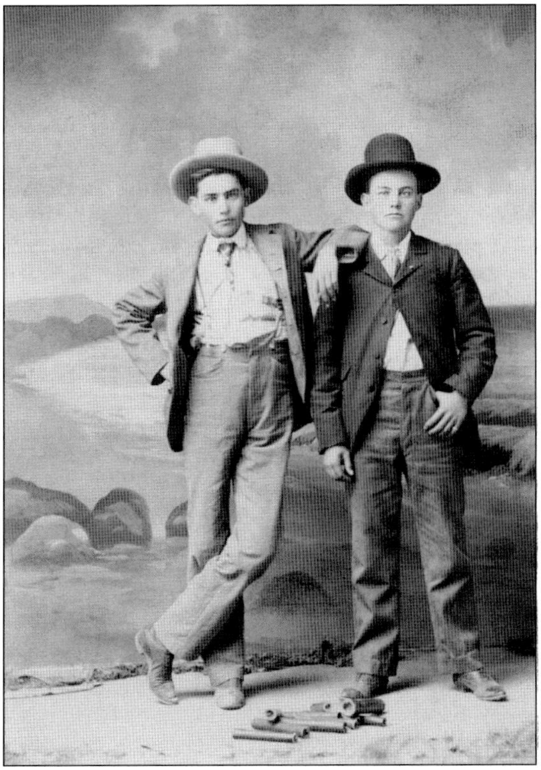

Henry Tilden Belcher's younger brother Charlie Calloway Belcher (right) is pictured with an unidentified friend. Charlie married Attie Catherine Gentry. The two grew up as students of the Union school of the Pigeon community. They had seven children and spent their entire lives in the Huckabay area. Active in Democratic Party affairs, Charlie was Precinct 1 Erath County commissioner for several years beginning in 1935. (Jan Jennings.)

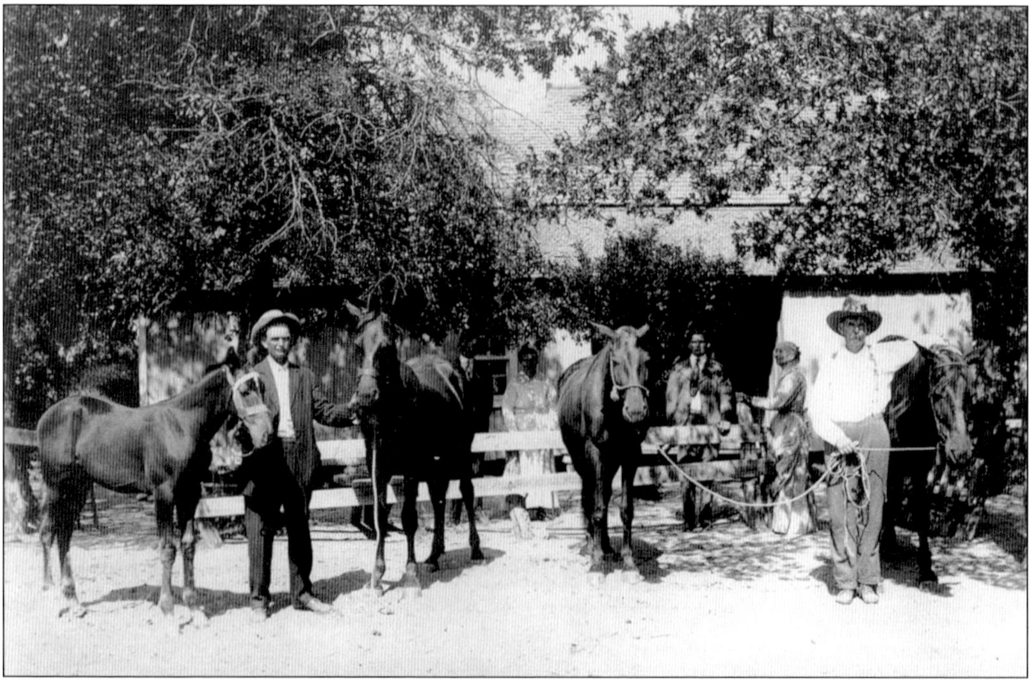

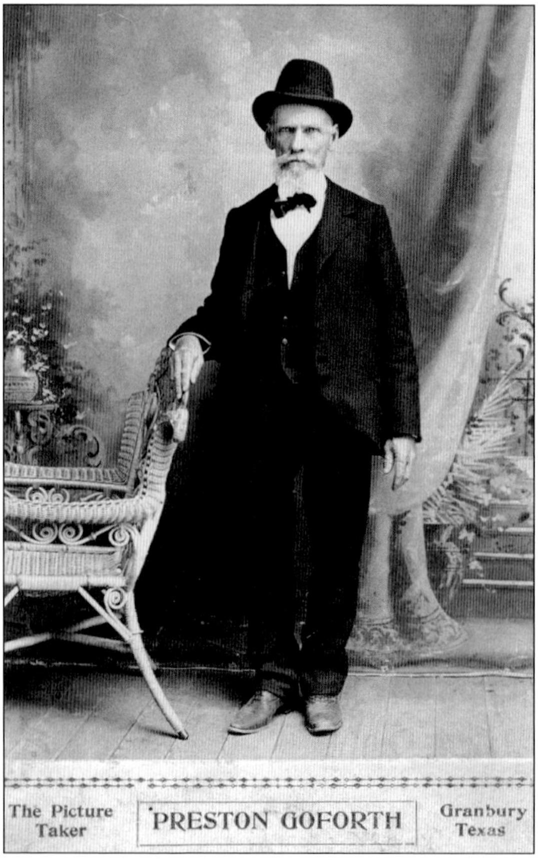

In 1856, Henry Clark settled in Rockfalls, between Allard and Elmgrove. The name Rockfalls was changed to Sisk when the post office was established in 1903, with William Taylor Long serving as the first postmaster. Mail service was discontinued there in 1921 and diverted to Johnsville. Pictured at the Long homestead and post office are, from left to right, "Ike" Isaac Henry, Herbert C., Minerva Ann Clark, Conda Toliver, unidentified, and Long. (SHHM.)

After serving with the Georgia 6th Cavalry, 26-year-old John Madison Hendon returned to his young family in Cleburne County, Alabama, to farm near his in-laws. A blacksmith, farmer, and landlord by 1900, he served as the postmaster for Iron City in Calhoun County, Alabama, from 1903 to 1914. After his wife's death, he joined some of his grown children who had settled near the Erath and Hood County line. (JBH.)

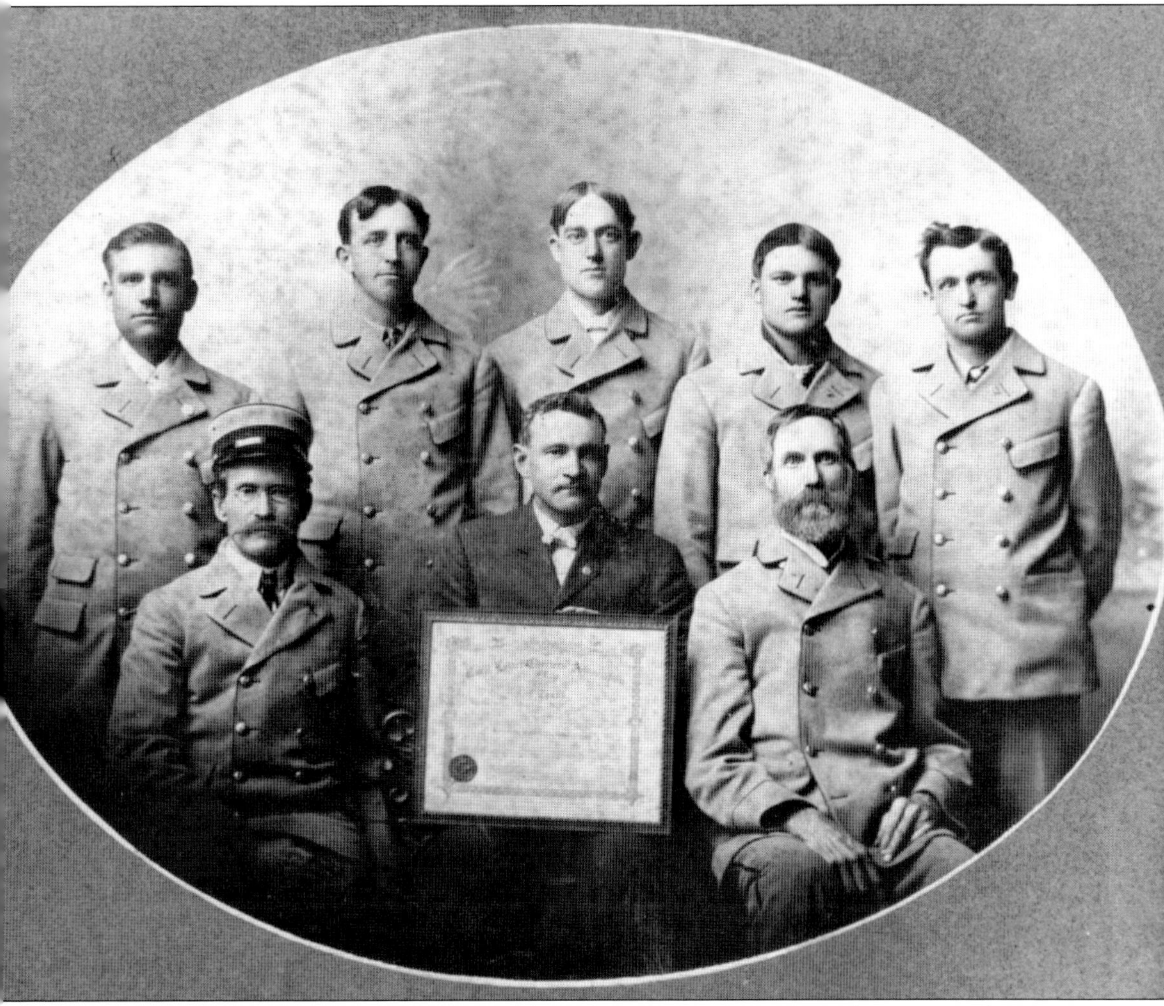

The *Dublin Progress* reported these 1907 Rural Mail Carriers Association of Texas members as, from left to right, (first row) E.M. Pollan, W.B. Andrew, and A.L. Morgan; (second row) Abram Gideon Howell, Columbus R. Hagler, Mark D. Warner, J. Lee Carlisle, Finis P. Ewing, and Davis Kiker. Their postmaster was H.H. Andrew. Route 1 served 184 families along Morgan's 24-mile trip from Edna Hill to Hazel Dell. Carlisle journeyed the 20-mile Route 2 for 105 families from Roch to St. George to Proctor. Pollan's 23-mile Route 3 served 150 families near Highland and De Leon. Howell's 27-mile Route 4 trip went to the Lingleville post office, west to the Cow Creek community, on to Highland, and back to Dublin, delivering to 143 families. Kiker made the 25-mile Route 5 to Kikers Gin and 155 families. Hagler did the 23-mile Route 6 to Harbin and Cottonwood. Warner carried mail to 120 Alexander and Palmer families on Route 7. Ewing's Route 8 circled 28 miles to 75 homes in Purves, Wilson, and Barbee. (Barbara Dalton Jones.)

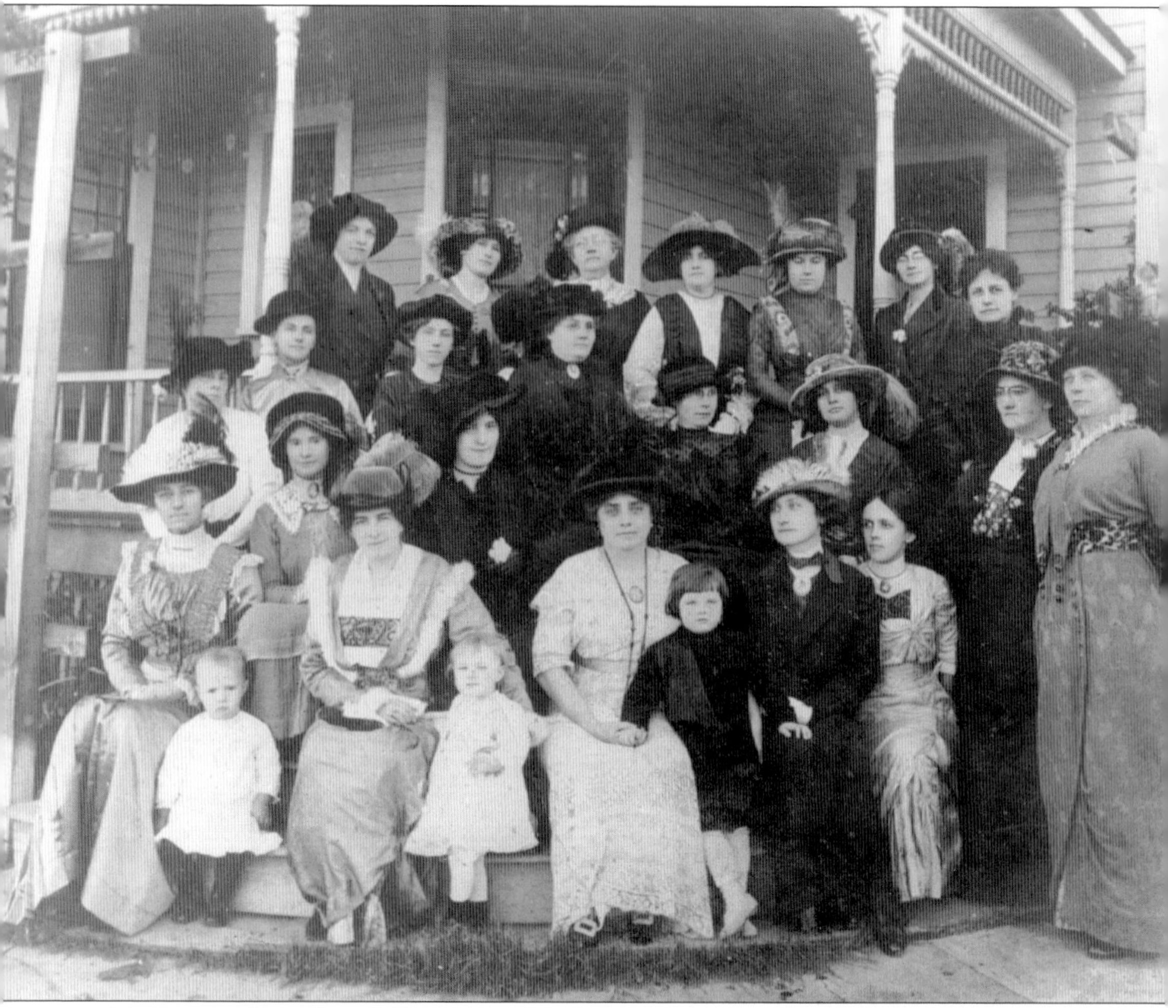

In 1914, members of Stephenville's Twentieth Century Club gathered at the home of Mrs. Baxter Ator. From left to right are (first row) Mrs. Hunt Perry and her daughter, Mrs. Ulpian Holt and her daughter Elaine, Mrs. Jay Collin George and Mary Marshall Ferguson (child), Mrs. Charles O. Blakeney, Mrs. Roscoe E. Cox, Mrs. W.P. Orr, and Mrs. Hill Perry; (second row) Mrs. Lee Young, Mrs. Willard Chamberlain, Mrs. Dave Deaton, Mrs. H.A. Mothershead, and Mrs. Ben Bassell; (third row) Mrs. M.J. Thompson, Mrs. Charles W. Froh, and Mrs. Millard F. Martin; (fourth row) Mrs. Joe Price, Mrs. John Cage, Mrs. Jack Crotty, Mrs. Marshall Ferguson, Mrs. Wallace Lyle, Mrs. Will Shelton, and Mrs. Baxter Ator. The occasion was a farewell party for Mrs. George, wife of J.C. George, the lawyer who persuaded John Tarleton to bequeath money for a Stephenville college. (SHHM.)

Married in 1870 in Freestone County, Julia Frances Adams and attorney William Watkins Moores later made Stephenville their home. Both were active in the First Methodist Church of Stephenville, and Julia was on the 1924 committee organized to write the church history. In 1934, the women's mission group honored her by naming the organization the Julia Moores Circle of the Woman's Missionary Society. She also served as president of the Twentieth Century Club. (SHHM.)

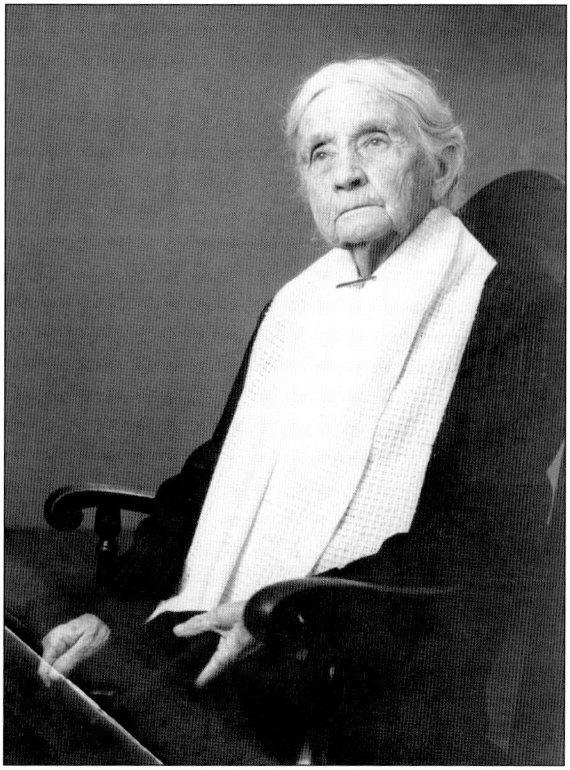

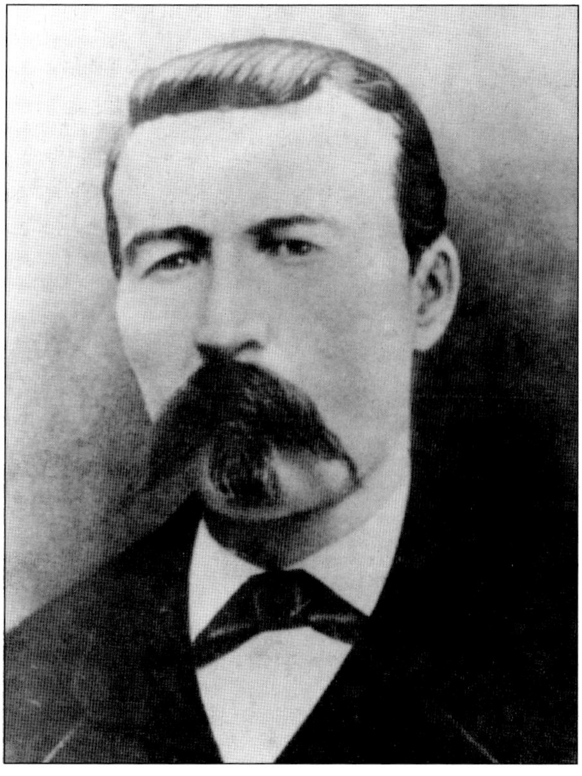

Virginia-born Daniel Fielding Smith headed west as a young man. Serving as an Indian scout, he helped establish the Butterfield Overland Trail. He lost an eye while serving as a Confederate scout. In Stephenville on Christmas Day 1882, he married Matty J. Murphy. He and Union veteran William Wilson built the Stephenville Presbyterian Church. He is listed as a carpenter in the 1894 Stephenville business directory. (SHHM.)

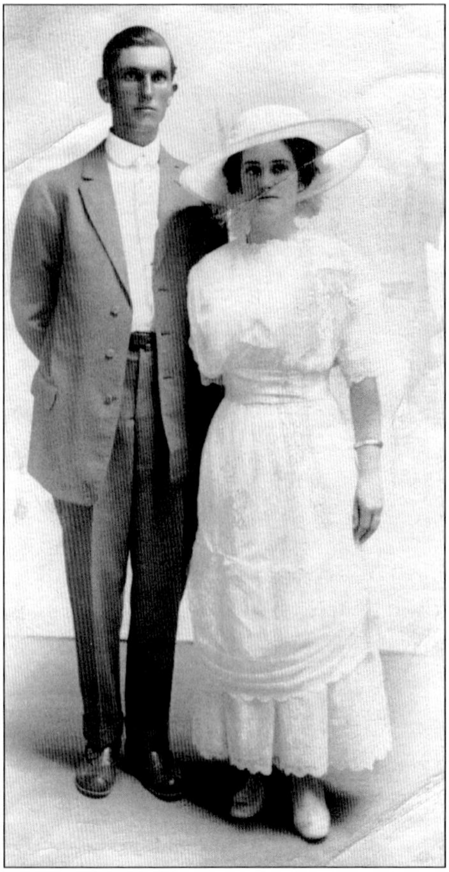

Pitching for the Hankins Normal College baseball team paid Arthur Warren Shoup's expenses for his 1911 teaching certificate. He is pictured with Lela Miller in their 1913 wedding photograph. Over 23 years, Arthur taught at Chalk Mountain and Lone Oak, and was principal at Greens Creek. Beginning in 1936, he worked exclusively with the Soil Conservation Service. Born near Duffau, he farmed his entire life. (Sandra Shoup Hammons.)

Arthur Shoup began soil conservation practices in 1916, assisting Erath, Hood, and Somervell County farmers to establish terraces to prevent soil erosion. He pioneered strip-cropping for soil conditioning. This 1939 aerial image shows alternating rows of sorghum and cowpeas immediately above terraces that empty into a channel between the fields and the farmstead. Shoup designed over 1,000 miles of terracing and 500 rural ponds and waterways. (Sandra Shoup Hammons.)

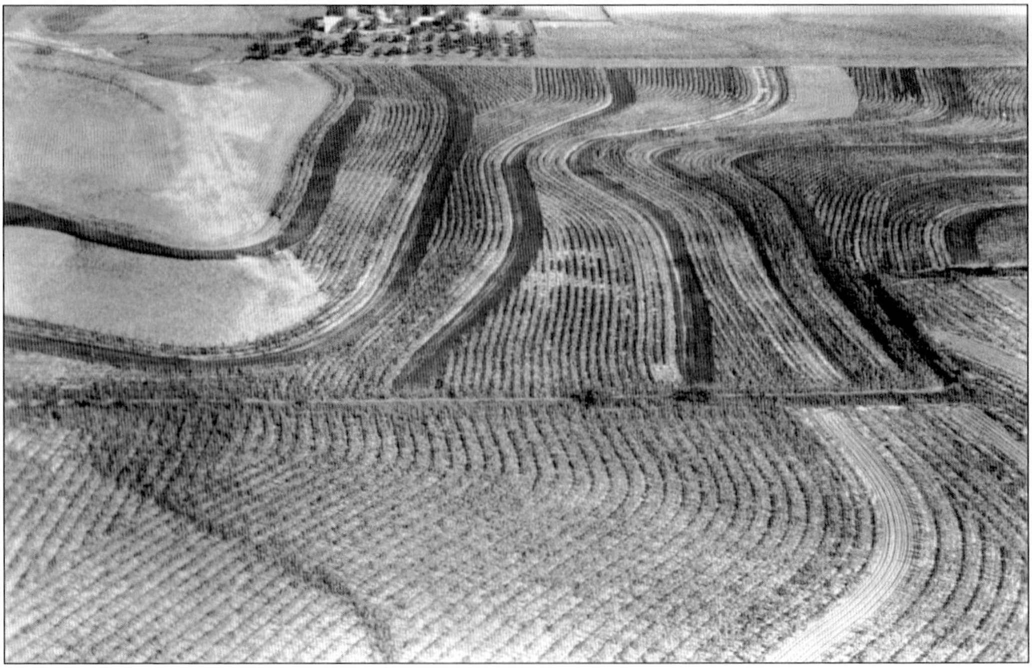

Seven

Strong Foundations

While spiritual energy accompanied travelers, once people settled in a place, many churches started in family homes. Baptist and Methodist faiths arrived in Erath first, followed by Christian, Holiness, and Presbyterian. In 1854, Baptist reverend William "Choctaw Bill" Robinson was the first to preach in the county. He organized several Erath churches, including those at Dublin and Stephenville. Freemason, Methodist missionary, and circuit rider Rev. Peter Gravis also established churches in Stephenville and Dublin. During the bleak Civil War years, Rev. Isaac Reed ministered to those on the home front. Reed coordinated several Baptist associations, including in Erath. Appearing during the turbulent Reconstruction era, Rev. Reuben "Comanche Rube" Ross arrived by oxcart in 1866. Ever vigilant of outlaws or violent encounters, Ross and his fellow "pistol packing preachers" were armed and rode a fast horse.

About 1870, a 21-oxen Alabama wagon train brought the extended families of Daily, Howell, Kiker, Morton, Ware, Whitfield, and others to the area. Settling Center Grove, Rev. Marshall James Morton and his family established Morton Chapel and cemetery. At Greens Creek, the Kikers began a Methodist group, while the Baptist Howell and Whitfield families met on Narcissa Howell's front porch. The two churches worshipped side by side, in members' homes, under the same brush arbor, and in the same log school before each constructed a building in the 1880s. Permanent structures such as tabernacles replaced the brush arbors; these were used for fairs, funerals, singings, reunions, and revivals. Erected in Alexander, Bluff Dale, Edna Hill, Greens Creek, Harbin, Huckabay, Johnsville, Lingleville, Little Mexico, Morgan Mill, Patillo, Pecan Cemetery, Purves, Round Grove, Stephenville, and Valley Grove, some of these structures remain standing today.

It was common for a single community house to serve as church, school, and social gathering place. Traveling evangelists, politicians, tax collectors, and voters visited that one centrally located property. Prior to state funding, subscription schools usually charged a fee, such as $1 per month per student. A single person taught all ages and all subjects. Many schools closed in 1861, as funds went to the Confederate war effort. The first free public school in the county opened in Stephenville in 1872. Church and school were community development entities.

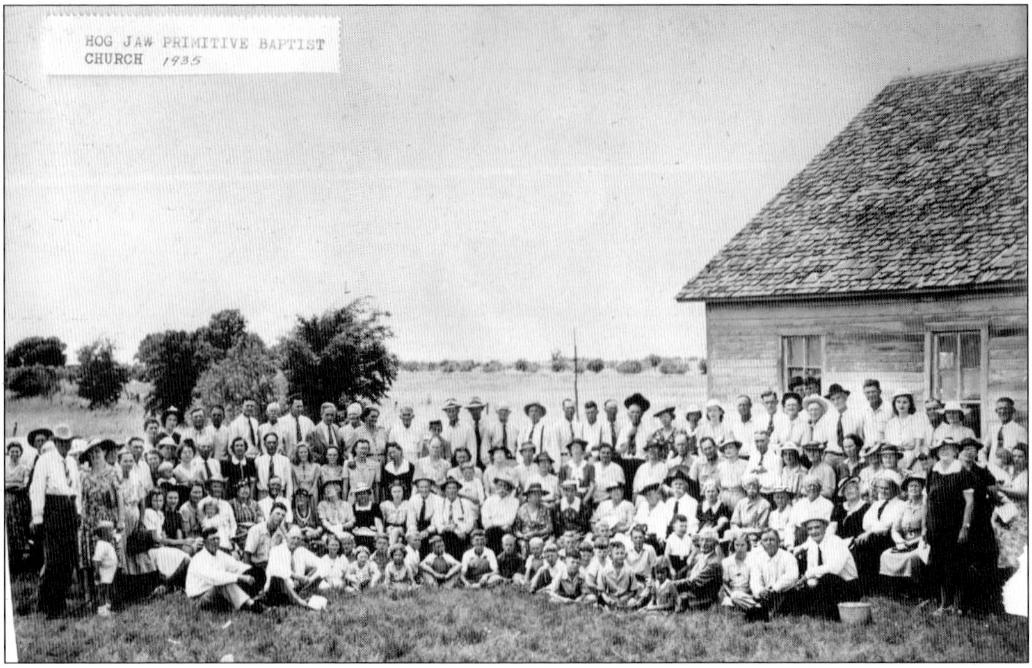

The Bosque Primitive Baptist Church was organized in July 1859 just north of Stephenville. Over time, for various reasons, the church moved to multiple locations before settling at Hog Jaw, southwest of Millerville and near Hico. In 1935, some 125 members gathered at the Hog Jaw Primitive Baptist Church for a homecoming. A school was there until about 1915, when it consolidated with Millerville and Slaterville. (SHHM.)

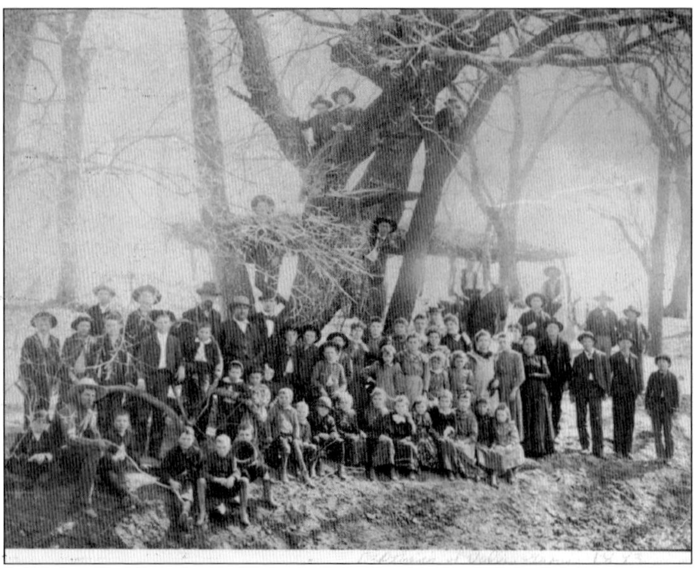

Valley Grove Baptist Church designated armed guards on horseback to protect from Native American raiders. A brush arbor (center) served as the meeting place until a two-room schoolhouse was built in 1877. Charter members included Margarete and John Henry Roberts, Sarah McCormick and James H. Roberts, Portia McCormick and I.N. Roberts, Sarah Thompson and Christopher Columbus Sharp, Joann and J.L. Walker, Sarah and James H. Parr, and Charlie Walker. (SHHM.)

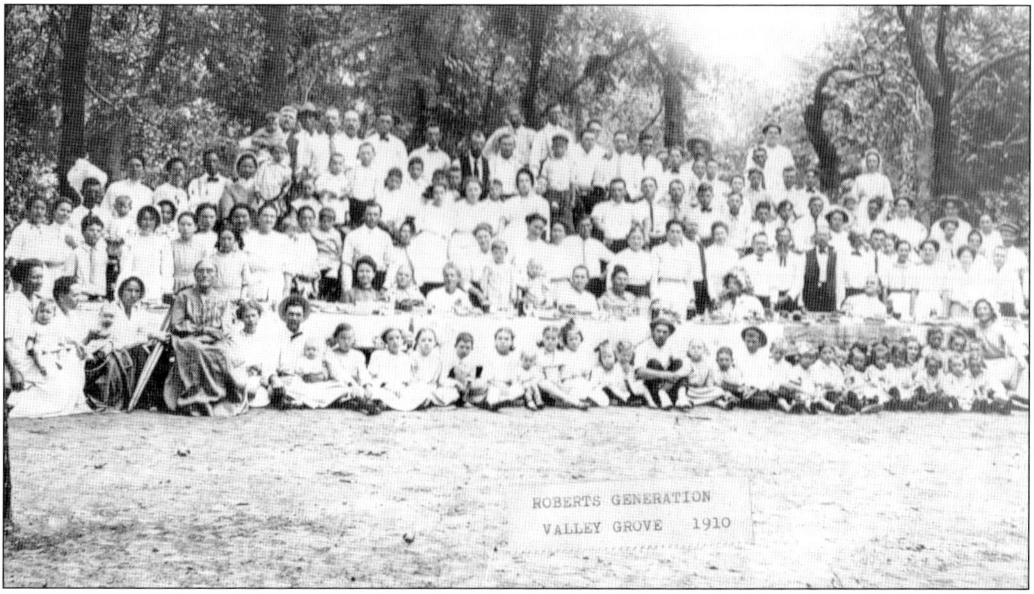

The descendants of John Henry Roberts gathered for a 1910 reunion. The family began settling along the oak-wooded southern banks of the Bosque River in 1856. The area was later called Valley Grove. John purchased enough acreage for each of his sons to homestead, although his sons Charles P., George W., and John Kyle died as young men. James Henry, Isaac Newton, Leonard Franklin, and Alexander and their descendants became pioneers of the county. (SHHM.)

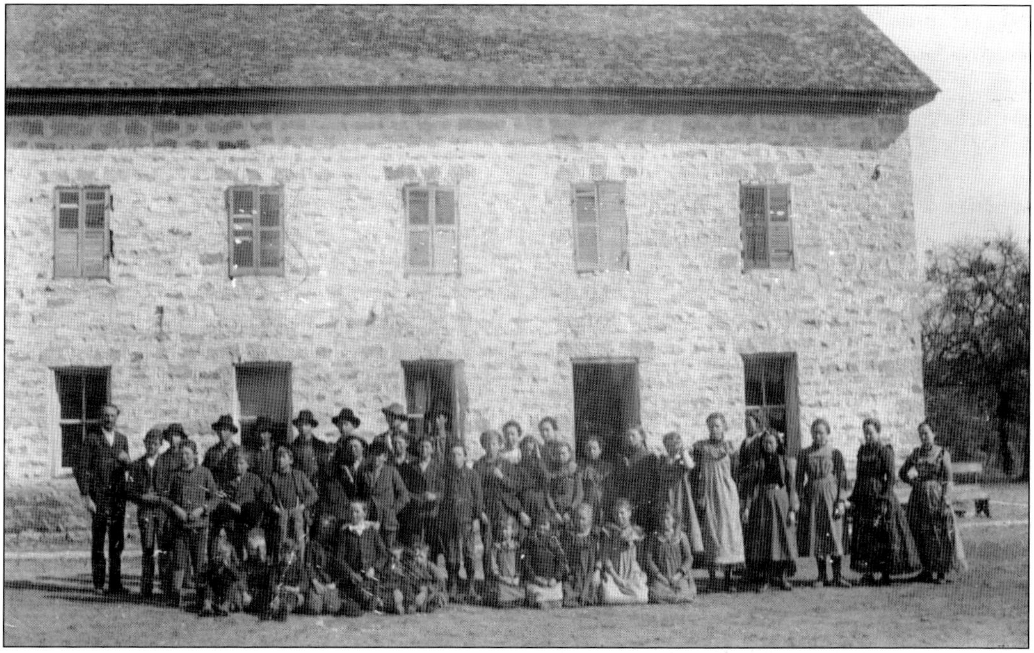

Jesse Caraway, Ike Cowan, Andy Jackson, John R. Jones, John and William B. Pate arrived from Tennessee in the late 1850s and settled in the valley between the Paluxy River and Richardson Creek. Johnny Birdwell, Jesse Brooks, Don Crites, Jake Nutt, Ben Tinnin, and Alex White soon followed. These men built and deeded the Methodist Rock Church, which served as a community center for education, faith, and social activities. (SHHM.)

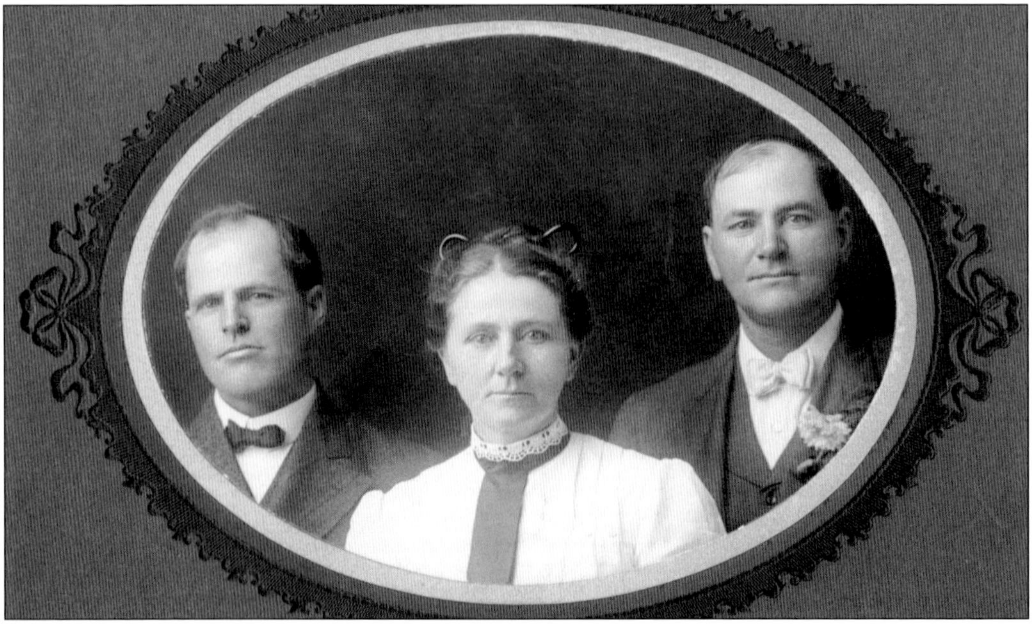

The Mary Jane Mayhew and James Riley Wallace family followed the McCluskey family from Kentucky to Huckabay in 1875. John Andrew (right) preached and performed ministerial duties. Lydia Victoria "Vicky" (center) married Andrew Jackson "Jack" Wells in 1879. They had eight children. Widowed in 1928, Vicky lived almost another 50 years. John and Lydia's younger brother, Edwin Ross (left), also became a preacher, attending Weatherford College. (Jan Jennings.)

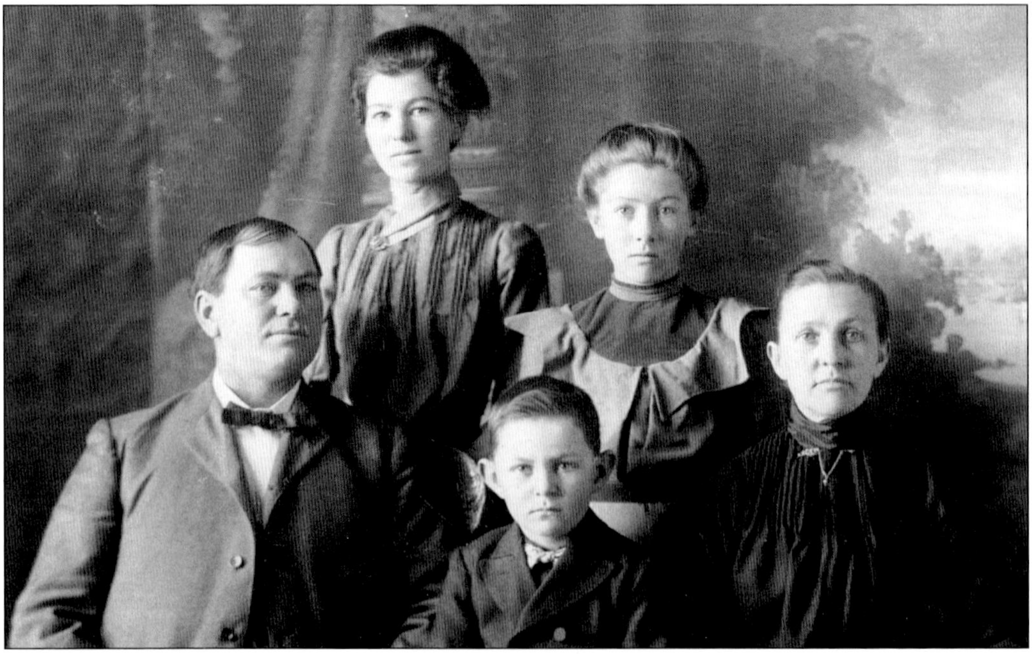

Examined in 1887 by the Quarterly Conference of Stephenville (Texas) Circuit, John Andrew Wallace was a deacon of the Methodist Episcopal church. Pictured here are, from left to right, (first row) John Andrew Wallace, Thomas Jefferson "Jeff" Wallace, and Louisa Alice Wells Wallace; (second row) Bertha Jane Wallace and Edna Lou Wallace. (Jan Jennings.)

Kentuckians Lucinda Victoria "Puss" Wallace (center) and her husband, John Edwin McCluskey, arrived in 1874. In 1900, Lucinda and her two youngest daughters, Alice McCluskey (left) and Ivy McCluskey (right) lived next door to her oldest child, John Riley McCleskey. John Riley adopted the new surname spelling. (Jan Jennings.)

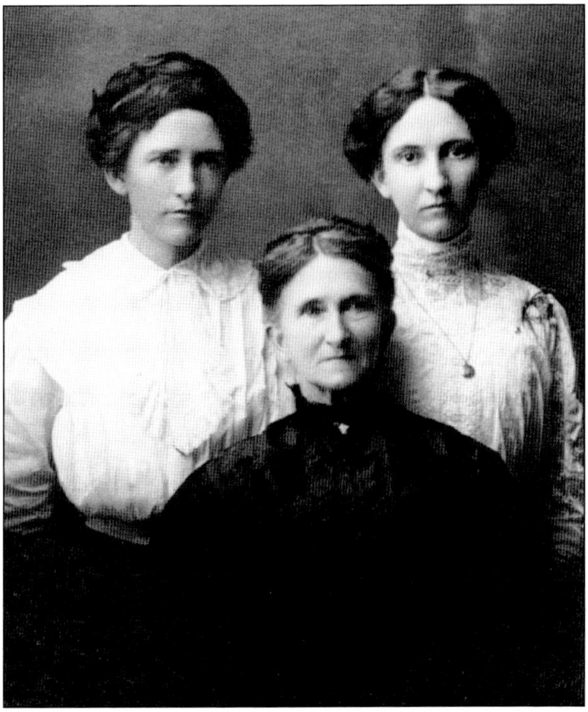

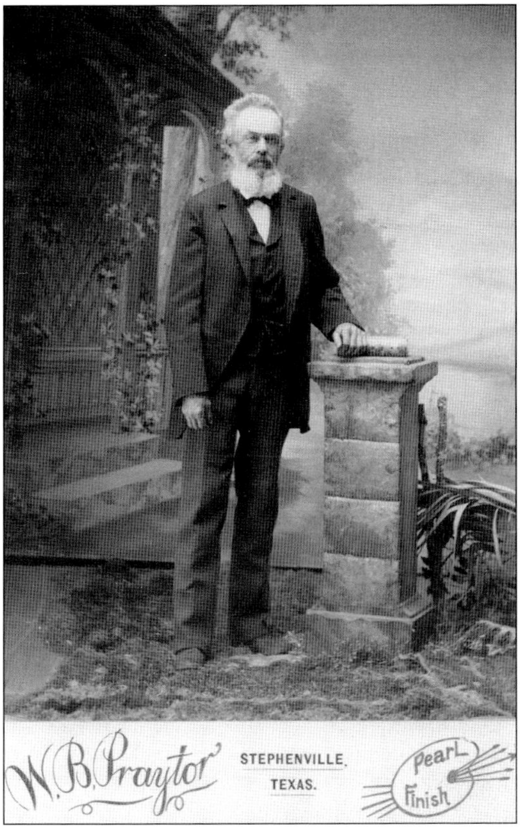

Having served in the Mexican-American War in 1846, Dr. W.P. Hatchett returned to Texas in 1855. Although he was an ordained Baptist minister, his medical practice kept him from pastoral work. He was instrumental in the 1880 organization of the Central Texas Baptist Convention. His children and grandchildren served Selden Baptist Church after its 1881 organization; his son H.S. Hatchett was the church's first pastor.

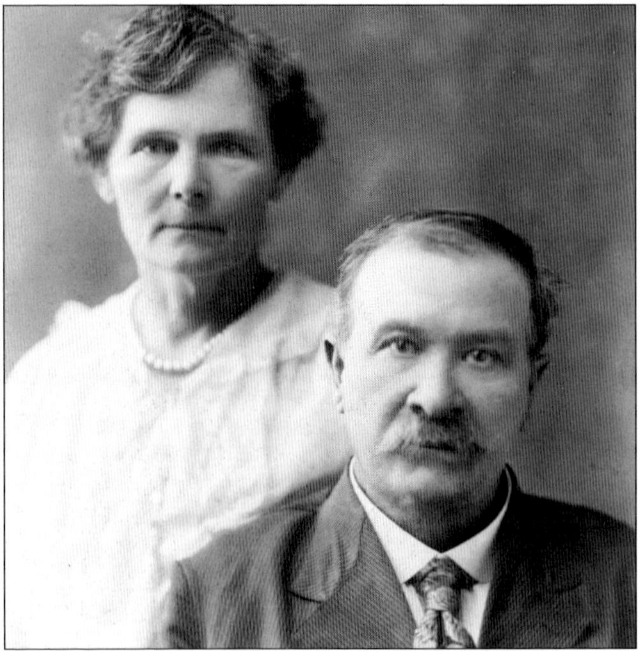

As a child born in 1860 near Pony Creek, Charles E. Darnell experienced multiple encounters with indigenous people. Once, while searching for his mother's geese, he hid and watched two of them carry the geese away. In 1876, he married Mattie Cargill and moved to Selden, where they were active in the Baptist church. In 1898, he purchased the Stephenville telephone system.

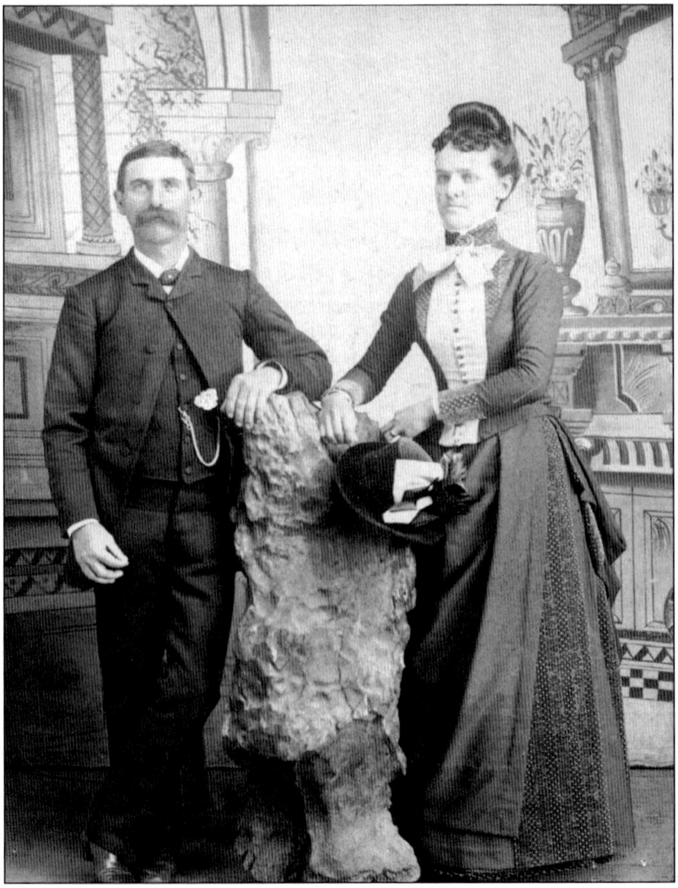

William H. Gentry and Dora Randolph Dryden got married in Lincoln, Missouri, and came to Erath County to farm. William served as second clerk of the Sims Creek Baptist Church (now Selden Baptist Church). In 1886, he sold the family farm and opened a grocery and dry goods store in Selden. He served as postmaster of Selden from November 1890 to October 1896.

Born in St. Louis, infant John F. Funk came to Texas by wagon train with his parents in 1857, settling on Sims Creek. In 1878, he and two of his brothers went west to Albany, and then Tom Green County, where they built the Funk Ranch. John returned to Erath and married Annie G. Poensalot in 1886; they made their home in Selden. He donated land for Selden Baptist Church.

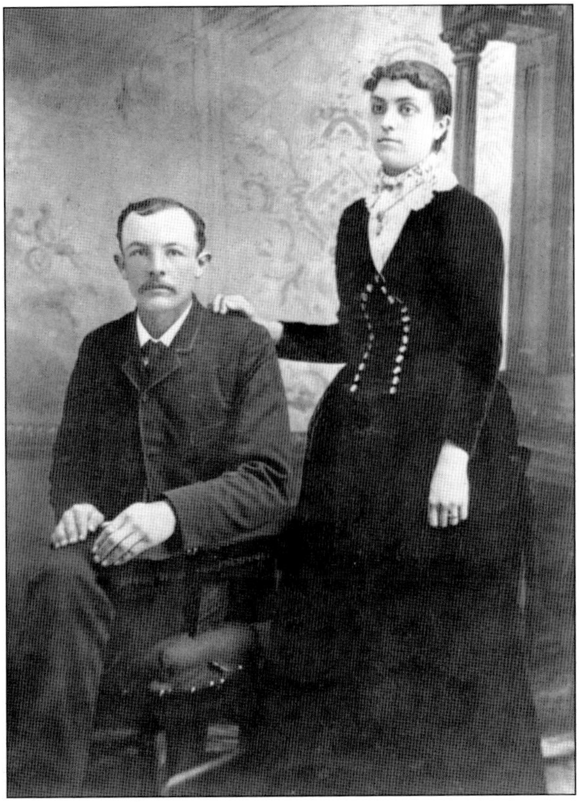

In this c. 1900 photograph taken on a Saturday afternoon after church services, a group of young people enjoy fellowship with a game of croquet. The lady with the "X" marked at her feet was Della Gentry (later Della Gentry Gardner). This picture was taken on the east side of the Selden Baptist Church building.

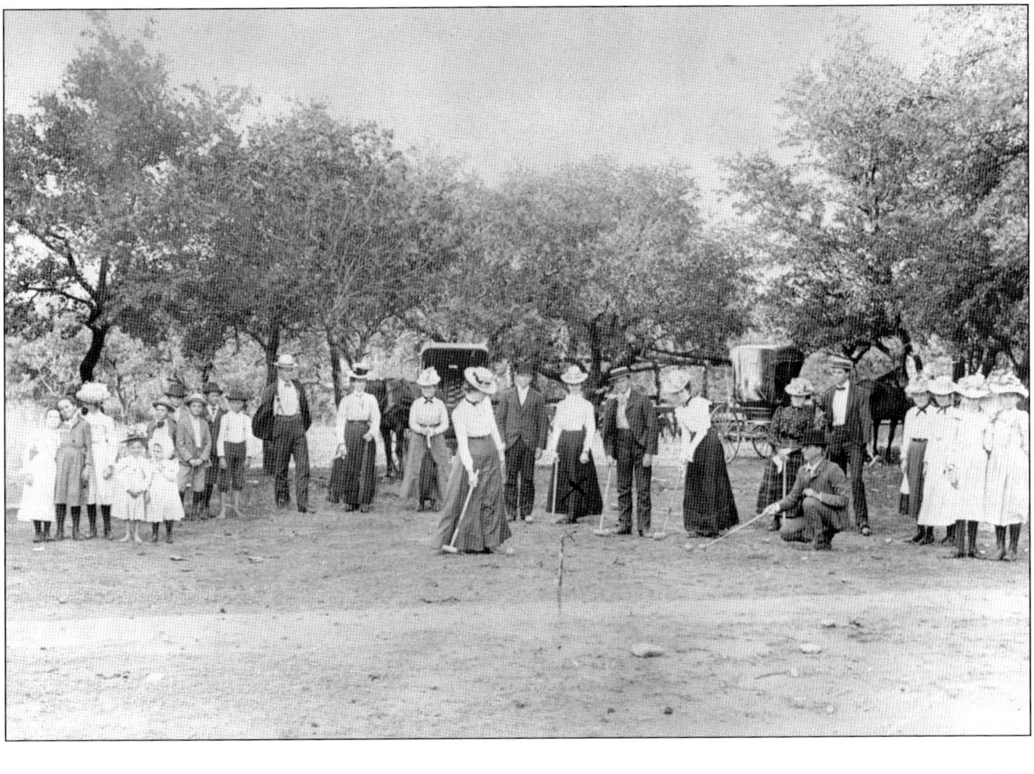

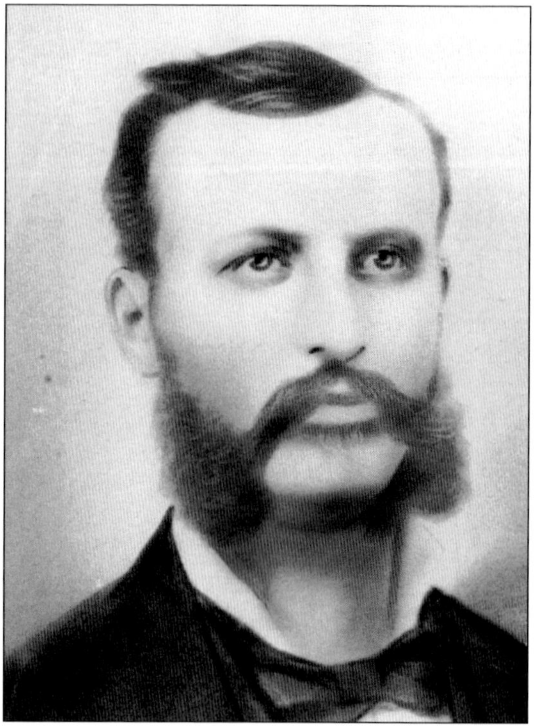

Rev. John Sharp and his wife, Sally Calhoun of Erath County, sojourned as Methodist missionaries to Jacksonville, Florida. When there was a yellow fever outbreak, John's Texas family asked him to return home, but he could not leave his congregation when they needed him. He succumbed to the disease and is buried in Florida. John and Sally's children were Lucia and John Sharp. (JBH.)

Lingleville's Church of Christ sponsored the Lingleville Christian College, providing advanced education to about 100 students. The white two-story structure was on the east side of town. Classes commenced in October 1901. In 1912, college president James F. Cox became president of Tarleton College; he later served as president of Abilene Christian College. After the Lingleville campus closed, the building was sold to the Lingleville Independent School District.

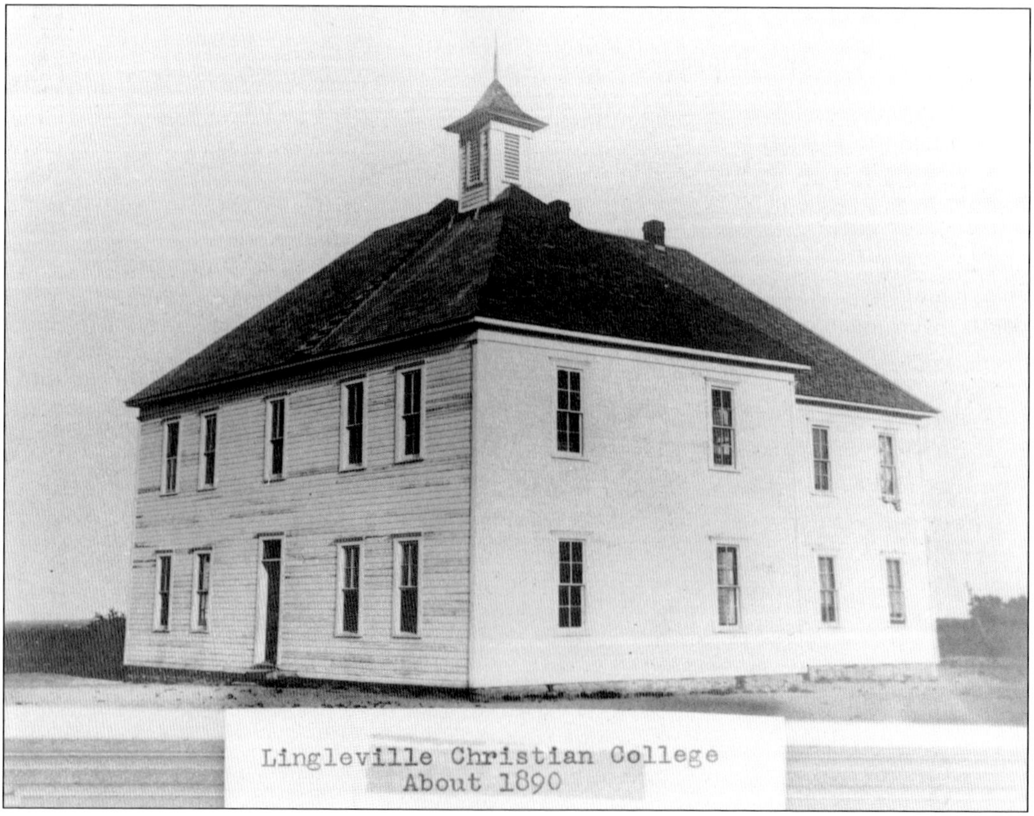

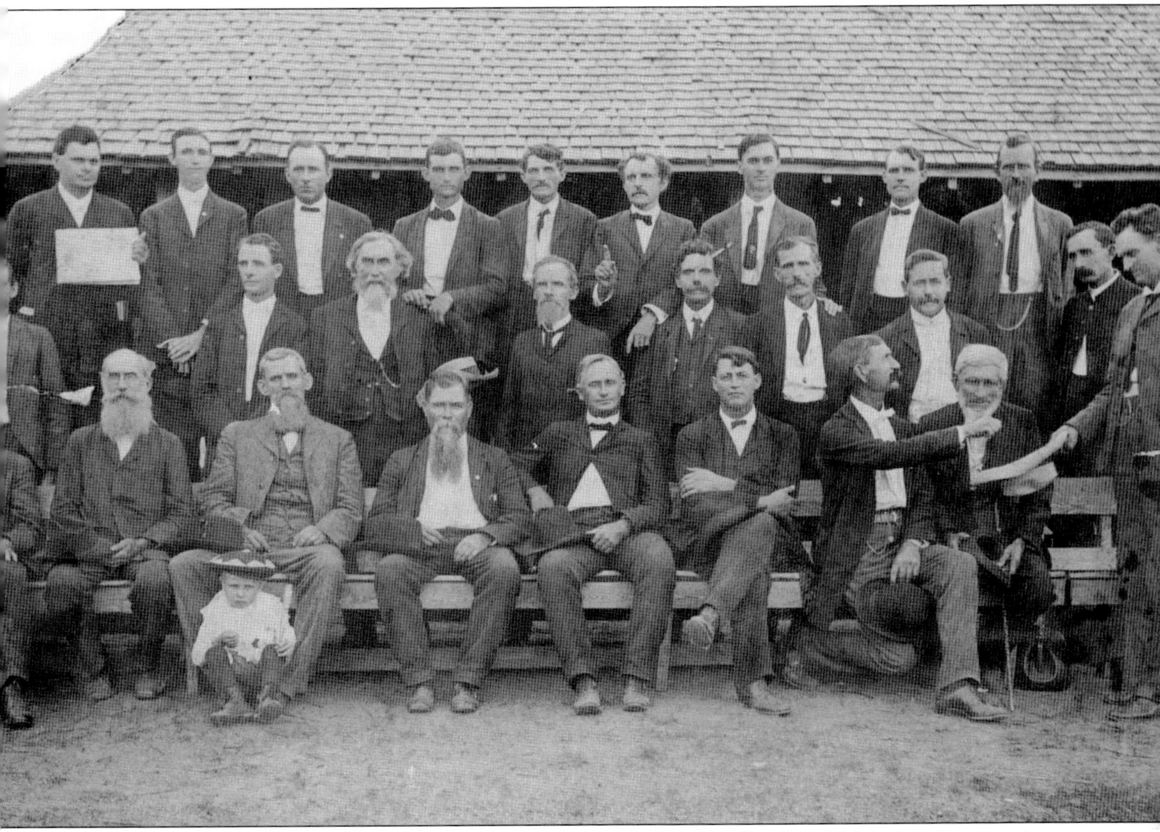

Baptist leaders met in Dublin from September 14 to 16, 1905, with over 3,000 people attending. Forty-three of the 48 churches were represented, reporting 4,064 members and contributions aggregating $15,572.64. New churches received were those at Liberty Valley, Palmer, and Rock Falls. First-time ordained ministers were L.Y. Brown, Y.T. Hillsman, and J.B. Riley. A successful year of mission work by I.M. Crutcher at Thurber and W.M. Green in the association was recorded. Speakers included J.B. Vinson, J.M. Gaddy, Dr. J.M. Carroll, Dr. George W. Truett. In his 1937 book *History of the Baptists in Erath County*, historian Rev. Donovan Duncan Tidwell notes that Baptists were among Erath's earliest settlers. Local Baptist beginnings reached the frontier's edge of the Brazos River Association. Bosque River, Comanche, Round Grove, and Erath County Associations formed with religious development of the region. Bluff Dale, Greens Creek, Harbin, Huckabay, Lingleville, Morgan Mill, Patillo, Pecan Cemetery, and Stephenville built tabernacles. The tabernacle was an advancement from the brush arbor. (SHHM.)

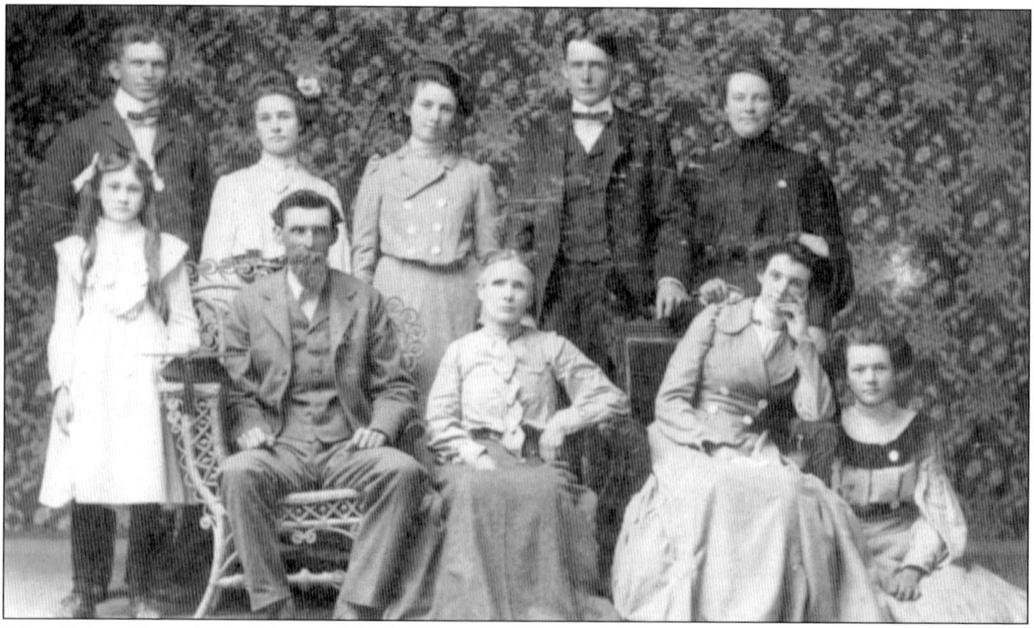

John Riley Chapel was active with the Erath Baptist Association, serving on the state missions committee in 1909. Pictured here around 1903 are, from left to right, (first row) Alice, John Riley, Mary Derida Conatser, Nova E., and Cora; (second row) Albert Lee King, Viola Paralee, Mary A., Jesse Alexander, and Danie Addison Boggs. Four of the women pictured here had died by 1909. (Connie Conatser McSpadden.)

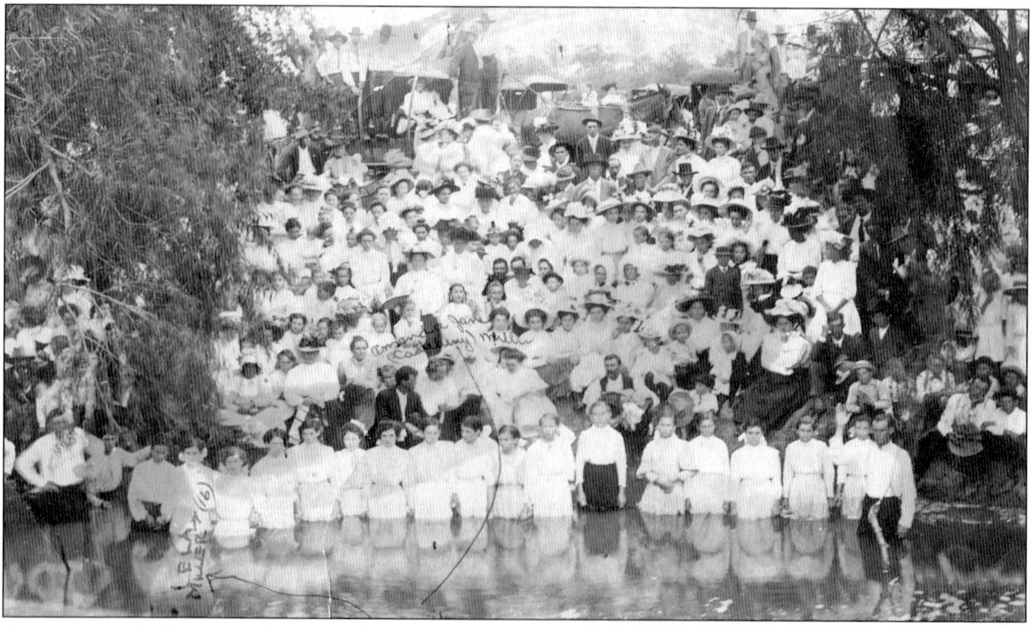

Greens Creek Baptist Church celebrated its 125th anniversary in 2001. Worshipers first met at the home of Narcissa Howell, then under a brush arbor. In 1880, money was raised to build a one-room log schoolhouse where services were also held. Prior to 1971, when a baptistry was added to the current building, baptisms were conducted at Smith Hole, including this one in 1909. (Sandra Shoup Hammons.)

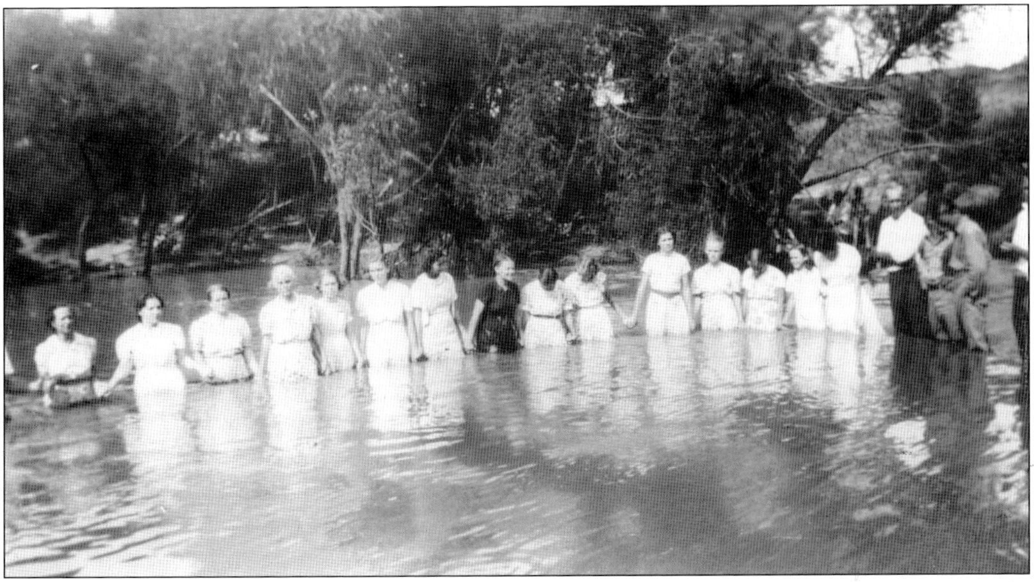

This image is labeled "Purves baptism" and may include members of Friendship Baptist Church, which organized in the Purves area in July 1884. Established in 1903, Purves Baptist Church consolidated with Friendship Baptist in 1914. Salt Branch Primitive Baptist Church met in a school building from 1886 until it bought the Bynum Methodist Episcopal Church South building. Fields School House Baptist Church held services from 1878 until 1923. (Linda Tolston.)

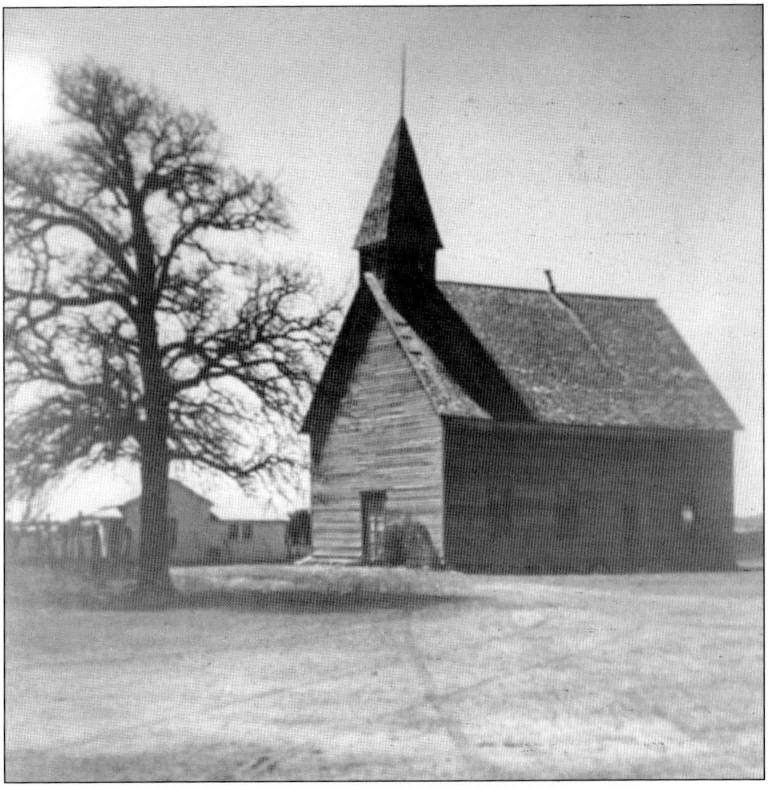

Harbin saw an influx of new arrivals after the Civil War, and a brush arbor served as place of worship until the Harbin Baptist Church building was erected. Harbin had a church and parsonage, a school, a post office, a railroad depot, a general mercantile store and grocer, a blacksmith, a barber, two doctors, and a cotton gin and mill owned and operated by Ben Everrenthus Robbins. (Judith Robbins Lemons; photograph by Myrtis Robbins.)

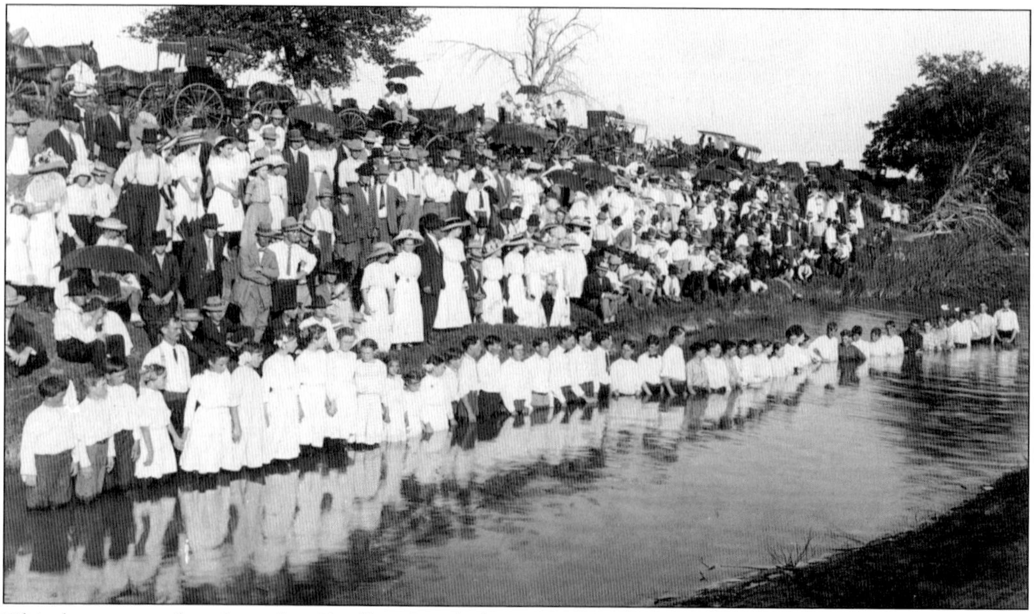

This large crowd gathered at Duffau Creek for a 1914 baptism held by Duffau Baptist Church. Elders A.W. Elledge, O.W. Hughart, and D. Shipman began this fellowship with 17 charter members in 1878. Soon after the church organized, its members furnished material and completed a sanctuary at this site. After a fire destroyed that building in 1935, a new structure, which still stands, was built. (SHHM.)

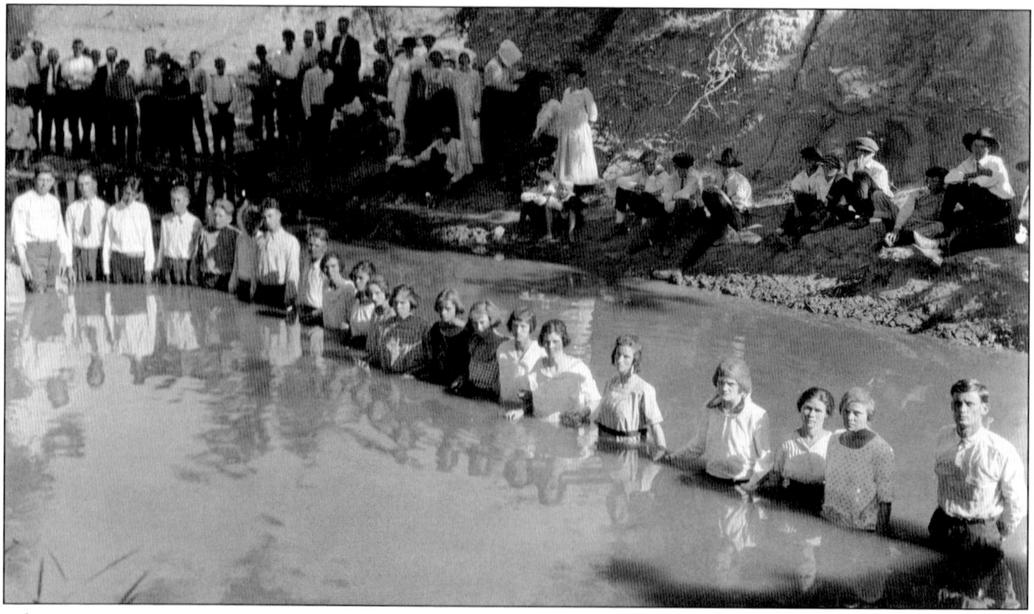

About 1930, near south Paluxy River's Nine Mile Bridge, Brother W.L. Daniels (standing in the water at far left) and Rev. William Cornelius Bramlett (far right) baptized, from left to right, two unidentified, Ira Henry Ratliff, Gordon Pierce, two unidentified, Olen T. Wood, unidentified, Trixie Norris Hawkins, unidentified, Lydia Spears, Essie McDowell Caldwell, Lou Ollie Spears Montgomery, Jewell Kilcrease Lindblade, Nettie Williams Engler, Zella Williams Smith, Alma Gardie Spears, Dorothy Norris Mayo, and unidentified. (SHHM.)

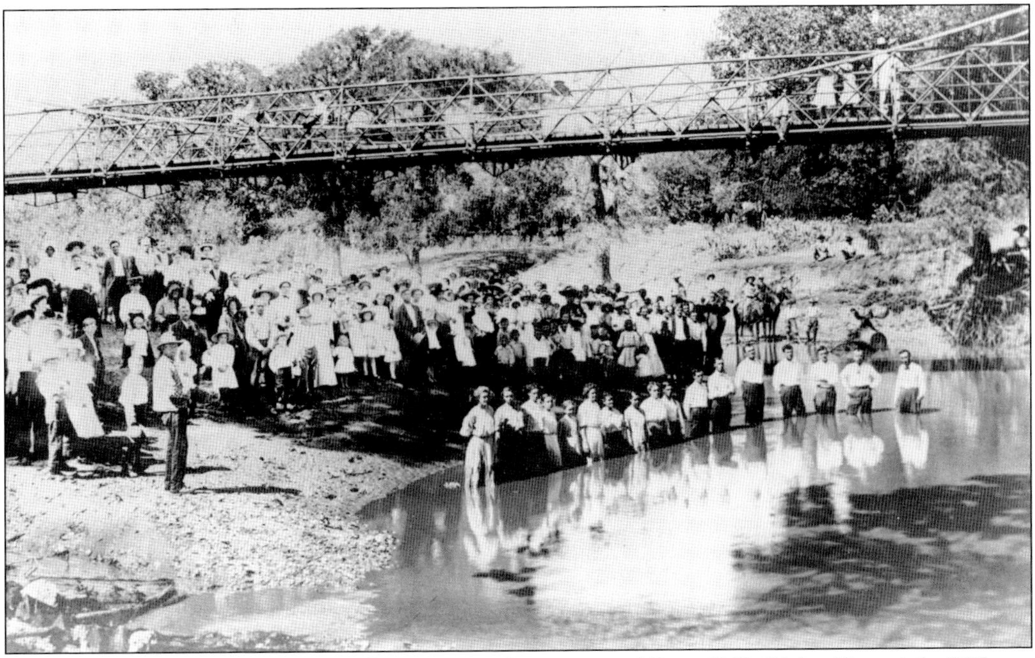

On April 26, 1935, the *Stephenville Empire-Tribune* printed Rev. D.D. Tidwell's article "Fifteen Session of the Bosque River Baptist Association." Along with providing annual statistics, Tidwell noted the large number of baptisms at churches in and near Alexander and Iredell. Alexander's New Hope had 65 additions by baptism, and Friendship had 17. Tidwell attributed these results to a great revival conducted by famous evangelist Major Penn. (Catherine Rampley.)

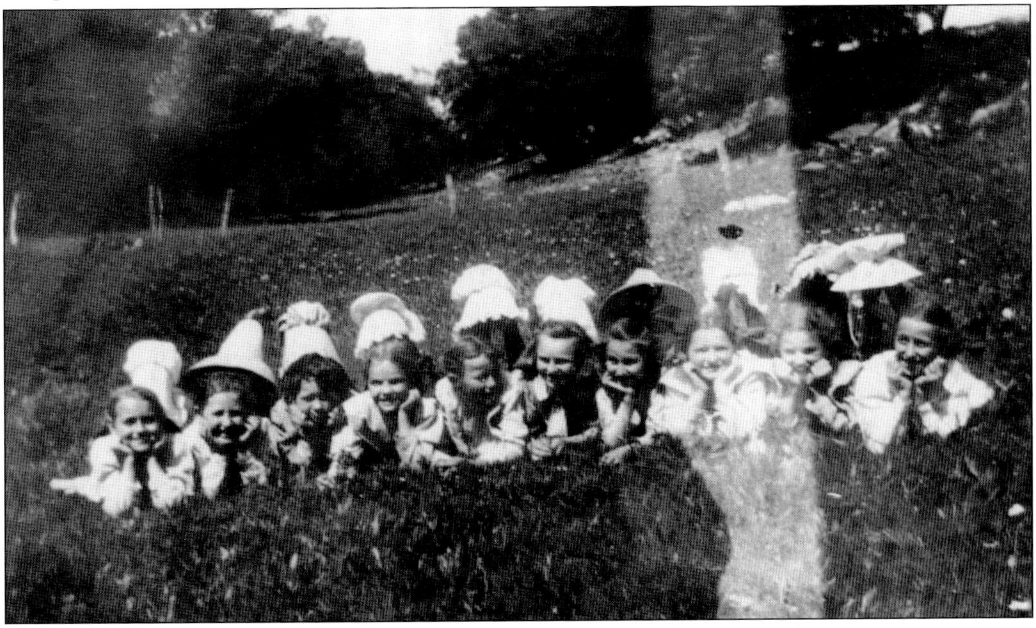

A well-dressed young lady often received a new bonnet for Easter, as a bonnet was necessary to protect one's skin. In this c. 1908 picture, these girls just wanted to have fun dangling their bonnets on their feet. Mabel Teresa Hickey (Conatser), daughter of Annie Ruth Holt and Will Hickey, enjoyed the day with cousins and friends. (Connie Conatser McSpadden.)

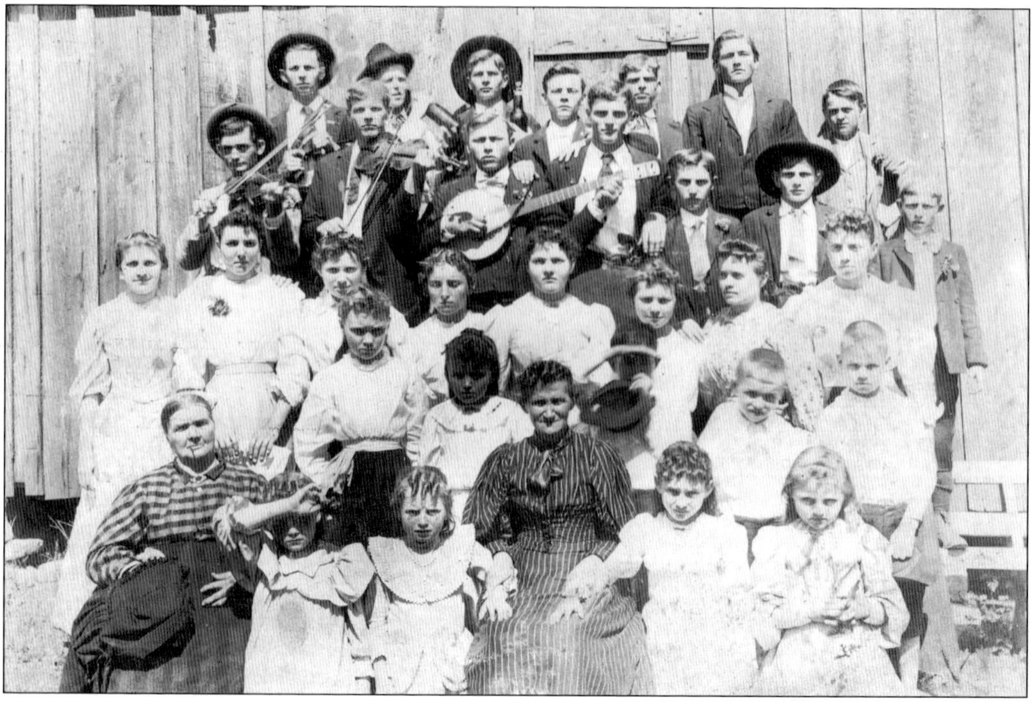

On March 24, 1899, the *Dublin Progress* reported that the Clairette singing class met at a Mr. Salmon's place. On July 21, 1922, the *Stephenville Tribune* described Clairette singing as "enjoyed at the Methodist church." This 1892 photograph was most likely taken at the Clairette schoolhouse built in the 1870s. (SHHM.)

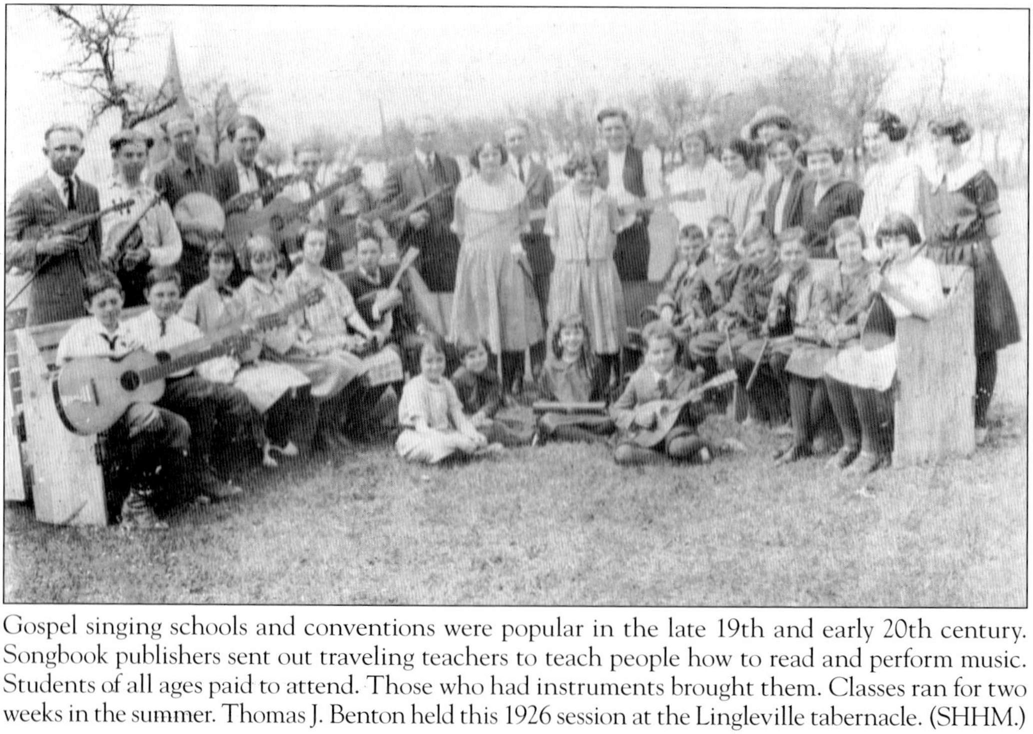

Gospel singing schools and conventions were popular in the late 19th and early 20th century. Songbook publishers sent out traveling teachers to teach people how to read and perform music. Students of all ages paid to attend. Those who had instruments brought them. Classes ran for two weeks in the summer. Thomas J. Benton held this 1926 session at the Lingleville tabernacle. (SHHM.)

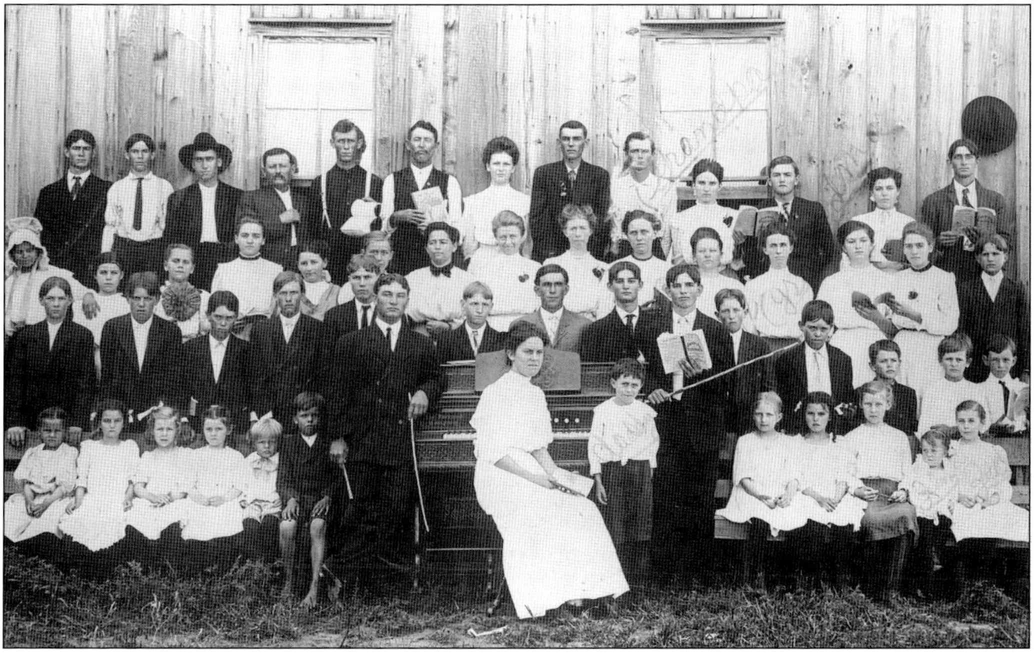

This group of children and adult students attended a 1908 singing school held at the Mexico schoolhouse located near the Comanche and Erath County line. With Grace Ewing on the organ, teachers Henry Eiland and Oscar Cox conducted the musical session. Note that long sleeves were worn in spite of the summer heat. (SHHM.)

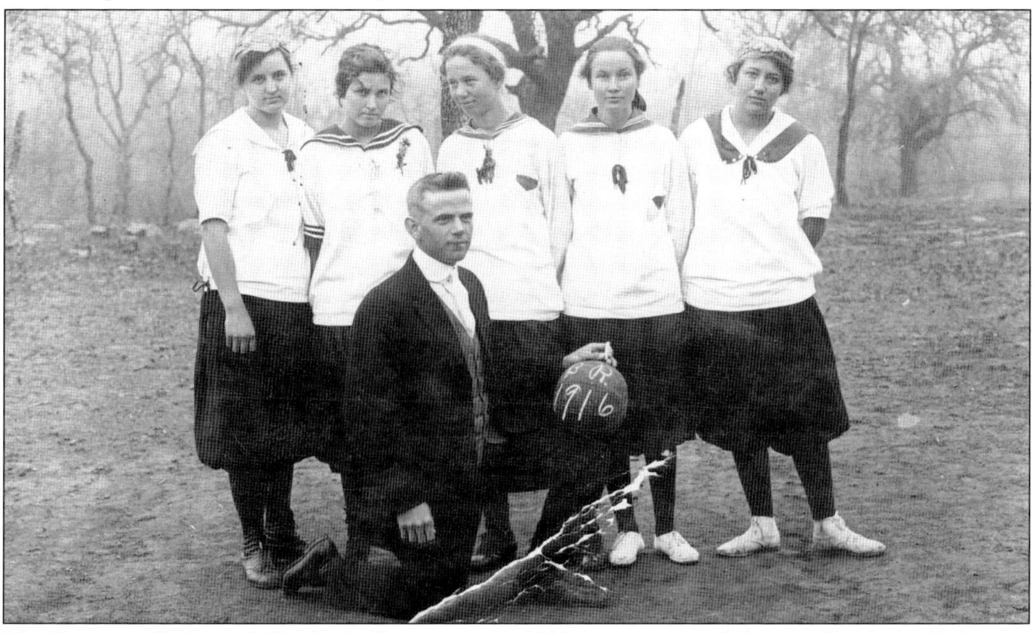

The Bowman Ridge girls' basketball team won a 1916 tournament, defeating Stephenville by one point when Tempe Sageser scored from 55 feet in the closing minute. Pictured here are, from left to right, Tennie Sageser, guard; Etta Jordan, guard; Lizzie Shuffield, forward; Eula McCann, center; and Tempe Sageser, twin of Tennie, goal pitcher. Kneeling in front is basketball coach and school principal M. Luther Kelley. (SHHM.)

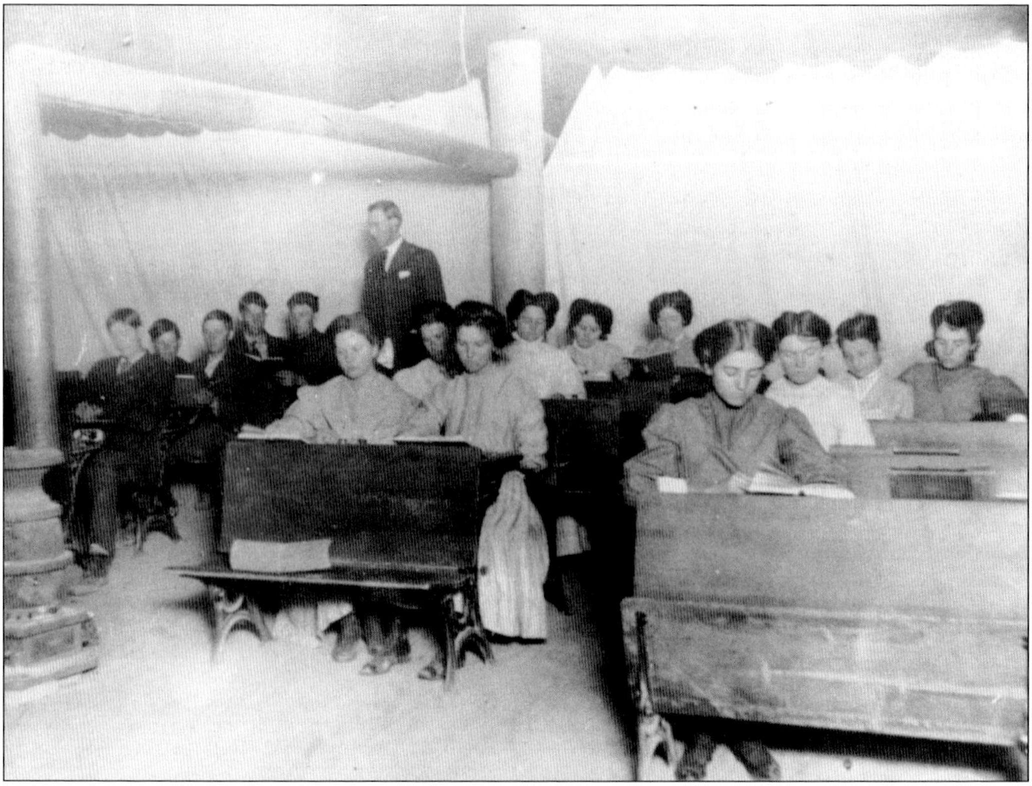

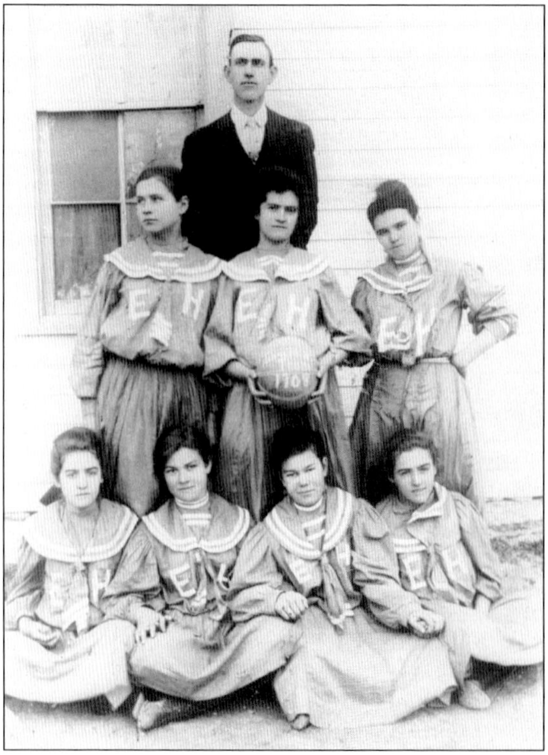

A school opened in Edna Hill in the early 1900s. Rural children usually had farm chores to complete before they could go to school for the day. It was common for a couple of the older boy students to arrive early to start the fire and warm the building. Warner Dale and Charles Don Bramlett remembered having this assignment in the 1920s. Children often brought their lunch in a saved lard or syrup bucket. Pictured here are a 1908 classroom (above) and the 1908 Edna Hill girls' basketball team. The team members pictured with coach Arthur L. Duff are, from left to right, (first row) Hettie Porterfield (Whisenant), Alice Dennis, Lena Barbee (Salyer), and Hattie Porterfield (Gilbreath); (second row) Sally Gilbert (Hatley), Frances Gee (Lancaster), and Allie Gilbreath (Luker). The Edna Hill school consolidated with the school in Dublin in the late 1940s.

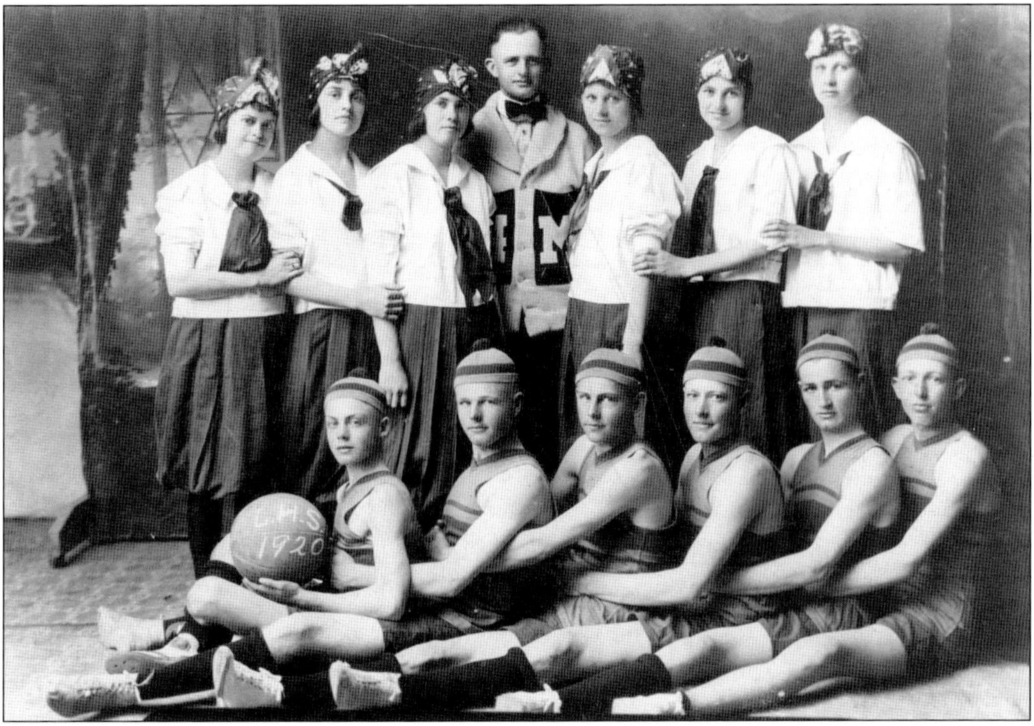

Lingleville had a public school in the 1890s and a private school earlier than that. In the 1890s, Lingleville had two colleges. A post office opened in 1885, and in 1920, the postmaster was Joseph H. Morris. In 1920, Lingleville businesses included a bank, blacksmiths D.C. Chandler and R.N. Whitworth, druggist Ivy Cutler, F.L. Grissom Dry Goods, Hilliard Mercantile, and leatherwork by B.F. Pinkard. The 1920 basketball students pictured above are, from left to right, (first row) Lyle Price, Walter Brandon, Buster Grissom, Albert Whitacre, and Neil Noah; (second row) Electra McMahan, May Wilcoxson, Demaris Leatherwood, Blanch Davis, Jettie Smith, and Hazel Carroll; the man at center is coach Jeff Duncan. The classroom photograph below is dated 1923.

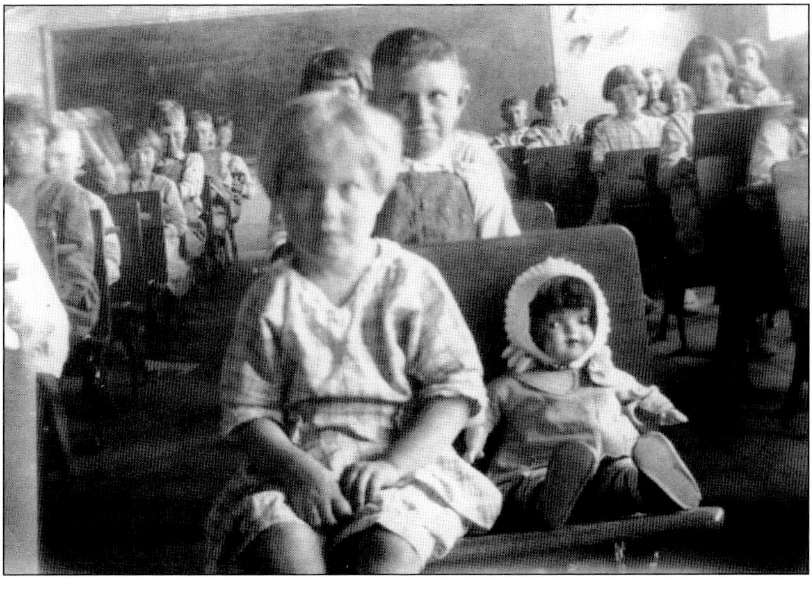

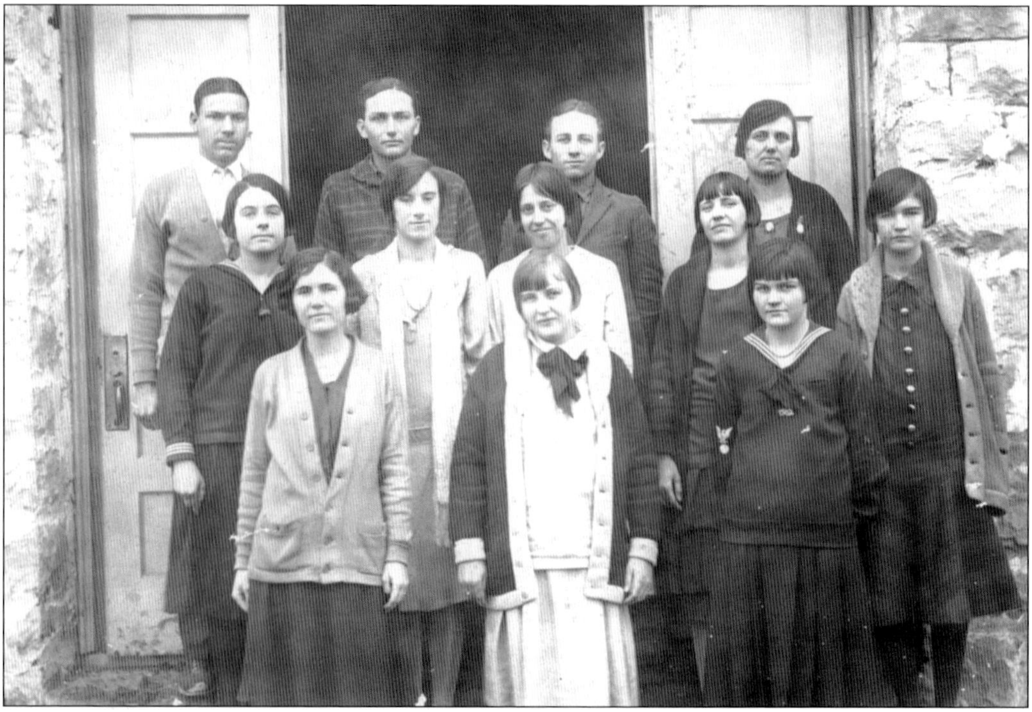

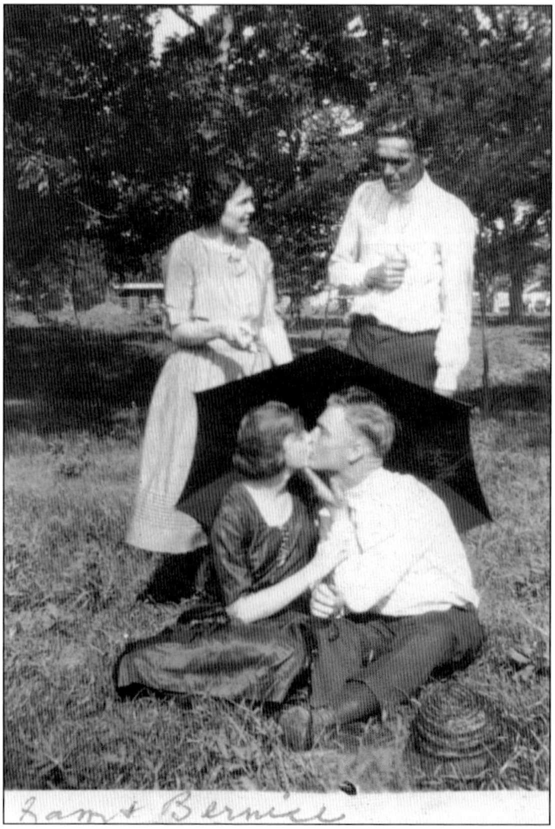

The Bluff Dale High School graduating class of 1926 gathered on the school steps for this picture. The back of this photograph lists the nicknames of these friends: Buddah, Priss, ALE, Beautiful, Jane, Cap, Duck, Quiety, Foal, Buzzard, and Brown Eyes. At far right in the first row is "Brown Eyes," Ida Lee Watson Kile Henderson. (Pamela Kile Pollock McDuff.)

She said yes! Bernice Maude Darnell and James Samuel "Sam" Watson of Bluff Dale got married on December 17, 1922. After a turn at farming, Sam operated a Fort Worth service station. He was a member of the Tarrant Masonic lodge. Sam and Bernice belonged to North Fort Worth Baptist Church. After rearing three children, they later had a number of grandchildren and great-grandchildren. (Pamela Kile Pollock McDuff.)

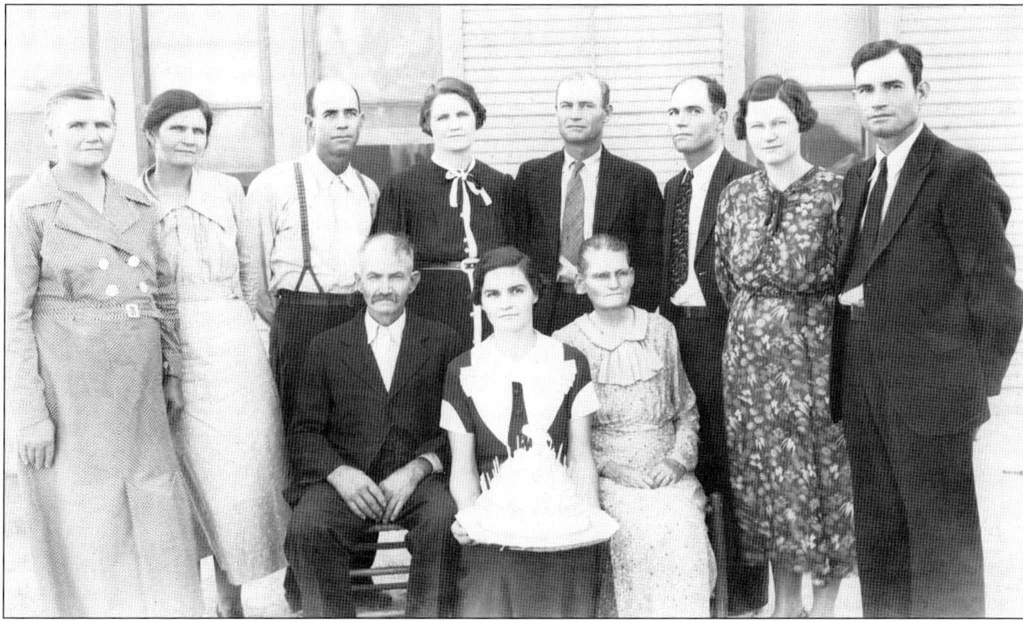

Orpah Iantha Jeanette Howell and Cornelious Samuel Watson married on October 14, 1886. They are pictured at their 50th anniversary in 1936 with their surviving children (from left to right), (first row, seated) Cornelious, Ida Lee Kile Henderson, and Orpah, (second row, standing) Martha Alice "Mattie" Stembridge, Matilda Safronia "Tillie" Howard, Hugh Robert, Eva Lena Baldwin, James Samuel, William Hunter, Lily Mae Glenn, and Walton Oren Watson. (Pamela Kile Pollock McDuff.)

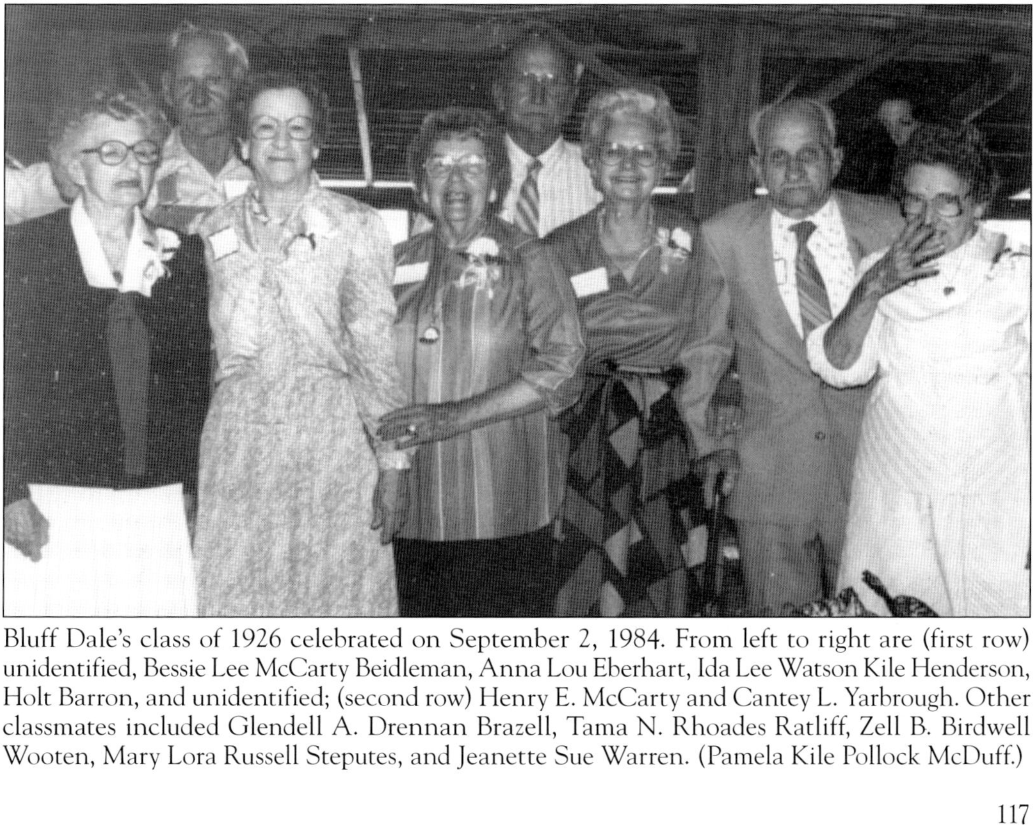

Bluff Dale's class of 1926 celebrated on September 2, 1984. From left to right are (first row) unidentified, Bessie Lee McCarty Beidleman, Anna Lou Eberhart, Ida Lee Watson Kile Henderson, Holt Barron, and unidentified; (second row) Henry E. McCarty and Cantey L. Yarbrough. Other classmates included Glendell A. Drennan Brazell, Tama N. Rhoades Ratliff, Zell B. Birdwell Wooten, Mary Lora Russell Steputes, and Jeanette Sue Warren. (Pamela Kile Pollock McDuff.)

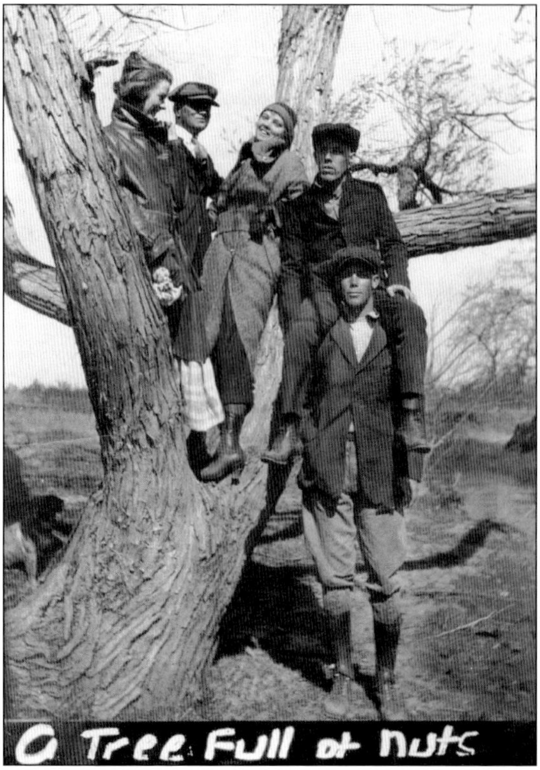

Courting was done among groups of friends. Many of these outings included activities such as picnicking, fishing, and enjoying the outdoors without doing physical labor on the farm. From left to right are Josephine "Joe" Augusta Billman, John Elliott Conatser, Mabel Hickey, and Kay and Paul Hickey. Joe and Kay eventually wed, as did John and Mabel. (Connie Conatser McSpadden.)

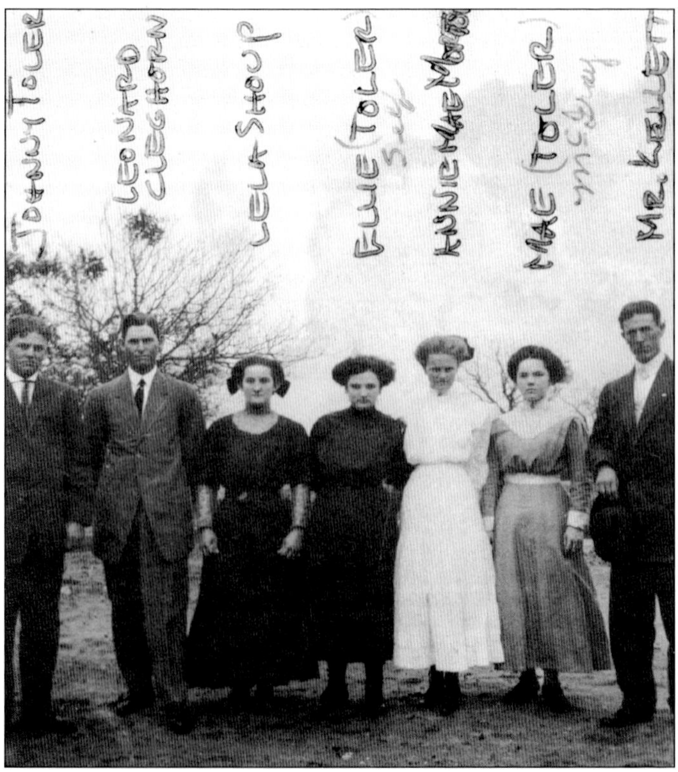

In this c. 1913 image, the courting friends are, from left to right, John Toler, Leonard Vincent Cleghorn, Lela Miller, Ellie Lucretia Toler, Annie Mae Morton, Ollie Mae Toler, and Prof. Edward Parker Kellum of Clarkston school. Lela Miller married Arthur Shoup. Ellie married Charles "Charlie" James Self in 1916 and lived to be 101 years old. Ollie married Edward Parker Kellum. Leonard and Edward served in World War I. (Sandra Shoup Hammons.)

Eight

Making a Difference

Whether by development or restoration, vocation or avocation, people helped one another. The midwife and physician risked personal safety while traveling in all seasons to care for residents. Some villages had a doctor or druggist by the 1890s, but it was also common practice on the frontier to visit a neighbor who was sick or in need. Sarah Palmer of Purves and Lavina Ford Moody of Huckabay midwifed for many mothers. Physician and druggist Dr. Hardy L. Holt had the first drugstore in Bluff Dale. In 1914, Altman's Dr. Thomas Joseph Laird transitioned from traveling via horse and buggy to getting around on a motorcycle. Thousands of unheralded and selfless actions increased the general welfare of the region.

The *Texas Pacific*, *Dublin Enterprise*, *Alexander Tribune*, *Erath County Enquirer*, *Texas Mining and Trade Journal*, *Erath Appeal*, *Central Texas Journal*, *Texas Miner*, *Erath County Democrat*, *Thurber Journal*, *Bluff Dale Sun*, and *Dublin Weekly Telephone* were newspapers that existed during Erath County's first 50 years.

For centuries, purposeful organizations have played a part in the successful growth of a community through benevolent and social activity. Freemasonry served as an Erathian influencer, with the first lodge in the county established in 1860. Alexander, Armstrong, Berlin, Bluff Dale, Chalk Mountain, Clairette, Dublin, Duffau, Johnsville, Lingleville, Morgan Mill, and Thurber also chartered Masonic lodges. Like the Independent Order of Odd Fellows, the Knights of Pythias sought to foster humanitarianism through self-improvement and helping others. Dedicated to helping their fellow men, Woodmen of the World had lodges organized by at least 20 communities in the county. Through annual reunions, the Dublin-Comanche Ex-Confederate Association and Grand Army of the Republic chapters sought social and charitable consideration of Civil War veterans. Addressing agrarian economic, educational, and social hardships was the objective of agricultural societies such as the Grange and Farmers' Alliance.

Such groups furnished an avenue for altruistic contributions and personal enrichment. Singularly and as a unit, the populace worked to build a better place to live. The physical and intellectual stamina of the people led to a harvest of community prosperity. These are a mere sampling of the measures that improved the quality of life in Erath County.

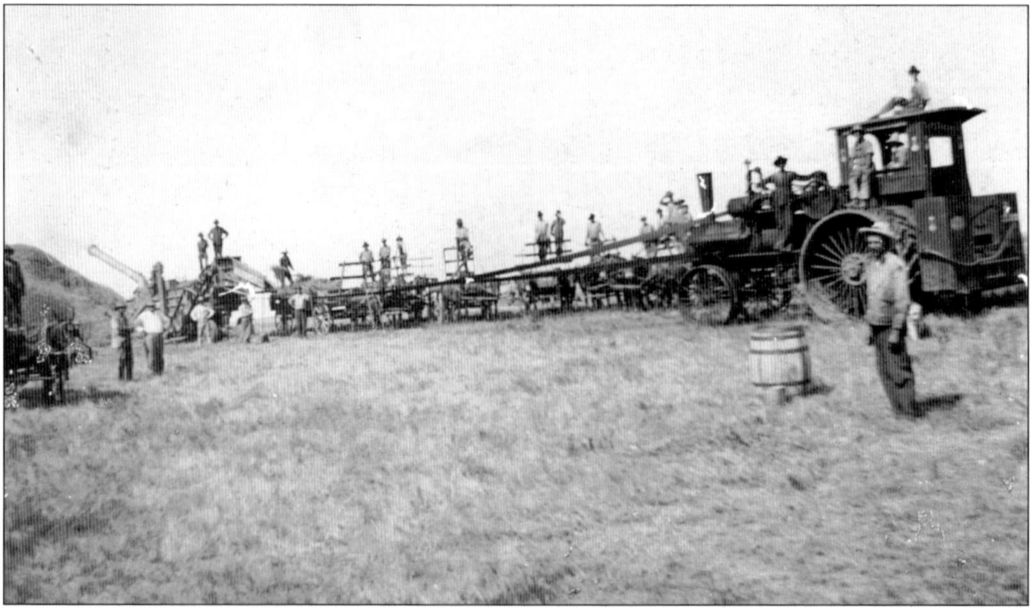

This thresher crew was working near Clairette in Jacob Andrew "Jake" Carter's field in the early 20th century. Wagons pulled by mule and horse teams brought the crop to the large thresher, which was powered by a tractor motor. Neighbors and relatives normally helped one another at harvest time. Day laborers were generally paid by the day or half day rather than by the hour.

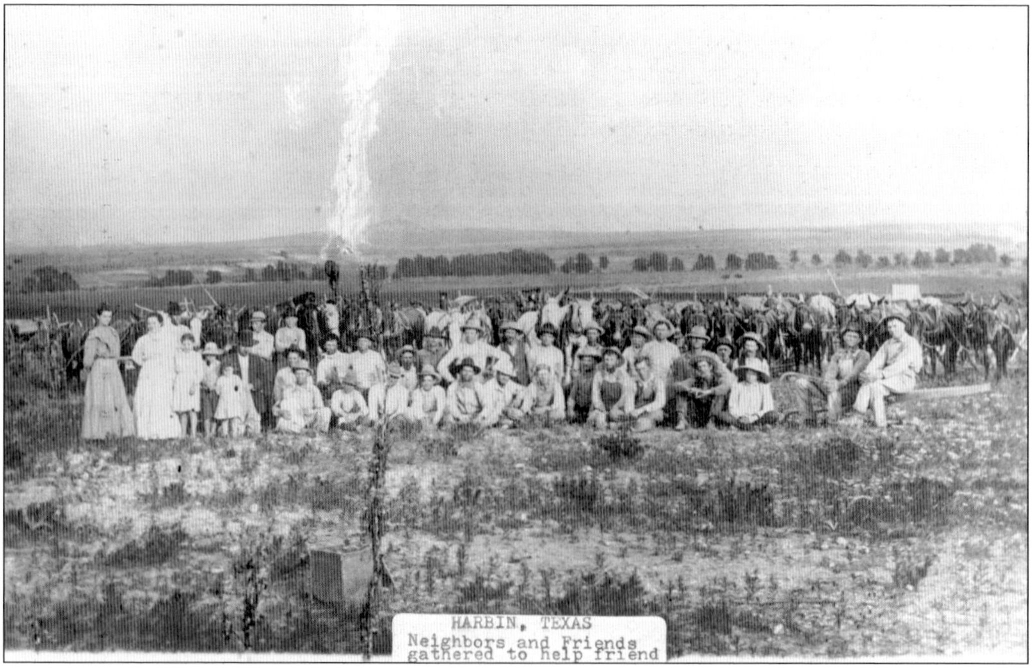

In March 1910, the *Stephenville Tribune* reported that as Henry Miller and Jack Smith from near Greens Creek and Harbin had fallen behind on farm work due to family illness, neighbors were determined to help. Fifty-four teams with plows and stalk cutters prepared 75 acres for planting. After Woodmen of the World proposed the idea, other neighbors joined in. (SHHM.)

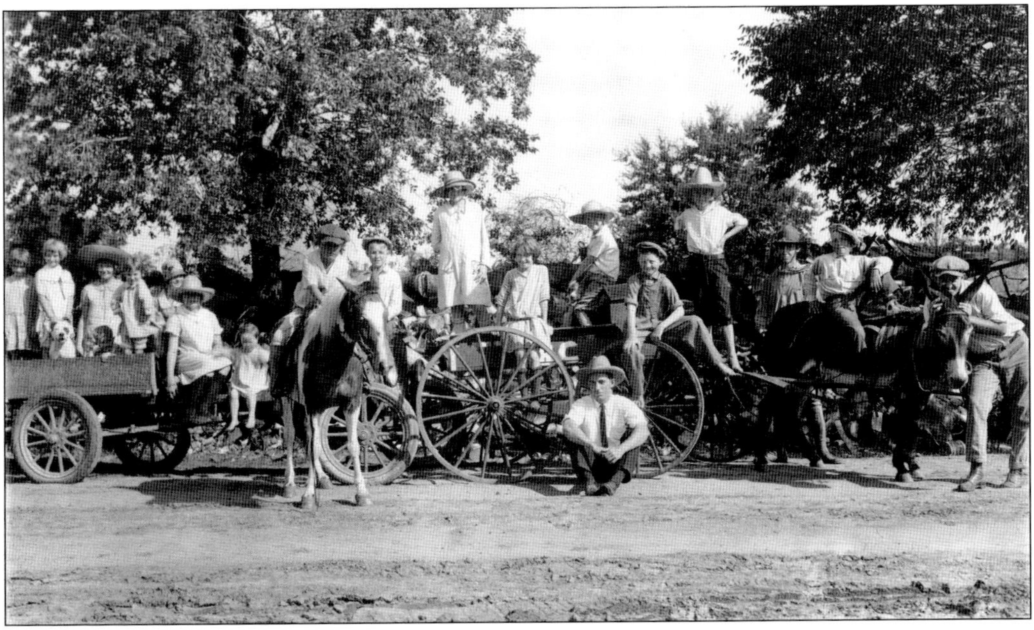

In 1917, the American Red Cross created an auxiliary, the Junior Red Cross, to engage youth in charitable efforts supporting those affected by World War I. In May 1917, Pearl Wylie Cage organized an Erath County Red Cross society. Women knitted wool items, held sewing parties, and conducted classes on how to prepare surgical dressings. A theatrical production was held at Crow's Opera House on the courthouse square to raise money for the Red Cross. Pearl Cage, Bamah Crow Young, and other local leaders set up a Junior Red Cross chapter. Children collected salvage materials such as paper, rags, rubber, iron, tinfoil, and all kinds of metal. Pictured in these photographs are the dogs, ponies, mules, wagons, and vehicles accompanying the Erath County children who gathered the materials piled behind them. (Both, SHHM.)

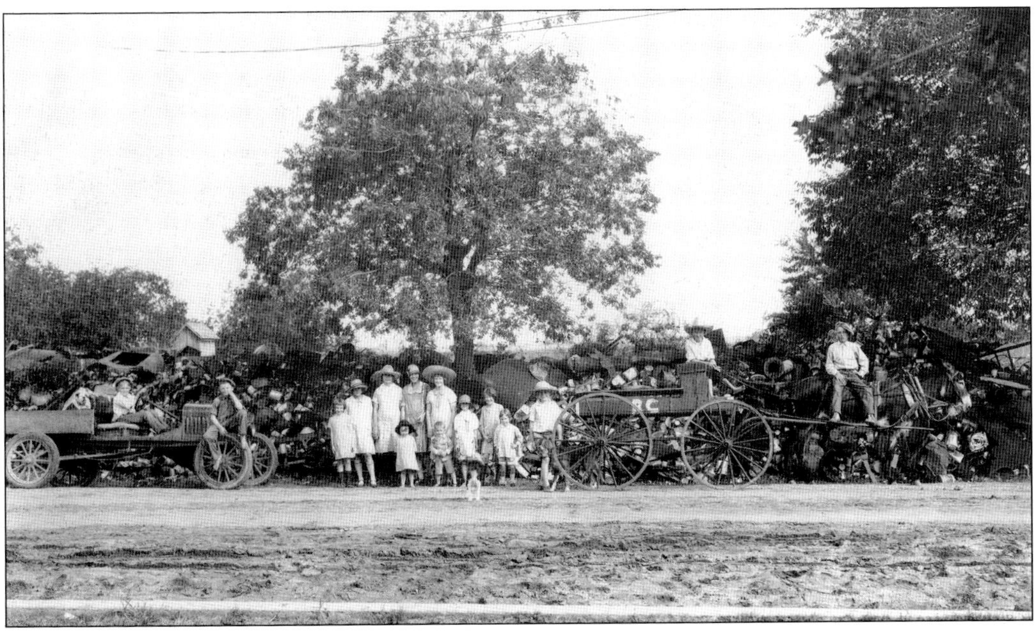

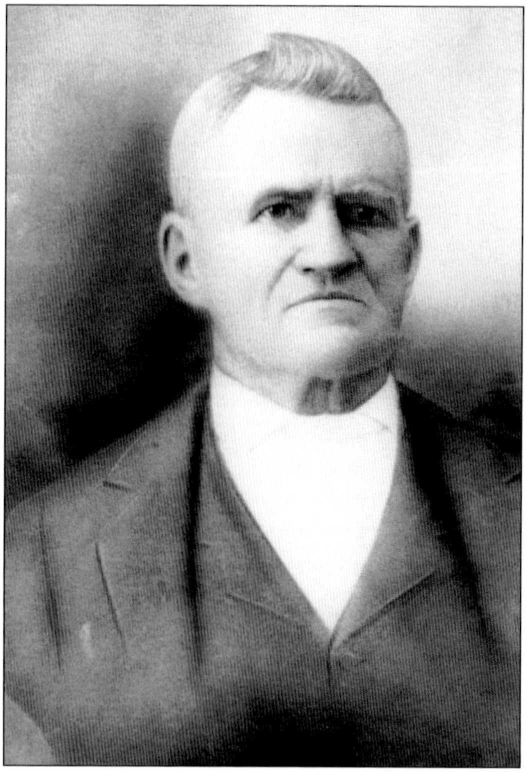

Arriving in 1854 with his father-in-law John M. Stephen, Dr. William W. McNeill was the first physician, druggist, postmaster, and county clerk. He organized the Methodist church with 10 members, including John Carmack and his wife Susan Carr, Henry Carr, William Painter, John M. Stephen, and himself. He was a charter member of Stephenville's Masonic lodge and served as secretary of that organization. (SHHM.)

Ivy William Cutler came to Erath with his widowed mother in 1878, and they settled near Greens Creek. After graduating from pharmacy school in 1905, he worked for several drugstores; he went on to own stores in Plano, Munday, and Lingleville. He is pictured at left in 1905 in his Lingleville Drug Store. (Carla Stacy Trussell.)

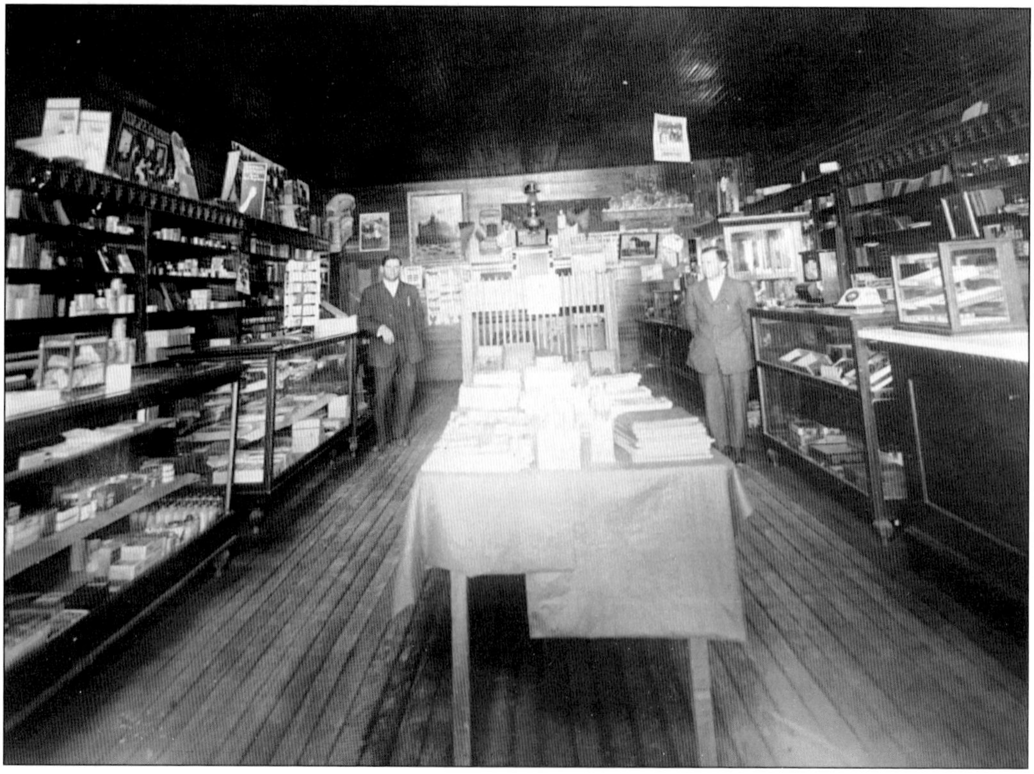

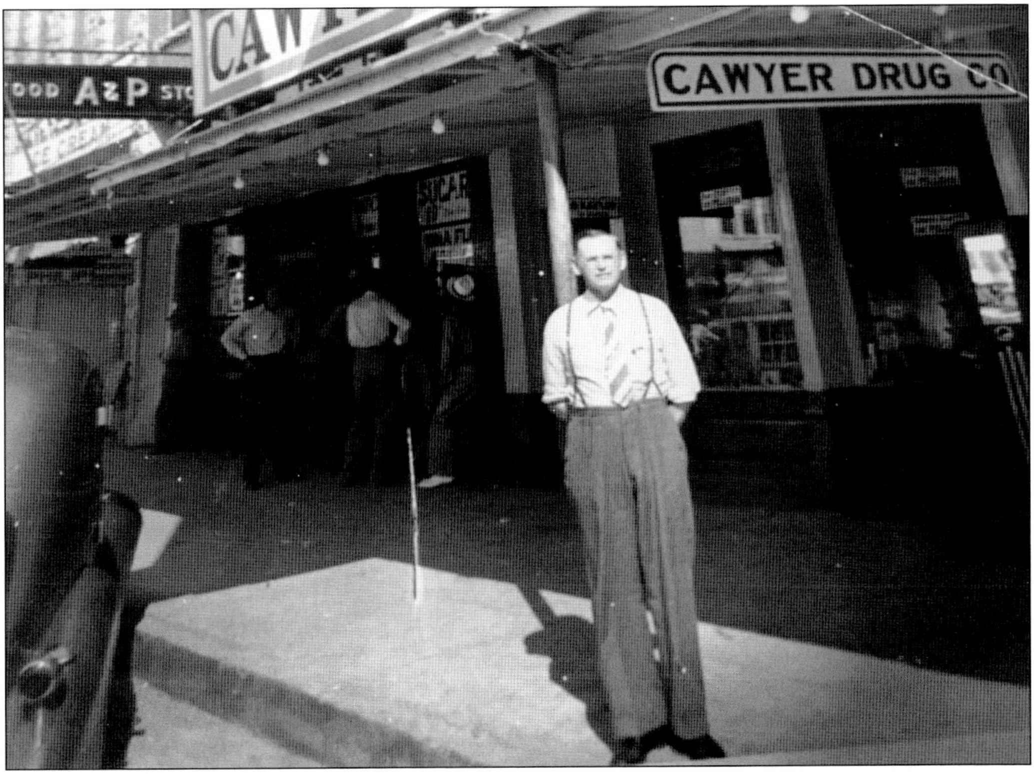

Ivy Cutler is shown standing outside Cawyer Drug Store on the north side of the courthouse square where he worked in the 1940s. Civic-minded druggist Telefus Beverly Cawyer served in leadership with the Boy Scouts, American Heart Association, American Cancer Society, Stephenville Rotary Club, Stephenville Chamber of Commerce, and city council. He was also a minister and conducted hundreds of funerals and marriages. (Carla Stacy Trussell.)

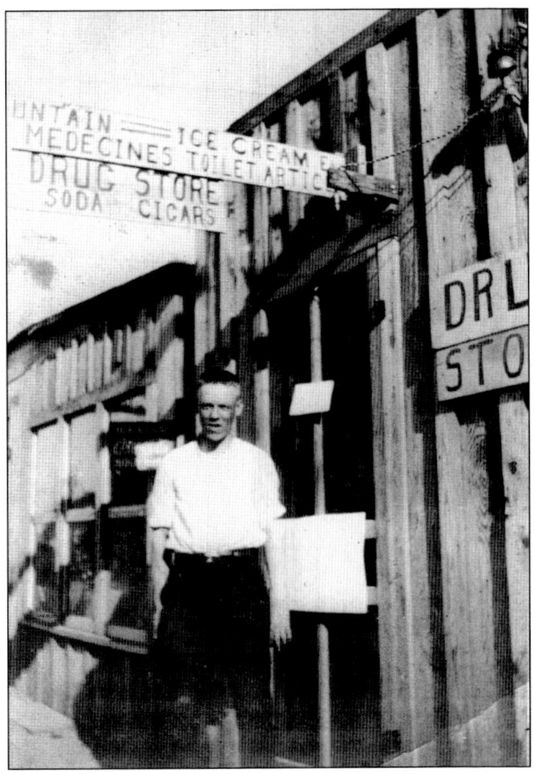

Erath native and pharmacist Carson Kay Hickey is pictured outside Hamilton's drugstore around 1917. While in Hamilton, Kay married Josephine "Joe" Augusta Billman. Kay was born in 1894 to Annie Holt and William Newton Hickey. In 1912, he served with Company L, 4th Texas Infantry. He worked at drugstores in Port Arthur, Breckenridge, Mineral Wells, Graham, and Stephenville. Kay was known for having a pet monkey. (Connie Conatser McSpadden.)

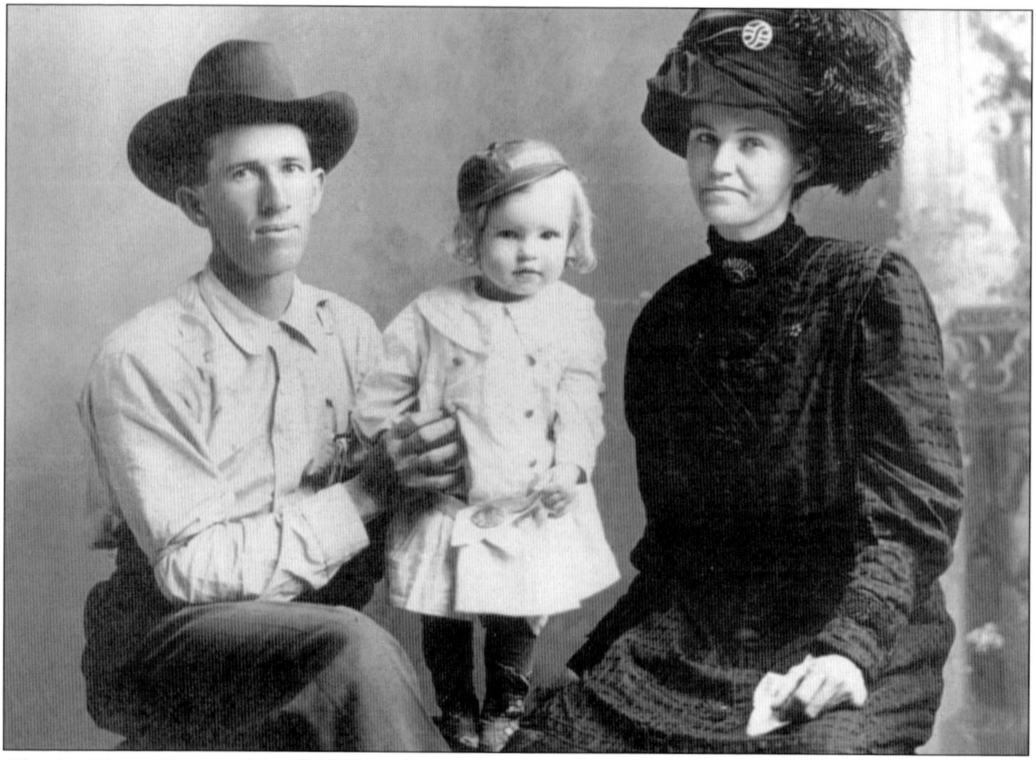

Charles Elmer II, son of Dr. C.E. Clendenin, is pictured around 1911 with his son Alvis B. and his wife, Carra Alameda Price. While a student at Lingleville Christian College, Charles met Carra at a revival. After he became a pharmacist, he had his own drugstore in Victor. (Nelda Blankenship Keever.)

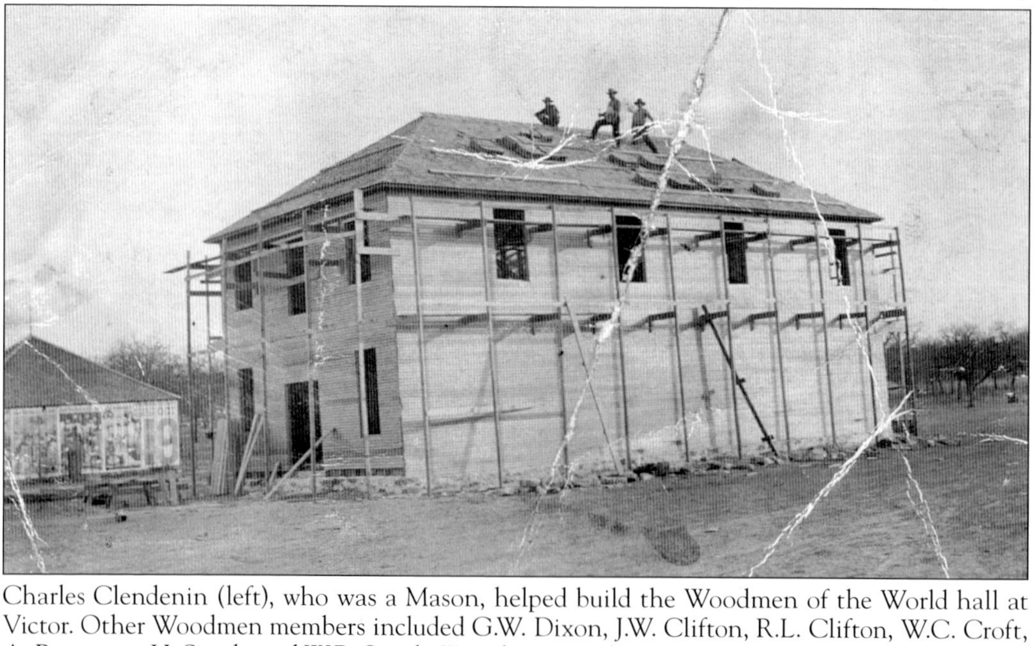

Charles Clendenin (left), who was a Mason, helped build the Woodmen of the World hall at Victor. Other Woodmen members included G.W. Dixon, J.W. Clifton, R.L. Clifton, W.C. Croft, A. Browning, H. Smith, and W.B. Smith. Woodmen conducted funerals for their fellow members and held ceremonies to unveil monuments honoring their graves. (Nelda Blankenship Keever.)

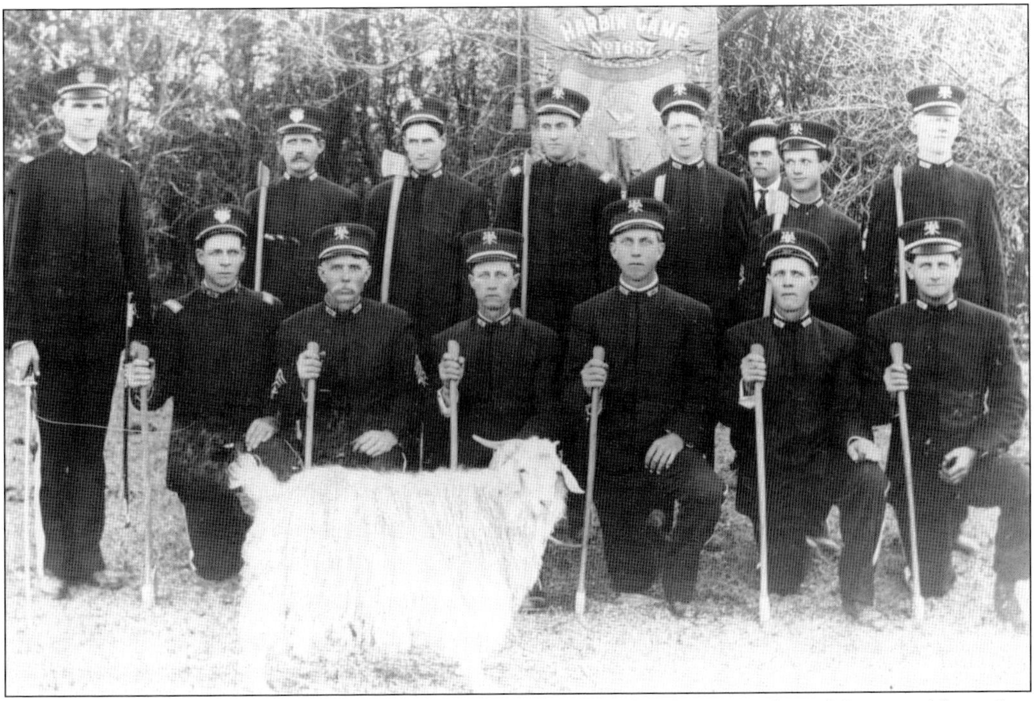

Members of Woodmen of the World were eligible for social, educational, and financial benefits. Woodmen in Alexander, Bluff Dale, Chalk Mountain, Clairette, Dublin, Duffau, Edna Hill, Exray, Flatwood, Greens Creek, Harbin, Hico, Highland, Lingleville, Morgan Mill, Oakdale, Purves, Shiloh, Stephenville, Thurber, Victor, and possibly other locations established camps. Camp organizers collaborated with each other and other groups like the Masons and Odd Fellows. The camps featured classes, speakers, box suppers, picnics, and conventions. In June 1904, an estimated 3,000 attended a grand all-day affair held by the Alexander Odd Fellows and Woodmen. The event included a band, a parade, baseball, and addresses before an elaborate dinner on the grounds. The Harbin camp had uniforms, a long-haired goat for a mascot (above), and at least 14 members. In 1907, men from Edna Hill, Purves, and Shiloh met for the group photograph below. Some of the projects undertaken by these groups included presenting flags to schools, furnishing hospitals, awarding youth medals for proficiency in US history, and placing historic markers.

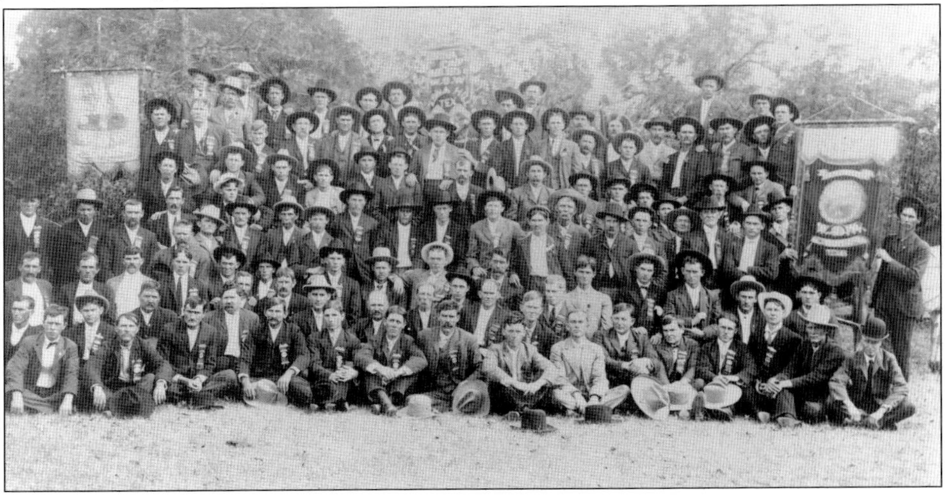

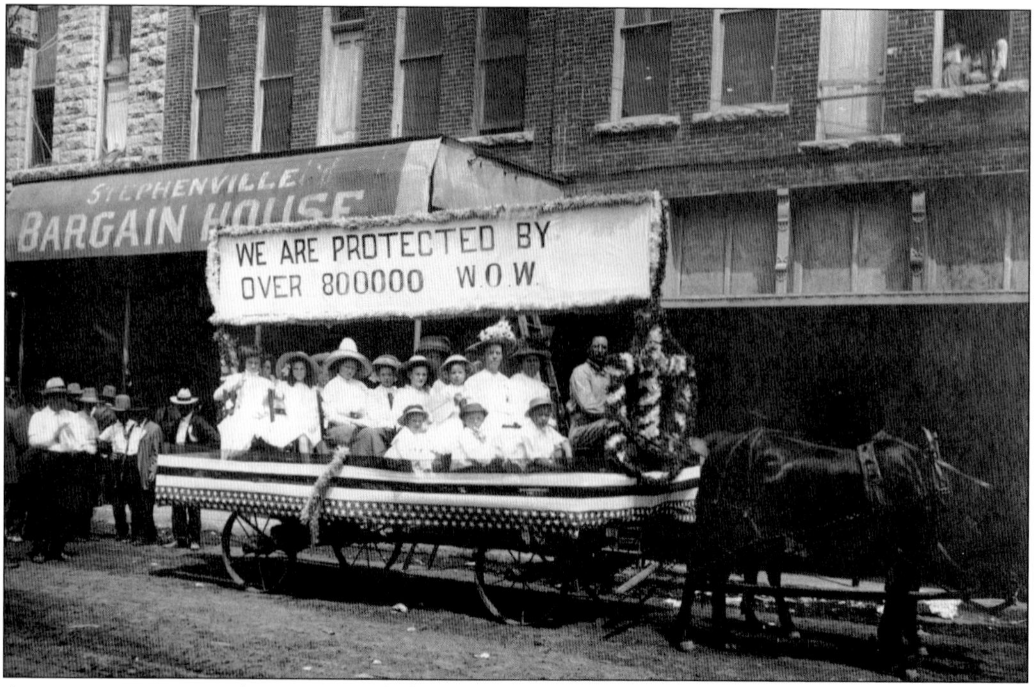

Any community social activity, including this parade from the late 19th or early 20th century, was a special event. These Woodmen families were enjoying the Fourth of July in grand style. Note the onlookers at right enjoying the excitement from the second floor. The appearance of a "WOW" poster in another second-floor window may indicate that this building on the courthouse square was the group's local office. (Connie Conatser McSpadden.)

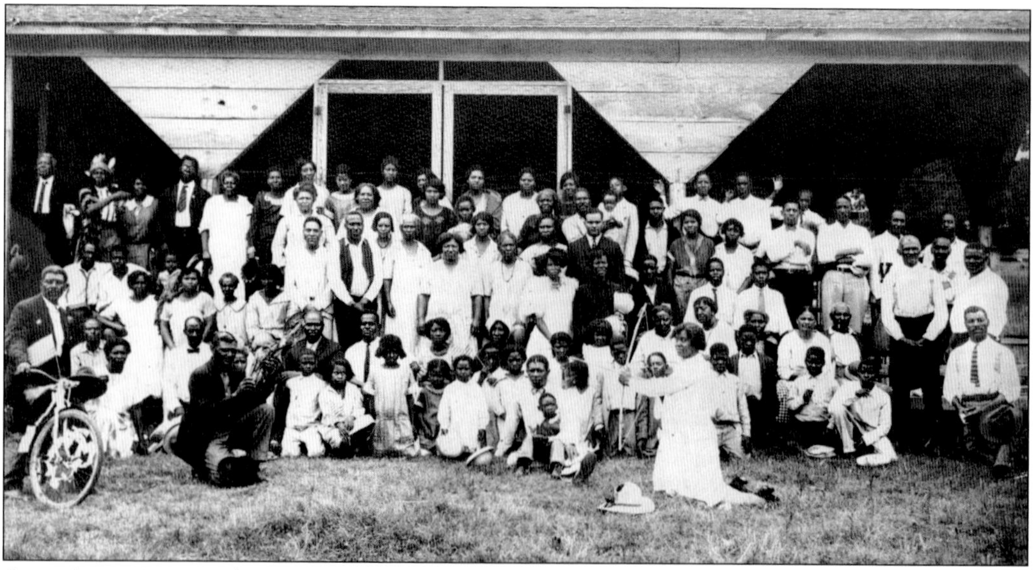

As early as 1931, Stephenville hosted an elaborate celebration of Juneteenth, with visitors from nearby counties coming together for a downtown parade and city park dinner. For several years during the 1930s and 1940s, a rodeo was included. Juneteenth, held on June 19, commemorates the day Union general Gordon Granger arrived in Galveston, Texas, in 1865 to announce the emancipation of enslaved African Americans. (SHHM.)

Bibliography

Awbrey, Jon A. *Legends of Dublin: Personalities of the Irish Capital of Texas*. Dublin, TX: *Dublin Citizen*, 2009.

FamilySearch. The Church of Jesus Christ of Latter-day Saints. www.familysearch.org/.

"Handbook of Texas." Texas State Historical Association. www.tshaonline.org/handbook.

Knight, Sherri. *Vigilantes to Verdicts: Stories from a Texas District Court*. Stephenville, TX: Jacobus Books, 2009.

McCool, Billy Dee. *This Here Book: History and Stories of the Settling of Comanche and Surrounding Counties*. Hamilton, TX: CreateSpace Independent Publishing Platform, 2017.

"Portal to Texas History, The." University of North Texas Libraries. texashistory.unt.edu.

Pylant, James. *Sins of the Pioneers: Crimes & Scandals in a Small Texas Town*. Stephenville, TX: Jacobus Books, 2019.